Portugal

The Portuguese have the oldest settled borders in Europe. With the Americas to the west, continental Europe to the north and Africa to the south, Portugal has been a trading nation from Phoenician times onward.

After 47 years of stagnant and repressive dictatorship, Portugal finally emerged as a democracy in 1974, following a bloodless coup by the army. At the same time, she granted independence to colonies such as Mozambique and Angola, bringing to an end costly colonial wars, which had raged for over a decade.

Today Portugal is coming to terms with its new identity – as a member country of the European Economic Community.

In *We live in Portugal*, the people themselves give us a vivid picture of what life is like in their country in the 1980s.

Minho River

Viano do Castelo

Lousado

*Atlantic
Ocean*

Oporto

Regua

Douro River

SPAIN

Aveiro

Guarda

Coimbra

Nazaré

Fatima

Tagus River

Santarém

Sintra

Altentejo

Cascais

Lisbon

Estoril

Setúbal

Évora

Algarve

Portimão

Pechão Monte Gordo

Quarteira

Faro

San Vincente

we live in
PORTUGAL

Ana de Skalon and Christa Stadtler

The Bookwright Press
New York · 1987

Living Here

We live in Argentina
We live in Australia
We live in Belgium and Luxembourg
We live in Brazil
We live in Britain
We live in Canada
We live in the Caribbean
We live in Chile
We live in China
We live in Denmark
We live in East Germany
We live in Egypt
We live in France
We live in Greece
We live in Hong Kong
We live in India
We live in Indonesia
We live in Ireland
We live in Israel

We live in Italy
We live in Japan
We live in Kenya
We live in Malaysia and Singapore
We live in Mexico
We live in the Netherlands
We live in New Zealand
We live in Pakistan
We live in the Philippines
We live in Poland
We live in Portugal
We live in Saudi Arabia
We live in South Africa
We live in Spain
We live in Sweden
We live in the U.S.A.
We live in the Asian U.S.S.R.
We live in the European U.S.S.R.
We live in West Germany

First published in the
United States in 1987 by
The Bookwright Press
387 Park Avenue South
New York, NY 10016

First published in 1986 by
Wayland (Publishers) Ltd
61 Western Road, Hove
East Sussex BN3 1JD, England

© Copyright 1986 Wayland (Publishers) Ltd

ISBN: 0–531–180883
Library of Congress Card Number: 86–70995
Phototypeset by Kalligraphics Ltd
Redhill, Surrey
Printed in Italy by G. Canale & C.S.p.A., Turin

Contents

"A ship ran aground here once"

Porfirio Sousa, 47, has been a lighthouse keeper for twenty-seven years. Four years ago he was promoted to senior keeper and was posted to the Aveiro lighthouse.

There are 278 steps in my lighthouse.

Lighthouse keepers are technicians now. The image of us checking the wick in the oil lamp is long out of date. We don't even have to stay up nights anymore!

My lighthouse is 69 meters (226 ft) high. You have to trudge up 278 steps to get to the crystal and lamp at the top. During the day we draw the curtains so that the heat of the sun's rays won't explode the lens. We have electricity here, but we always keep a gas light on standby in case of power cuts or generator failure. Living on the premises, as I and my family do, isn't much different from living in a town.

Apart from the lighthouse, I also look after the gas-operated buoys that mark the sea lanes in the Aveiro lagoon. The Vouga River carries sediments into the sea, and these form small islands between which ships have to pass. The western side of the lagoon is impeded by a long, sandy spit, which is intersected by a channel. On both sides of this channel there are small beacons, which I also have to supervise. A ship ran aground here once and

two of its crew died.

There are 26 lighthouses along the coast of Portugal. To the north of Aveiro, in the mouth of the Douro River, there is a lighthouse dating back to the sixteenth century. Up there the coast is very rocky – a contrast to the sandy beaches that stretch from here down to Nazare. Between Nazare and the Cape of San Vicente – the most southwesterly point in Europe – the coastline is high and rugged. At San Vicente, a lighthouse has been incorporated into the tower of the San Francisco convent!

The Aveiro lighthouse, which guards the entrance to the Aveiro Lagoon.

The coast continues high and rugged all the way along the Algarve, until Quarteira, where wide, sandy beaches take over again.

There are 177 lighthouse keepers in Portugal, Madeira and the Azores. To qualify as a keeper, candidates have to attend a three-year course at a *marinha* (navy) school. Very few people want to be keepers, though. That's why more and more lighthouses are being automated.

"We carry on the tradition"

Carlos Duarte Pimentel, 28, is a potter and ceramics designer at a factory near Coimbra. His craft goes back a long way in Portugal.

Paints and glazes for the pots are no longer made from local materials.

Portugal has been manufacturing pottery and ceramics for many centuries. There isn't a province that doesn't produce some pottery, and here, in Condeixa-a-Nova we carry on that tradition. Condeixa-a-Nova is 10 km (6 miles) away from Coimbra. It's a very fertile area in which rice, corn, olives and vineyards abound. It's also an historic town with many big stately homes dating from the eighteenth and nineteenth centuries. The area is famous for its limestone which can be seen in the façade of many local buildings. There is also plenty of clay, which explains our tradition in pottery and ceramics.

I work in the Ceramica Conimbriga factory, painting and glazing the pots made here. Imitation seventeenth-century pots are in greatest demand. The design is either a straight copy or an original. We buy our glazes from abroad now, but when the factory first started – thirty-five years ago – the glazes were made out of local materials and stones.

It takes me two or three days to decorate

a big vase and about a day to do a dish. Each piece is baked twice – first at 1,040°C, (1,904°F), after the pot has been "thrown," then at 980°C (1,796°F), in order to set the glaze. The ovens are now electric, but we started with a wood fired stove!

At Ceramica Conimbriga we also make and decorate tiles. Most are decorated with original Dutch Delft designs. Ornamental tiles – *azulejos* – were introduced to Portugal in the fourteenth century. Many tiles were imported from Seville, in Spain, until the sixteenth century. After that we started to manufacture our own. Some tiled surfaces look like huge jigsaw puzzles, with each tile forming part of the design that covers an entire wall. They are found in offices, churches, railroad stations and in many other buildings, and they usually depict great moments in Portuguese history or life in the regions.

Clay is found nearly everywhere in the country, and especially in the Tejo and Sado river valleys. Lisbon, Oporto and Setubal produce pottery on an industrial scale. And at the Vista Alegre factory, near Aveiro, they produce china. We are also fortunate in having a thriving export trade – mainly to the United States, Japan and West Germany.

Carlos takes about a day to decorate a dish.

"Folk dancing is dying out"

Augusto Manuel Peçes, 22, worked on a building project before becoming a dancer. He now lives in Lisbon and performs mainly for the tourist trade.

I have been a dancer for several years now. I first joined a *rancho* (dance group) in Alentejo, where I was brought up. The Alentejo people are regarded as being poor dancers, but I think one of the most beautiful Portuguese dances comes from this region – the *saias* – which means skirts.

When I was seventeen, I came to Lisbon to live with my oldest brother and his wife. I got a job in the restaurant where he danced – in the Bairro Alto district, an area traditionally associated with clubs and nightlife. It's a very old part of Lisbon.

Every night, except Sundays, I arrive at 9:00 p.m. to get ready for the show. We perform dances from the Minho, Estremadura, Ribatejo and Algarve provinces. There will also be dances that originated here in Lisbon and several from the island of Madeira. Each of my dancing costumes represents a different region too.

In the sheer variety of Portuguese dance it is possible to trace the influence of the different cultures that settled here. Before

The influence of different cultures can still be seen in many Portuguese dances.

Christianity there was a rich pagan culture, a mix of Roman and Moorish traditions. The remnants of these cultures can still be seen in various dances – especially those performed at the Christian *festas* (festivals) such as S. Joao on June 24. This celebration coincides with the summer solstice – continuing an old pagan custom. At this sort of event I might dance the *mourisca*, which is of Moorish origin and which symbolizes the struggle between the Christians and the Moors, who stayed in Portugal for nearly five centuries.

But I know many other dances as well. There is the *malhao* from the Minho province and the *vira* from Nazare in the Estremadura – both celebrate the work of fishermen. And in the Ribatejo there is a dance called the *fandango*, an old Spanish routine that took root in Portugal. One of its main features is the *despique*, a sort of duel of steps between two male dancers.

But it can also be considered a dance of seduction in which a man and a woman try to outdo one another by creating new and more complicated steps.

In the Algarve they have the *corridinho*, a traditional dance first performed in the cities and then taken to rural areas where it was transformed into what it is today. It is danced to a polka rhythm.

In Madeira many dances are associated with winemaking. People dance barefoot and pretend they are treading grapes!

Nowadays these dances are still found at some festivals. But folk dancing is dying out in Portugal, along with many other traditions. These days there aren't that many places where you can dance, though I still find work in restaurant-clubs catering mainly to tourists.

Each costume represents a different region of Portugal .

"Our olives are the best in Portugal"

Ana Paula vas Fraga, 22, has worked in an olive processing plant in the small town of Cachão for seven years.

Each morning I have to drop my daughter off at the crèche before going on to work. I have to be there by 8:00 a.m. As I live nearby, I usually walk, though most of our 800 workers catch the factory bus.

My job is to process olives – sometimes bottling the oil, sometimes stuffing them with almonds and peppers. But we also process fruit, vegetables and dairy products. Alcohol is distilled here for port and wool is prepared for weaving. All these different products come mainly from local farmers.

The industrial estate dwarfs Cachão, which is only a small town.

Washing the bottles before filling them with oil.

I think the olives here are the best in Portugal. They come from the Zona da Terra Quente (hot land), which takes in parts of the Doura and Tua river valleys. In winter the weather is mild and rainy, but in summer it is sweltering. These are ideal conditions for the olive tree which, like many other Mediterranean plants, has very long roots enabling it to get moisture from deep down. Olive trees can be found nearly everywhere in Portugal but mostly in central and southern regions.

Harvesting olives can be hard work. Equipped only with long sticks, the workers shake the branches, causing the olives to fall into canvas sheets and the women's skirts. Green olives are picked in October and black olives in early winter. Black olives are brought to the factory for oilmaking. They are washed and then crushed to a pulp. The pulp goes into a centrifuge, which separates out the oil.

The oil is then filtered and stored in big tanks. This process is only undertaken for three months of the year – between January and April. These days it is all highly automated – a far cry from the times when olives had to be ground under a stone to produce oil!

This week I have been working in the bottling section. Yesterday we bottled 20,000 liters (4,400 gallons) of oil. Today we've been washing the bottles that we'll use tomorrow.

I am looking forward to 6:00 p.m. because that's when we finish and I can go home. My daughter and I live alone, as my husband is a policeman in Lisbon and can only spend the weekend with us. After I have made my daughter something to eat and put her to bed, I will settle down to watch the Brazilian soap opera on TV!

13

"I'd much rather have a beer"

José Pereiri Lopes, 35, is an agricultural technician. For the last four years he has worked for Ver Coope, a wine-makers' association, which buys, bottles and sells wine both in Portugal and abroad.

Wine has always been part of my life. I was even born in a wine-producing area. Yet I don't like its taste or smell. I'd much rather have a beer.

I live in Lousada, a small town in the Minho province. The Vinhos Verdes region stretches from the Minho River — the northern limit of Portugal — down to the Douro River and the city of Oporto. This area occupies about 10 percent of the country.

Vinho Verde vines get their character from humid and rainy weather, mild temperatures and granite soils. The grapes don't get as much sun as they would in other parts of the country — consequently they have a lower sugar content. A Vinho Verde wine made from mature grapes is slightly acid and not very strong — precisely because of the absence of sugar. We produce both red and white Vinhos Verdes, although in this area we nearly always serve a white wine with our meal.

Winemaking goes back a long way in Portugal. Vines were first introduced into

Washing down the wine press.

14

Vinho Verde vines get less sun than vines in other parts of the country.

Portugal by the Phoenicians and then organized on a commercial scale by the Romans. Once, it was forbidden to grow vines on good agricultural land. This meant that vines could always be found mingled with the trees forming the boundary of a plot of land – though now we rarely pick the grapes from these vines. We call this *enforcado* culture and it makes for a lot of hard work when we harvest the grapes. The commonest vine culture on my father's land is the traditional *ramada* (or trellis) method, which is a tunnel of vines covering the paths that lead to the corn fields. Nowadays this is being replaced by *cruzetas* (cross-shaped supports), because this method permits mechanization.

We start grape picking during early October. Men and women are employed from the neighboring areas and they spend seven to ten days picking the grapes. On average we produce about seventy 500-liter (109-gallon) containers a year. But I don't usually get involved in this side of the business. I advise on the quality and think up ways of improving the yields. Vine growers buy plants from us in order to get better crops.

Our region has about two million inhabitants. Of these, a staggering 300,000 are Vinhos Verdes producers. But only 15,000 of these actually make a living from winemaking. Most of them work in factories – this is a highly-industrialized area – and tend their vines in their spare time.

But I think I must be the only person around here who doesn't have a glass of wine with his food!

"Our industry is on the decline"

Daniel Tiago Soares, 60, has been a fisherman all his life. For many years he lived in the Portuguese colony of Angola. Since his return to Portugal in 1975, he has lived and fished at Portimão, on the Algarve. He is due to retire next year.

Fishing has a long tradition in Portugal. Our shoreline yields up a rich harvest. We Portuguese eat most of our own catch — either fresh or salted. But we also have an important fish canning industry, which is geared mainly to export.

I have been a fisherman since the age of eight. My father was also a fisherman. I lived in Angola for many years, though since my return to Portugal, in 1975, I have

Portimão is one of the most important fishing ports in the Algarve.

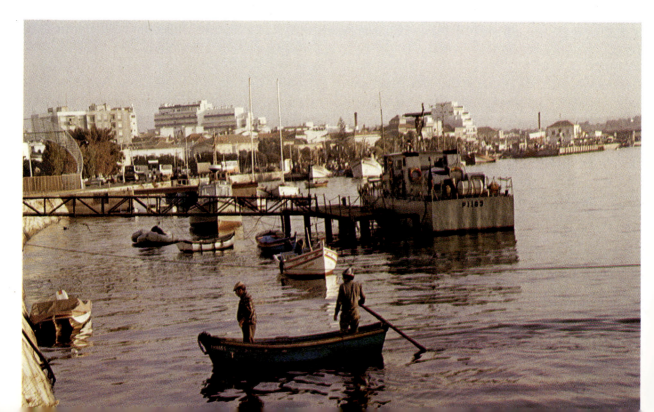

Returning to port with a good catch.

lived here in Portimão. Although there are many bigger fishing ports along our coasts – Leixoes, Lisbon, Aveiro – Portimão is one of the most important on the Algarve. It's a well-protected port, which means that boats can come and go at any time of the day, and can unload their catches even in bad weather.

In summer – our best inshore fishing season – we put out at about 7:00 p.m. each evening and return about 6:00 a.m. In winter we leave earlier and return later. Unfortunately the catch isn't anywhere near as good as in the summer.

The fish are caught in red *cercadora* (encircling) nets. One end of the net is tied to the stern of the boat and the other to a small rowboat. When it is full, we pull the net and it closes like a string shoulder bag. The fish are sorted and sold at the port to wholesalers or to one of the market stall owners. Then we have to mend our nets before putting out again that evening.

My dog Caca is an invaluable member of the crew. He starts running up and down the boat as soon as he spots a shoal nearby. Up to a few years ago, we had no electronic equipment on board, but now we have sonar, which makes our task a lot easier.

There are also bigger boats – known as *arrastoes* – operating out of Portimão. They have holds and can stay at sea for many months. They usually go to Nova Scotia, where they trawl for cod.

Our industry is on the decline – despite the extension of fishing limits to 345 km (220 miles) offshore. My fear is that we will be swamped by imported fish, which will further deplete our fishing fleet. Perhaps it's just as well that none of my children wanted to be fishermen!

"Extracting salt is very hard work"

Dionisio de Sousa Milharo, 19, works in the saltpans of the Algarve. He was born in Maputo, the capital of Mozambique, and arrived here four years ago. Because his father is Portuguese, he now has Portuguese nationality.

I've been working in these saltpans for three months now. Extracting salt is very hard work and I don't like it much. It's especially bad working during August, which is the hottest month of the year here in the Algarve.

Two different kinds of salt can be found in Portugal – sea salt and mineral salt. Sea saltpans exist all along the coast. The oldest are in Aveiro, where you find a great

Most workers in the saltpans are Africans.

many salt marshes. To extract salt from the sea, saltpans are built in the open air, then the sea water is pumped into them. The sun dries the water out and the salt remains at the bottom of the pan. We wash it, using the remaining water, then remove it. Women carry it to the tractors in 15 kg (33 lb) baskets.

It took me just three days to learn my job. After washing the salt, I shovel it from the tractors into the storage area. It stays here till the buyers take it away to be refined. I work eight hours a day, usually under a blazing sun, as sea salt can be extracted only during the summer. What's worse, my job can only be done manually!

On average we extract between 20 and 30 tons of salt a day. About 19,000 tons are taken out of Faro each year. But the biggest area of production is in Setubal, near Lisbon.

As for mineral salt, this is found in underground mines. Tunnels and galleries have to be constructed to get it out. The biggest mine of this kind is in Loule, which is also in the Algarve province.

Dionisio works hard shoveling salt into one of the storage areas.

Both types of salt are used for cooking, for industrial use, and to preserve fish. One of our national dishes is *bacalhao* – salted cod.

Most of the workers in Portugal's saltpans are Africans from former colonies – Cabo Verde, Guinea-Bissau, Angola and Mozambique. They come here on a two-year contract. The Government allows them a work permit but doesn't help to find them work. As a result they can only get low-paying jobs – on building projects, in mines and, of course, in the saltpans. When their work permits have expired, they have to leave the country. If they don't, they are usually repatriated by their embassies. There are a great many immigrants who don't have work permits.

I'll be leaving this job soon. This year I am due to start compulsory military service. I hope to qualify as an electrician after my two years in the army. Then I'll be able to do more interesting work!

"We're the world's leading cork producer"

Horacio Ferreira, 28, trained as an agricultural engineer. For the last four years he has supervised the production of cork for Torres Pinto Lda.

51 percent of the world's cork comes from Portugal. That's a lot. It makes us the leading international cork producer!

In the Alentejo they have a saying: "Anything that stands is a cork oak, anything that moves is a pig." The Alentejo is full of cork oaks – *sobreiros*. They are the second most common tree in the country. Nearly a quarter of all Portuguese forests are comprised of cork oaks. Oddly

The bark of cork oaks awaiting processing.

This factory has the highest output of manufactured cork in the Algarve.

enough, though cork is grown mainly in the south, the factories that process it are found mainly in the north and along the coast. Our factory has the highest output of manufactured cork in the Algarve. It is located in Faro, the capital of the province.

Nine years have to pass before the bark of the cork oak can be removed. But if it is left beyond its eleventh year, it starts to deteriorate and attracts parasites. The first bark to be taken is called natural cork and subsequent layers are known as amadia cork. Because it takes so long for the bark to mature, farmers usually divide their land into three parts and remove the bark on each plot every three years. They sell it to us in its raw state – though we also buy processed cork sheets from them.

We produce natural and agglomerated cork sheets, bottle stoppers and tiles. As far as tiles are concerned, we cook the raw cork at 80°C (176°F), then pass it through cold water. This makes the bark more flexible. Next it goes to be cut, where it is separated according to its thickness and consistency. After cutting, the different pieces are put together and beaten into a sheet, mainly by women, who make up the majority of the work force at this plant and, indeed, in the industry as a whole. The sheet is then pressed and coated with varnish or candle wax. The finished tiles are generally used for sound insulation. To cover an average-sized room, the bark of two trees is needed!

The bits and pieces that are left over are minced and used for making agglomerated cork. They are cooked with glue at 120°C (248°F) and made into 50 kg (110 lb) blocks. They are then cut into sheets and end up in the stores as economy tiles.

95 percent of our output is exported to Europe, Japan and the United States. Among our European customers, West Germany is the biggest buyer.

"Most schools here are overcrowded"

Susana Baptista, 14, was born in Lisbon, although her family moved before she could start school there. She is now a pupil at the Escola Secundaria de Avelar Brotero in Coimbra.

This is my first week at a big secondary school. I like it, though I must say it's very noisy. No wonder – there are 3000 students crammed into a building designed for only 800! Most secondary schools are overcrowded in Portugal. Furthermore, there are still those who cannot find a place and who miss out on valuable schooling. Not everyone can afford a private education!

The entrance to Baptista's school in Coimbra.

I have thirty-one hours of classes a week. Some days I study in the morning, other days in the afternoon. School starts at 8:30 a.m. and finishes at 6:15 p.m. In the evening the adults arrive for their vocational courses. These are usually people who had only their six years of compulsory schooling. All children in Portugal have to have four years in elementary school and two years in pre-secondary school, though this is available only up until the age of fourteen.

Next year I will start my tenth year. Then I'll have to decide on my specialist subjects. Six will be compulsory and three vocational. They will determine what I can study when I leave school and, indirectly, my future career.

These days you have to work hard to get into college. At the end of the twelfth and last year, we sit our final examinations. They are set by the Ministry of Education and we take them in June and July. We are marked not only on the results of

Most classes in secondary schools are overcrowded.

these exams but also on our performance during our last two years at school. We can attain anything up to 20 points, though for some careers – such as medicine – the entrance qualification can be as high as 18.5 points. If we fail, we can retake the exam twice. The two subjects students seem to find most difficult are math and English!

I want to study economics at college, but I know it's going to be a problem getting accepted. For one thing we cannot afford all the books I need. Because my father died recently, my mother – an elementary school teacher – is the sole wage earner. On top of that, libraries aren't always well-stocked.

But university is a few years away yet. For the time being I will go on studying French and English and practicing for the inter-school swimming competitions.

"I couldn't wait to get back"

José Abanteiro Alminhas, 43, is married and has five children. After three months of work in West Germany, he returned to his home in Regua on the Douro River to open a restaurant.

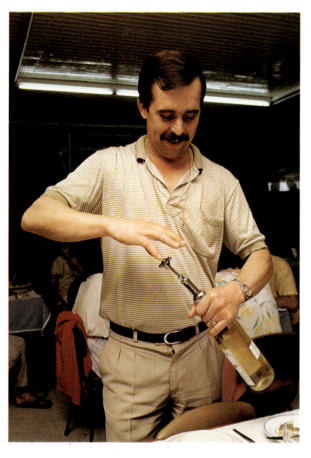

José opens a bottle of local wine for a customer.

There are about four million Portuguese emigrants around the world. Over a quarter of these are to be found in Europe. I was one of them, but I came back after just a few months. Today, thirteen years later, my wife and I own a restaurant in Regua.

I've had to do all sorts of jobs in my life. I've driven trucks, delivered gas cylinders and worked in factories. But I was always poor. That was why I emigrated to West Germany — to seek my fortune, to make some money, so that in a few years time I could return with plenty of cash.

Since 1960 emigration has risen dramatically. Most emigrants come from the poorer, northern areas of Portugal. Like myself, they have small plots of land but cannot make a living from them. So they go to the industrial centers looking for work. However, they don't bargain on the high level of urban unemployment, and in the end they have to go farther afield – that is, abroad.

Many emigrants cannot settle in their new countries. It is estimated that some

400,000 people will have returned home in the decade 1980–90. Either they are homesick, or they want their children to go to school here, or they can't get work in their adoptive countries. I couldn't wait to get back.

After I returned, I decided to risk my money on buying a derelict house and turning it into a restaurant. My wife does the cooking and my oldest son and I see to the customers. Each day I go to the market to buy fresh fish, vegetables and fruit. I also buy 20 kg (44 lb) of meat from the local butcher. Our bread comes from a traditional baker, who makes corn and rye loaves in wood-fired ovens.

Our dishes are varied. My wife creates new recipes all the time, most of them based on regional cuisine. Most meals begin with soup – eight out of ten Portuguese consider they haven't had a complete meal without soup. As for the main course, they favor pork, roast kid (goat's meat) and beef. Fish is another favorite. Personally I have a very sweet tooth. I like our *ovos moles*, which is made with egg yolks and sugar.

The restaurant can serve eighty people at a time. During the week it is usually full of traveling salesmen. They nearly always have a local wine with their meals, and they usually end with a *bica*, a small cup of strong, black coffee.

I don't regret returning to Portugal. There's no place like home.

The oldest son of the family helps out in the restaurant.

"Sometimes the traffic is completely chaotic"

Maria de Moura Magolhaes, 26, joined the Seguranca police force five years ago. After training, she specialized in traffic control.

I have been a traffic cop for four years now. It's sometimes very tiring standing on high heels for three hours at a stretch in Oporto's cobblestoned streets!

Oporto has 600,000 inhabitants and is the second largest city in Portugal. It is situated in the northwest, at the mouth of the Douro River, which once formed a natural barrier to the territory to the north. These days three bridges link the city to the opposite shore. One of them, the Dona Maria Pio Railroad Bridge, was built by Eiffel, the famous French engineer: it is made entirely from cast iron. The Don Luis I Bridge serves both the upper and lower parts of the city and carries two roads across the water. And the 270-meter (886-ft) Arrabida Road Bridge – the one nearest the sea – was once the largest single-span concrete bridge in the world.

I've never had to direct the traffic on either of the road bridges. The main road from the second bridge runs north into a wide double avenue where the main squares and the Town Hall are found. I

Maria directs traffic in Oporto's busy shopping and commercial center.

The Don Luis I Road Bridge in Oporto.

usually direct traffic in the city's main shopping and commercial area. Actually there are very few wide roads in Oporto: the old town center is a maze of steep and narrow streets. Sometimes the traffic is completely chaotic – especially in winter when the streets are wet and the cars skid and bump into each other. During August 1985, there were 360 accidents, though few were fatal. Fortunately, there isn't much drunken driving here, as there is in Lisbon.

Policewomen work in shifts, six hours a day, from Monday to Friday. Women have been part of the Portuguese police force for only thirteen years. Today they represent 1.9 percent of the force – a higher proportion than on some other police forces. In Oporto the police force comprises 2,000 people, of which 130 are women. Women not only direct traffic – they also go on patrol, though usually with a male colleague.

In a city the Policia de Seguranca Publica is accountable to the *Gobernador Civil*, who represents the central government in the province. In small villages it is the Guardia Nacional Republicana (GNR) that supervise traffic control.

My daughter has just started walking. It won't be long before I start teaching her road safety. It could save her life.

"I take part in thirty bullfights each year"

Antonio Ribeiro Telles, 22, has been a bullfighter since he was a child. He lives with his father on the family ranch in Coruche, where he helps to train horses for the bullfights.

Today I have come to Santarem to take part in a bullfight. Santarem is the capital of Ribatejo province and overlooks a vast plain. The *Ferira da Piebad* is famous for its afternoon bullfights. Here they have held bullfights dating from medieval times, when it was a sport practiced only by kings and nobility.

I took part in my first contest as a *cavaleiro* – horseman – when I was twelve. I became a professional *cavaleiro* three years ago – after that time I was able to wear the special colored *cavaleiros* jacket in the ring. Until then I could only wear

Antonio trains his horse to get used to bulls.

the standard black jacket.

On the average I take part in thirty bull-fights a year. My father and older brother are also *cavaleiros*. In fact our family is known as a family of *cavaleiros*. Both my brother and I are taking part in today's contest. We drew lots and were each given two bulls to fight. Ribatejo bulls are the bravest bulls in the country.

After a procession around the ring, the *cavaleiro* starts the fight. My style is very different from my brother's. From the very first moment I call the bull and challenge him. My aim is to try to wear him down. Only then do I strike and bury the *farpas* – long and short spears – into the muscles on the bull's back.

Finally the *pega* begins. I give way to eight fighters called *moco de forcade*. Their leader has to seize the animal by the horns. The others help to distract the bull – one of them pulling him by the tail! The leader is often wounded – some leaders have even been killed.

The Cavaleiros *come into the ring.*

When it is all over, the bull is led away by a herd of *cabrestes* – castrated bulls – accompanied by *campinos* (cowboys). We never kill the bull in the ring as they do in Spain. The bull is sent to the slaughter house the next day.

So far I have never fallen off a horse during a bullfight. If I am riding a young horse, I ride it only when I am using the long spears, changing to a more experienced horse for the short spears. It takes about three years to train a horse to be good in the ring. It isn't just the steps the horses have to learn – they also have to know how to square up to a bull! Palhaso – a horse I rode today – is a good fighter. He is a thoroughbred English horse. Portugal has its own breed of horses – the Alter – but I prefer either English or Arab breeds.

I love being a *cavaleiro* and wouldn't want to do anything else.

"Our rooms are booked all the year"

Tourism is a big currency earner in Portugal. In 1985, 10 million people visited the country. Carlos Alberto Barroqueiro, 41, is a hotel manager in the Algarve, the popular tourist province in the south of the country.

I have been working in the tourist trade since I was sixteen. I have been a manager at hotels in Brazil and here in the Algarve for fourteen years. I was appointed manager of the Alcazar Hotel three years ago.

The Alcazar is in Monte Gordo, a resort well known for its white sand beaches and pine woods. The town was once a prosperous fishing port, but now tourism has taken over.

The most important area of tourism in Portugal is the Costa del Sol (Sun Coast), which extends west from Lisbon and includes Estoril and Cascais, but the Algarve is catching up fast. The Algarve derives its name from the Arabic *Al-Garbhe*, meaning "The West." Until the thirteenth century, it was under Moorish control. Here the weather is the main attraction: the average temperature is 20.8°C (70°F) throughout the year, and in the summer it can soar above 30°C (86°F).

Tourism is relatively new in this country. Since the 1960s, though, the Algarve has seen the construction of a

Hotel managers rarely have a chance to sit down for long.

staggering 39,580 hotels, motels and boardinghouses! In Monte Gordo itself there are only five hotels, which together hold about 2,500 tourists.

he Alcazar Hotel in Monte Gordo is one of the Igarve's many luxury hotels.

At the Alcazar we have 227 beds and 6 suites. Most of the rooms are booked hroughout the year: the tour operators rrange 95 percent of all our bookings. In vinter, most of our guests are British. In ummer, the British still predominate, but ley tend to be younger. We have 130 staff, ost of whom are employed all year ound. Besides making sure the hotel inctions on a day-to-day basis, I am also responsible for long-term planning.

Unlike the prices in Spain, our prices are not regulated by the government, which means that each hotel can charge what it likes. A couple staying overnight can expect to pay about 3,900 escudos ($27). But, of course, there are much cheaper places. You can stay in a boardinghouse for as little as 350 escudos ($2.40) a night.

I think Portugal's entry into the EEC will be of great benefit to the tourist trade. In a few years time the Algarve could be an even more important resort than it is now.

"The vision revealed herself as the Virgin Mary"

Portugal is a Roman Catholic country and between 60 and 80 percent of its people go to church every Sunday. Maria da Silva Ferreira is Mother Superior of the Sanctuary of Our Lady of Rosaria in Fatima.

A young Portuguese girl carries a banner celebrate the apparitions of the Virgin of Fatima.

There are certain special places to which God and the Virgin Mary grant favors. One such place is Fatima, where the Virgin Mary chose to make her six apparitions at the beginning of the century. My order — Servants of Our Lady of Fatima — was founded about the time of these apparitions and we exist solely to devote ourselves to her work. There are nineteen nuns in our order and we live in one of the fifty convents in the Fatima Sanctuary.

The first apparition occurred on May 13, 1917. Three children had a vision of a lady who promised to return on the thirteenth of each month until October of that year. She would then reveal her identity. In October thousands of people gathered to see the apparition, although no one except the oldest of the children, Lucia, saw her. Lucia said that the vision revealed herself as the Virgin Mary and that she ordered a chapel to be built on

Thousands of people come on pilgrimage to Fatima from all over the world.

he spot where she appeared, so that people could come and do penance for their sins. A few years later Lucia became a nun and is now in a convent in Coimbra. The other two children died three years later and are buried in the Basilica of Fatima.

In 1930 the Roman Catholic Church decided that the apparitions were miracles. As a result Fatima has become a place of pilgrimage and each year thousands of people come here from all over the world — especially between May and October. On August 13, Portuguese expatriates arrive from the far-flung parts of the world where they live and work. It's very moving to see them turn up with baskets full of wheat for Communion bread. This year over thirteen tons of wheat were collected.

My order was founded only a few years after the Portuguese Republic was estab-

lished in 1910. At that time we were persecuted by the authorities. So our founder decided that we should dispense with our habits – to avoid being detected – and we have worn ordinary clothes to this day. We started our work in the impoverished districts of Lisbon and now we run schools, and health centers, and help organize baptisms, weddings and funerals throughout the entire country. We also have missions abroad – in Mozambique, Canada and Belgium. Here in Fatima we look after the Basilica and Sanctuary and cater to the needs of those who come here for a spiritual retreat.

I will be staying on in Fatima for at least two more years. And I am looking forward to every minute of it!

"It's a journey through a time tunnel"

Antonio Peixeira, 44, has been a streetcar conductor for eight years. He believes there is no better way of seeing the most interesting and historical parts of Lisbon.

The fare is cheap, and I think the electric streetcar – the *electrico* – is a real bargain. There are twelve different routes in Lisbon, and I have worked on most of them. At the moment I am assigned to the Estrela route – No 28.

The first electric streetcar made its maiden journey on August 31, 1901. But trolleys had been pulled by horses for the previous thirty years. There are 94 km (58 miles) of track running through Lisbon, and about 300 trolleys running along them. I can think of worse ways of seeing our capital city!

Lisbon took over from Coimbra as capital of Portugal in 1255. Exactly five hundred years later 40,000 of the city's inhabitants were killed in an earthquake. Before the earthquake it was difficult to get around, because of the many alleys and cul-de-sacs. Modern Lisbon was conceived under the Marquis of Pombal's administration, in the eighteenth century.

Although the trolleys are old and slow, people enjoy riding on them.

Whole districts were rebuilt and buildings and streets were constructed on a much grander scale. Many new squares and parks were incorporated into the design of the city.

On my line there are 11 trolleys running at 6-minute intervals. The route is 8 km (5 miles) long – a 35-minute journey through a "time tunnel." The trolley starts from Largo Martin Munis, a part of modern Lisbon, then climbs to Alfama, the old medieval centre. On this route humble cottages stand next to palaces. We go through a labyrinth of narrow streets and alleys that cannot be reached by other forms of public transportation. There are places where the passengers can touch the washing hanging out of the windows!

Most of my passengers are women and children. The trolley gets crowded at rush hours. Accidents can happen when the streets are busy. In the past eight years I have been involved in fourteen accidents, though only five of them were my fault.

Despite the fact that trolleys are old and slow – they rarely exceed 20 km per hour (12 mph) – people seem to enjoy riding on them. In 1984 nearly 74 million people traveled this way.

Aside from streetcars, Lisbon's public transportation system consists of the railroad, the subway, buses and "lifts," for the most part administered by the Companhia Carris de Ferro de Lisboa. Lifts take people up the south-facing hills sloping down to the Tagus River. There are four lifts in the city – the Lavra, the Carmo, the Bica and the Gloria. The Gloria celebrated its centenary in 1985.

But it's trolleys I know most about. I hope I will be driving them for many more years to come!

Antonio's trolley on the route which takes in the historic S. Vincente district of Lisbon.

"I even decorated my own house with marble"

Manuel Monteiro Polido, 54, is the owner of a marble quarry near Sintra, in the Estremadura province. Although he bought the quarry in 1969, he did not start extracting the stone until 1985.

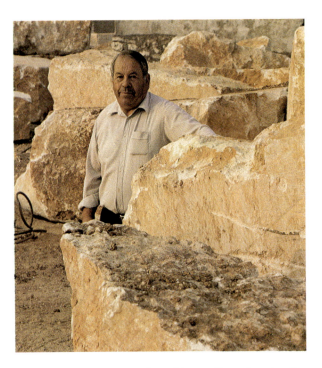

Red marble is mined at Manuel's mine in the Estremadura province.

I've just returned from the port of Setubal, where I sent off a consignment of marble to Japan. Another will be leaving soon – this time for the United States.

Basically there are two kinds of marble in Portugal – white marble from the Alentejo province and the red variety from here in the Estremadura province. It's an important industry, accounting for 17.3 percent of total mineral extraction.

In order to cut marble from the quarry, I use an electric cutting machine, which works like a chain saw. The sawing edge is water-cooled so that the chain doesn't snap. It takes about half an hour to cut an average-size slab.

Marble can also be cut using steel wires. This involves adding sand and water in order to provide the friction necessary to make any inroads into the stone. This method is primitive and it can take over a day to cut a piece of marble.

Marble is used mainly for building or ornamental purposes. I even decorated my house in Odrinhas with it. In Mafra, a town not far from here, they have a monastery whose basilica is made of marble. There is also a lot of marble in the buildings of Sintra.

Preparing to cut more stone from the quarry.

Sintra was built on the granite Serra de Sintra, a small mountain range. The unique climate of the Serra is a mix of Mediterranean warmth and heavy Atlantic rain. As a result, a dense, exotic, almost equatorial vegetation covers the hills. It was the Romans who gave Sintra its name, *cyntia*, meaning moon, which the Romans worshiped as a god. On one of the hills stands the Palacio da Pena, built in the nineteenth century on the ruins of an old convent destroyed by the 1755 earthquake. Members of the Portuguese monarchy often spent their summer vacations here.

As a one-time cyclist, I think I've seen most of what Portugal has to offer. But in my opinion the Estremadura province is by far the most beautiful part of the country. The poet Byron thought so too!

"Older factories need to be modernized"

Amelia da Conçeicão Albuqueruie, 39, has been working in the textile industry since 1970. She joined Clarcoop in Coimbra in 1977.

The textile industry is Portugal's oldest form of manufacturing. Until 1975, it was also our most important, but since then it has been superseded by the chemical industry. Today there are 203,294 people employed in textiles and clothing, most of whom are women. 27 percent of our total exports are textiles.

The woolen industry was developed in the eighteenth century, during the administration of the Marquis of Pombal. Before then only carpet making was of any importance, due mainly to Jewish refugees, who had settled in Arraiolos in

Most of the textile workers are women.

Amelia's job is to prepare the warp for the loom.

he Alentejo.

Woolens were first established on the lopes of the Cordillera (Central) Mountains, an area with many of the natural dvantages necessary for a thriving textiles industry, including sheep and abundant water. Covilha became the main enter and flourished between both world wars, at a time when there was ample heap labor. In 1940 two-thirds of all the ountry's woolens came from this town. y 1960 this figure had dropped to a third, ue largely to outdated machinery.

In Coimbra, cloth making began at the an Francisco Convent on the Modego iver. In the nineteenth century the convent was taken from the Church by the beral government and sold to a usinessman. He then put local textiles n an industrial footing.

I work at Clarcoop. During the 1974–76 ationalization, the factory was abandoned by its owner. The workers decided o take it over and turned themselves into cooperative.

Here I've learned all the processes involved in weaving. Now I specialize in preparing the warp for the loom. Most of the wool I warp comes from Australian or South African sheep. Portuguese wool is rarely used in cloth making nowadays.

Apart from weaving woolens and polyester cloth, we also make trousers. Recently we started buying cotton fabrics in order to produce light summer clothes. We export a great quantity of these, along with bedding and bathroom towels.

The cotton fabrics industry was initially developed in coastal areas – Lisbon, Aveiro and Coimbra – perhaps because 70 percent of our raw cotton was imported from Angola. Today the focus of the industry has shifted to the northwest – to Oporto, Braga and Guimaraes. In the last ten years, large new textile factories have sprung up here.

Old plants like ours needs modernizing, if only to make us more competitive in the world market. Next year we will move to new premises and soon we hope to be buying the latest machinery. It is up to us to make our cooperative work.

"The shipyard employs 2,000 people"

Joao Boaventura e Silva, 46, is a naval engineer at Estaleiros Navais in Viana do Castelo. He has been working there for eleven years and is now in charge of designing fittings for new vessels.

About 2,000 people work at the yards in Viana.

You'll find Estaleiros Navais in Viana do Castelo, at the mouth of the Lima River. Shipbuilding here dates back to the fourteenth and fifteenth centuries. Craft were built here with wood from the *Carvalho* tree, very common in these parts.

In 1944 some officials from Lisbon came to investigate the possibility of opening a shipyard that would build steel vessels. A year later the project got underway and today we are regarded as the largest construction unit after the Lisnave and Setenave yards at Lisbon and Setubal. At present we are building two chemical tankers for Brazil. We designed them too, as we do all ships built here. It takes us thirty months to build a tanker and costs around 35 million U.S. dollars.

We have just finished another coaster for the Soviet Union – the twelfth. We have been building dry cargo vessels of this type for the Russians for ten years now and we have just signed a new contract for more.

Since the 1970s, shipbuilding has been

in decline in Portugal. Very few oil tankers and other big ships are built anymore. And our merchant and fishing fleets rarely commission new ships, preferring to buy secondhand ones from abroad. If worst comes to worst, we could always do more repair work. At the moment we have two repair docks and on an average take 100 dockings a year.

Design materials, furniture and indoor paints are about the only Portuguese products we use. Everything else is imported. We have to buy foreign iron ore because we don't have enough of our own. And we also have to import finished steel and electronic equipment, the latter coming from Sweden.

Viana do Castelo is a town of around 20,000 people. The shipyard employs 2,000 of these. Most of them are also small-scale farmers who grow fruit and vegetables for their own consumption. If I had more spare time, I'd do the same!

One of the tankers for Brazil being built at the shipyard.

"Guarda station is busy 24 hours a day"

Joaquim dos Santos, 58, has been Guarda's stationmaster for eleven years. In all he has spent thirty-five years on the railroad and is due to retire soon.

Portugal had to wait until 1856 for its first railroad track. This ran between Lisbon and Carregado – 36 km (22 miles) in all. Many different companies – with mainly French and English backing – have constructed new lines since then. Several of them were taken over by the government in 1947 and the network was nationalized in 1975. Caminhos de Ferro Portuguesa

The railroad lines at Guarda Station are always busy.

(Portuguese Railroads) controls 4,720 km (2,933 miles) of track, although only 3,611 km (2,243 miles) are used.

Guarda Station is on the Beira Altra line. The track was started by a French company and finished in 1882 by the Companhia Real e da Beira Alta. It runs between Figueria da Foz, on the west coast, and Vilar Formoso on the Spanish border. It is a very beautiful line, traversing the Bussaco Forest – known for its 400 different varieties of trees – and the Mondego River. It is 225 km (140 miles) long.

At 1,056 meters (3,464 feet) above sea level, Guarda is the highest city in the country. Our station is busy 24 hours a day. Apart from the passenger and freight trains that pass through, there are four daily international trains running between Oporto, Lisbon and Paris. There are two other international lines – one that goes to Vigo in Spain, and another that goes through Alentejo to Madrid.

The Lisbon–Oporto line and Lisbon's suburban lines have dual tracks and are

A freight train, about to leave on its way to Figueira da Foz.

electrified. The rest of our network has single tracks and the coaches are pulled by diesel engines. Portuguese and Spanish railroads have a wider gauge than most European countries.

The rail network is much denser on the coast and north of the Sado River, which are areas of greater economic development. In the Algarve, tourism has been responsible for a good railroad system. The Douro, Tejo and Mondego valleys are also well served, and there are plans to modernize the Lisbon–Faro route. In the rest of the country public transportation is barely adequate.

The Portuguese love traveling by train – 72 percent of our services are passenger-only. As far as freight is concerned, we face stiff competition from road transportation. But we still carry all the really bulky materials such as wood, fuel, cement, oil and grain.

"I usually deliver the calves myself"

Antonio Pires Varela, 28, is in charge of the dairy unit on a farming cooperative in the Alentejo. He is married and has two children.

The Agrarian Reform of 1974–76 was very important for Portuguese farming. It allowed small farmers to band together to form collectives and work land that had not been exploited for a very long time.

The cooperative produces milk to a very high standard.

Historically, Portugal's farming methods have always been backward. One of the reasons was land distribution. In regions like the northwest, land was either badly fragmented or in the hands of big absentee landowners. In the Alentejo province – the largest, most sparsely populated and most fertile area of Portugal – the government put the land into the hands of the local collective production unit. The land is now administered by those who work it. 500,000 hectares (1,930 sq miles) of Alentejo land have been organized in this way, and 22,500 people, most of them women, are employed on them.

Our own collective covers 700 hectares (2.70 sq miles) and employs 420 people. We grow all kinds of grains – wheat, barley, corn, oats – as well as fruit and vegetables. We raise goats, sheep, pigs and cows – in all more than 10,000 animals. At the dairy unit we have 200 milking cows and 220 heifers and calves. Milk production started here eight years ago. In the beginning we had 40 cows, but they

weren't much good and so we had to milk sheep and goats. As the quantity and quality of the milk increased, we were able to buy better cows and improve our production. Each day a truck arrives to take 2,300 liters (607 gallons) of milk to a pasteurizing factory in Lisbon. We produce milk of a very high standard now.

My favorite cow is *Boneca*, which means Dolly. She's a Torina, a mix of English Friesan and Canadian Holstein. She gives 25 liters (6½ gallons) of milk a day. On average cows produce only 16 liters (4¼ gallons) during their two daily milking sessions. I delivered Boneca myself, and now I deliver her calves. I usually deliver all the calves unless we need the vet for a difficult birth.

Antonio inspects a young calf.

Most cows give milk for ten months a year, followed by two months rest, just before the birth of their next calf. We allow the calf to drink its mother's milk for the first five days only. After that, they get powdered milk. When they are three months old, they start eating adult food. Cows are artifically inseminated two months after their previous pregnancy. A cow can have about nine calves during its lifetime.

85 percent of milk production is undertaken by cooperatives now. There are 34,500 milking cows and 1,500,000 beef cattle in Portugal and the Azores. From this figure it is clear that the people much prefer eating meat to drinking milk!

45

"I've dedicated my life to television"

Maria Manuela Furtado, 50, is one of an increasing number of women who work in Portuguese television. Her colleagues claim that foreign TV executives say she *is* Portuguese television.

Television is the most important means of communication in Portugal. Radio Televisão Portuguesa (RTP) was founded twenty-eight years ago. It is state-owned and has two channels – RTP 1 and RTP 2. I have worked in the International Relations Department for the last twenty-five

The offices of Radio Televisão Portuguesa at Lisbon.

years. Now I am Under Director of this section. My job involves working with foreign television crews, making contacts with international broadcasting companies and representing Portugal at Eurovision events.

Today women work in most areas of the economy – in industry, where employment of women ranges from 69 percent (textiles) and 36.5 percent (food); in agriculture, where the average wage is 24 percent lower than a man's; and in education, the largest employer of women in the country. There are also a few women MPs (Members of Parliament) and we have had a woman Prime Minister. And, of course, there are women in the media! But there is still much illiteracy among women – particularly among the older generation and those living in rural areas. On top of that, very few women have reached the important decision-making posts.

I have had to work hard to get where I am. I have dedicated my life to television. But I am by no means the only one. There

are some good women journalists working here. In fact most interviews are conducted by women.

RTP has two broadcasting centers – one in Lisbon and one in Oporto. RTP 1 reaches 98 percent of the country, while RTP 2 reaches only 76–78 percent. In the islands of Madeira and the Azores, their local television stations compile programs with special material that we send to them. The news is transmitted to them via satellite.

During the week RTP 1 broadcasts from midday to 11:30 p.m. On Saturdays and Sundays it broadcasts all day. RTP 2 channel doesn't broadcast for quite so long. The news attracts the largest audience – four million people. The Brazilian soap opera gets good ratings too. But if there is

Maria is one of the few Portuguese women to have an important, decision-making job.

a soccer match – especially one between Portugal and another country – then everything stops and people sit glued to their TV sets.

In Lisbon there are three times as many TV and radio sets per 1000 people as in the rest of the country. Nearly all newspapers, weeklies and magazines, as well as other important publications, are produced in Lisbon or Oporto and sold mostly in the big cities along the coast. The best libraries, museums and theaters are also found in Lisbon and Oporto. So it is left to RTP – and the Catholic-owned radio station in Renasenca – to cater to the people in the rural areas.

"We want to restore and preserve our buildings"

Abilio Dias Fernandes, 47, ran as a Communist Party candidate in the first local government elections held in fifty years. He is now president of Evora City Council.

Evora is the capital of the mainly agricultural province of Alto Alentejo. It is thought to be the most important city in the south of Portugal. The Camara Municipal de Evora – the City Council – administers the local affairs of its 50,000 people. Most of them live in the city itself with some 10,000 in the surrounding countryside.

I have been President of the City Council

The Roman Temple of Diana at Evora.

since 1976. There are seven of us on the Council – in proportion to the number of voters in Evora. We carry out the programs and proposals agreed by the Municipal Assembly.

Ten years ago Evora was little more than an old historic center surrounded by thirty shanty towns. There was an acute water shortage and in most places there was no electricity or system of sewerage disposal. We have tried to develop our city to modern standards – often a slow and difficult task. We still have 1,200 families with housing problems. And without the support of the national government – responsible for all Portugal's eleven provinces and eighteen districts – we cannot hope to achieve our goals.

But a start has been made. We have built recreation centers, play areas and crèches. We organize cultural events involving local and national artists and performers.

The cathedral at Evora, the most important city in the south of Portugal.

We also collect the city's trash and look after the parks and cemeteries.

In 1982 we launched our conservation project. The historic core of Evora has changed little since medieval times, when a 4-km (2½-mile) wall was built around the city. Evora was conquered and settled by Romans, Arabs and finally by Visigoths, who arrived in the twelfth century. We want to restore and preserve our buildings, streets and squares, and to uncover the remnants of all the different cultures that are part of our heritage.

We have also started a whitewashing campaign. If owners and tenants want to brighten up their houses, they can apply for whitewash and paintbrushs from the Council. Sometimes we even do the job ourselves!

"We controlled most of the Indian Ocean"

Alzira Costa, 55, is the curator of Portugal dos Pequenitos, a model village in Coimbra. Its role is more educational than at first might be supposed.

Our model village tells the story of Portugal since the time of Prince Henry the Navigator. The buildings here – the houses, workplaces, churches, cathedrals, universities and forts – are scaled down to a convenient size. Children like them because they don't feel dwarfed!

I started here as an assistant to the nursery teachers in the crèche. That's many years after the establishment of the model village in 1941, though when I arrived the

The model village of Portugal dos Pequenitos was established in 1941.

section devoted to our ex-colonies had not been finished.

Portugal is fortunate to be near to both the Atlantic Ocean and Africa. In the fifteenth century we began to send vessels down the African coast. Then the explorer Vasco da Gama opened up a passage to the East Indies. By the mid-sixteenth century we controlled most of the Indian Ocean, establishing an arc of naval bases around the coast. We had also started to organize sugarcane plantations in Brazil, and we took slaves there from Africa to work on them. But by the early nineteenth century many of these possessions had either gained their independence or had been lost to other European powers.

Although Angola, Mozambique, Guinea and Cabo Verde became our colonies only at the beginning of this century, their people had started to press for freedom by the 1960s. For more than 10 years we were involved in a costly colonial war in which thousands of Portuguese and Africans died. Eventually these African colonies achieved their independence after the

The village is an original and interesting way of teaching children history.

Salazar/Caetano régime was brought to an abrupt end by the April Revolution in 1974. Today only one colony remains – Macao, in the Far East.

The man responsible for Portugal dos Pequenitos was Dr. Bissaya-Barreto, a Professor of Medicine at Coimbra University. He saw it as an original and arresting way of teaching children history. The village was built in stages and involved architects, artists and draftsmen from all over Portugal. After studying different buildings around the country, they then had to reproduce them here. They also had to decide on how best to show our overseas territories. Originally Angola and Mozambique were represented by two *cobatas* (straw huts), but later two forts were built, demonstrating Portuguese repression in these countries.

I get great pleasure out of telling children about our history. I hope my stay will be a long one.

"The Algarve is like a sieve"

José de Jesus Viegas, 42, was born in the district of Faro, part of the Algarve province, and has worked on the land since he was 17. He owns farmland around Pechao, which used to belong to his parents.

When I first started to work we grew mostly vegetables. I was one of the first farmers in the region to grow vegetables in greenhouses, known as *estufas*. Nowadays the majority of green vegetables are grown in this way, as are tomatoes, peppers, lettuce and even bananas. Most of this produce is sold at the market in Lisbon, but some is exported to other European countries, including Britain. We also grow flowers – more and more each year – which we export to the rest of Europe.

More recently I decided to start growing fruit, mainly citrus fruits such as oranges, tangerines and lemons. Portugal's cultivation of fruit began to develop in the sixties, and besides citrus fruits you will find peaches, figs, melons, strawberries, apples and pears. However, apples and pears do not grow so well in hot weather, so they are mostly found north of the Tejo River in the districts of Guard, Viseu and Castelo Branco.

The Algarve is ideal for growing citrus fruits, which need a hot climate and are very sensitive to frost. Nearly 60 percent – about 150,000 tons in 1985 – of Portugal's citrus crop comes from here. And our oranges and tangerines are sweeter than those from Lisbon, Santarem and Coimbra, because the high temperatures

The lack of water in the area is a very big problem for José.

in the Algarve allow the fruit to ripen earlier and at the same time develop a higher concentration of sugar. Yet in spite of this, Portugal imports oranges from Brazil which sell at prices cheaper than we can compete with.

The biggest problem we face here is lack of water. Although there is plenty of it, underground, it is not easy to reach. The Algarve is like a sieve – there are holes everywhere! As many as twenty new wells a month are dug and water is drawn up by pumps from a depth of about 200 meters (650 ft) into a system of irrigation channels. However, I believe the government could help us here, by building more reservoirs to take advantage of the rain that falls in the surrounding hills.

A farmer working on his own does not have the resources to sell and distribute his crops in the best way. Traditionally, middlemen have looked after this side of the business for us, making profits for themselves from our hard work. A few years ago a group of us got together and formed UNIHORTA, an association that deals collectively with the sales of our own produce. Not all farmers have organized themselves in this way, though, and they are bound to suffer from competition now that Portugal has joined the EEC. I don't know what will happen to them.

Planting seedlings can be backbreaking work.

"There is scope for improvement"

Maria Araujo Cunha, 48, is a nursery school teacher. She has been head of the Paraiso Infantil School since graduating from teachers' training college twenty-five years ago.

It was my mother who suggested that I open a private nursery school. She has been an elementary school teacher all her life and during that time came to realize there was an urgent need for nursery school education.

When I first started, there were no training schools for nursery teachers in Oporto. Now there are a few. Over three-quarters of all school teachers are women. But in nursery teaching there are no men at all. This is because nursery schools are sometimes regarded as substitute homes and nursery teachers as surrogate mothers. In 1985 the first two male teachers graduated from the Piaget Institute. But I think it will be difficult for them to find employment.

Usually children start attending nursery school at two. We have three age/ability groups here – a total of sixty-one children. They stay until they are six, when they start their elementary school education.

Nursery schools are still seen as a luxury in Portugal.

Children usually start nursery school at the age of two.

Though schooling is only compulsory for six years, the average middle class child spends twice that time in the classroom – four years in elementary, two in a pre-secondary school, five in secondary, and one in the equivalent of the twelfth grade in an American school. They then have the option of going on to further education.

In the state sector, there is a shortage of schools and teachers. Thousands of school children above the elementary level will not be able to start classes this year. The situation is worse in rural areas where there are even fewer schools and public transportation is unreliable. Children there often have to rely on *Telescola* (TV School).

The figures speak for themselves. In 1983, of the 168,501 children who finished elementary education, 11 percent did not continue with their studies. Today, nearly a quarter of the population is illiterate. It is estimated that 61 percent of those unable to read or write have received no schooling at all.

It says in our Constitution that private education should receive state support. But this doesn't happen. As a result, our fees have to be high and only a few parents can afford to send their children to us. Nursery schools are still seen as a luxury rather than as a necessary part of every child's education.

"Our parliamentary democracy must be defended"

Fernando Alves de Figueiredo, has been a Member of Parliament since 1975. He is a representative of the Social Democratic Party.

At dawn, on April 25, 1974, the Portuguese Armed Forces Movement, led mainly by young officers, carried out a bloodless coup and put an end to forty-seven years of dictatorship. The following year the first elections were held. I ran as a candidate for the PPD (Partido Popular Democratico) – now PSD (Partido Social Democrata). We spent our first parliamentary session writing the new republic's constitution, which was finally passed on April 2, 1976.

Our Assembly sits at Lisbon's seventeenth-century Palace of San Bento, in the Great Hall. We are a one-chamber Parliament.

During the years of dictatorship, political parties were banned. The Communist Party existed as an underground organization, but my party wasn't formed till after the April Revolution.

During the elections held on October 6, 1985, 250 members were voted into the Assembly, 246 representing the mainland, the Azores and the Madeira islands, and four representing our Portuguese emigrants. I represent our emigrants living in Europe. Though members are chosen locally, they represent the country as a whole.

Normally each legislative period lasts four years. But if the government is defeated on an issue, the Prime Minister

The busy Member of Parliament in his office.

may decide to call a general election. Each new parliamentary session starts in October and normally runs till mid-June, though sometimes it can be extended.

If you want to be a candidate, you have to get your party to sponsor you. Occasionally we run in coalition with another party. The final makeup of Parliament is achieved using a form of proportional representation, – the *Hondt* system, which allocates seats according to the percentage of votes won by each party. At the moment there are five major political parties in Parliament: my own party has the largest number of seats – eighty-eight out of a total of 250.

In Portugal we are a republic. The head of state is the President, who run in a separate election. If the President weren't elected, he could not appoint or dismiss the Prime Minister.

Central government is made up of several component parts – the Assembly, where the laws are passed; the Government, where they are enacted; and the Courts, where they are enforced. All laws have to be passed by a two-thirds majority and always need the President's approval. If he does not give it, the bill has to go back to Parliament for amendment.

Since 1974, we have had at least sixteen governments, including six provisional ones between 1974 and 1976 when the Constitution was passed. But our parliamentary democracy must be defended. We can't go back to the years of darkness under a dictatorship again.

The seventeenth-century Palace of San Bento, where the Portuguese Assembly convenes.

Facts

Capital city: Lisbon. (Population 817,600)

Language: Portuguese. The language is rooted in Latin and incorporates Arabic. It is also the language of Brazil and is spoken widely in Angola, Mozambique and Guinea-Bissau.

Currency: One escudos = 100 centavos. 1,000 escudos = one eonto. Rate of exchange (1986): 148 escudos = one U.S. dollar.

Religion: The established religion is Roman Catholicism. There are some Protestants, who make up about 1 percent of the population.

Climate: Mediterranean in the south, temperate in the north. In Lisbon, the hottest month is August, 17–28°C (62–82°F), the coldest is January, 8–14°C (46–57°F); the driest month is July and the wettest is January.

Population: 9,794,100 (1981 estimate). The most populous towns are Lisbon and Oporto.

Government: During the two years after the fall of the dictatorship in 1974 there was great political turmoil, with no fewer than six provisional governments. Elections for the Constituent Assembly were held in 1975, followed by elections for the Assembly of Representatives in 1976. The Socialist Party of Dr. Mario Suares won 37.8 percent of the vote. In 1979, the Center-Right coalition (Democratic Alliance) formed a Government. In 1983, the Socialists went into coalition with the Social Democrats. In 1986, the Socialists once again secured an absolute majority.

Defense: All fit males are liable for military service, although conscription is becoming increasingly selective, due to de-colonization and the need for a more professional army. The current joint strength of the armed services is 57,000.

Education: Free and compulsory from the age of 7 for 6 years. In 1979, there were 1,860,000 pupils to 97,000 teachers. Secondary schools are under great pressure at the moment, largely because of overcrowding. There are three old established universities – at Coimbra (founded 1290), Oporto and Lisbon. In recent years three new universities have been built.

Agriculture: The chief crops are oats, corn, wheat, rye, rice, barley, potatoes, beans, onions, olives, oranges, lemons, figs, almonds, tomatoes, and grapes (for port and for table wines). There are extensive forests of cork, pine, eucalyptus and chestnut covering 20 percent of the entire country. The last ten years have seen the emergence of the cooperative as a way of organizing agriculture.

Industry and trade: The country has not yet been fully industrialized, although great progress has been made over the last few years. The main industries include textiles, clothing and footwear, electrical goods, chemicals, fertilizers, cement, cork, glassware, wines and food processing. There is a modern steelworks and an important shipbuilding industry (at Lisbon and Sebutal). There are also several hydroelectric and thermal power stations. Principal exports include textiles, fruit, fish, timber, cork, chemicals, wines and electrical goods.

Newspapers and broadcasting: There are nine daily papers in Lisbon and four in Oporto and three main weekly papers. There are two national TV channels (broadcasting in color) and five national radio stations (four of which are state-controlled).

Glossary

agglomerate Materials of different size and consistency processed into a whole.

artificial insemination Fertilization of a female animal by artificial means.

centrifuge A machine rotating at high speed and designed to separate solids from liquids, or liquids from other liquids.

ceramics Products made by firing clay or minerals at high temperatures.

collective A jointly-operated venture in which workers pool their resources and share their profits.

constitution The set of rules and laws by which a country is governed.

crèche A day nursery for infants.

curriculum A course of study.

democracy A form of government whose members have been freely elected by the people as their representatives.

emigrant Someone who leaves his or her country to settle in another.

European Economic Community Also called the Common Market. An association composed of most of the Western European countries, which cooperate in matters of trade and economic policy.

nationalization The transfer of an industry (e.g. railroads, coalmining) from private to state ownership.

pasteurization Partial sterilization by heating; a process developed by Louis Pasteur.

republic A state in which power is held by the people or its elected representatives, or by an elected or nominated president.

socialist Someone who believes that a country's wealth should belong to the people as a whole, not to individual private owners, and that the state should control and decide how these resources should be used.

surrogate A person acting as a substitute.

vocational A form of training which relates to a specific trade or profession.

Index

NOTHING IS IMPOSSIBLE

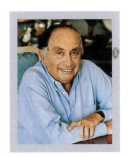

Gabriel Kune

Nothing is Impossible

THE

John Saunders

STORY

GABRIEL KUNE

SCRIBE PUBLICATIONS

MELBOURNE

Scribe Publications Pty Ltd
PO Box 287
Carlton North, Victoria 3054
Email: scripub@ozemail.com.au

First published 1999 by Scribe Publications

Text and cover design by Pauline McClenahan, Captured Concepts
Typeset in Perpetua by Captured Concepts

Printed and bound in Australia
by Impact Printing

National Library of Australia
Cataloguing-in-Publication data

Kune, Gabriel.
Nothing is impossible: the John Saunders story.
Bibliography.
Includes index.
ISBN 0 908011 41 5

1. Saunders, John, 1923–97. 2. Westfield Holdings Ltd.– Officials
and employees – Biography. 3. Businessmen – Australia – Biography.
4. Hungarians – Biography. 5. Hungarians – Australia – Biography.
6. Directors of corporations – Australia – Biography. 7. Philanthropists
– Australia – Biography. I. Title.

338.092

CONTENTS

Whatever you can do, or dream you can do, do it.

Boldness has genius, power, and magic in it.

GOETHE (1749–1832)

We must rethink the possibility of the impossible.

JACQUES DERRIDA (1930–)

The great pleasure in life is doing what

people say you cannot do.

ANONYMOUS

ACKNOWLEDGEMENTS

It would have been impossible to write this biography without the help and advice of many members of John Saunders' family, as well as many of his friends, business associates, and other individuals who came into contact with him during his extraordinary life. Everyone gave of their time and expertise freely. This was in itself an indication of the high regard in which John Saunders was held. However, any mistakes or errors of omission or commission are likely to be mine, and not made by those who provided the information.

I spent many hours interviewing John Saunders over an 18-month period, and subsequently carefully reviewing with him the first draft of this biography. He was extremely liberal and sympathetic towards my interpretation of events. At no stage did he suggest that I 'rewrite history', nor did he even vaguely or indirectly pressure me to adopt a revisionist view of past events.

His three children, Betty Saunders-Klimenko, Mark Saunders, and Monica Saunders, were most happy to be interviewed. They provided me with many important insights and subtle clarifications about their perceptions of their father's life. His sisters, Gita Klein and Lilly Somogyi, spoke about their brother's early life. His ex-wife, Klara Saunders, provided me with useful information.

Laczi Mizsák, who was one of John Saunders' employees in his woodworking factory after World War II, and who still lives in Sátoraljaujhely in north-east Hungary, took me around Saunders' home town in 1997. He also gave me invaluable information about life in the town just before and during the war, and after liberation.

John Saunders' close friend from the concentration camps of Garany, Auschwitz, and Dörnhau, Feri Vadász, as well as his partner Rózsa Lukács, provided me with invaluable information and clarification about life in Hungary just before and during the Second World War, as well as about life in the concentration camps. Dr Alfred Pasternak MD, now of Los Angeles, who was also with John Saunders in the Auschwitz and Dörnhau concentration camps, was most helpful in illuminating the noble behaviour of his friend whilst interned.

John's friend after escaping from Hungary, Cantor Michael Deutsch, talked about their time together after the war in Vienna and during their early days in Australia. Other early friends of John Saunders—Sam Moss, Andrew Lederer OAM, Joseph Brender AO, as well as Ervin Graf—were most gracious in talking to me about their long-time friend.

A special place in the acknowledgements goes to Frank Lowy AO, who was the co-founder of Westfield with John Saunders. His was the other half of a partnership that lasted for 33 years, and a friendship that remained after the two men's commercial separation. Frank Lowy gave me invaluable information and advice, and made constructive suggestions about several parts of the manuscript. I am most grateful to him for this.

In the same way, Neville Wran AC QC, and Bob Hawke AC, both long-time friends of John Saunders, gave of their time to be interviewed, and provided me with new insights and illuminations about several aspects of the life and character of John Saunders.

Several past executives of Westfield gave unstintingly of their time for interviews: these included Ben Nathan, John Bock, Brian Woolstone, John Biro, Bill Szabolcs, Jim Doe, and John Craig. Judy Hall, a current executive with Westfield, also spoke to me about her perceptions of John Saunders.

The executives of the Terrace Tower Group of Companies filled me in about aspects of the business life of John Saunders after his separation from Westfield. In particular I would like to thank David Dinte, managing director and chief executive officer of the group, as well as Sam Samuels, Bernard O'Hara, and John Davidson.

Rabbi Brian Fox, then of Temple Emanuel, Sydney, and now in Manchester in England, explained at length John Saunders' considerable charitable contributions to Jewry, in Australia and overseas.

Others who have talked to me about John Saunders include Sir Tom North, a previous chairman of G J Coles and Company, and Charlie Lynn, a member of the Legislative Council of the New South Wales parliament.

Professor Richard Rahe of the University of Nevada talked to me at length about the mindset of someone like John Saunders whose achievements were substantial in the face of major adversity, and also about what is now referred to as the 'gut-brain'—something that John Saunders utilised throughout his life with great success. Similarly, Angelo D'Amelio of Landmark Education in the USA and Dr David Miles, of Landmark Education in Australia, talked to me about the recipe for and the advantages and dangers of the so-called 'winning formula' which John Saunders utilised throughout his life.

The author Gillian Bouras explained to me some of the desirable elements of biography writing. I am grateful to Kay Ronai for editing drafts of the manuscript. Elizabeth Kennedy, LLM, advised me most wisely on anything I might have written inadvertently in the book that could have been interpreted as injurious to any person or organisation. My secretary of many years, Elaine Downard, typed the manuscript and its many drafts with her usual grace.

My relationship with the publisher, Scribe Publications, and in particular, Henry Rosenbloom, has been a happy and constructive one. We worked together in harmony to produce this book.

The Prime Minister of Australia, John Howard, was most gracious in giving of his precious time to be interviewed at length about John Saunders. Mr Howard also agreed to write the foreword to this book, an act which I appreciate immensely and regard as a great honour to the memory of the late John Saunders.

FOREWORD

John Saunders was a passionate Australian who exemplified the massive contribution made to post-World War Two Australia by a very special group of men and women born in Europe.

The life of John Saunders can be characterised as one of rising above personal tragedy and horrible evil, of optimism in the face of desolation, and of inspirational commercial skill and generosity.

Born in 1922, Jenö Schwarcz was the son of a small leather-goods shop owner in north-east Hungary. Jenö developed a keen eye for business at an early age. Two years after the untimely death of his father, Jenö took over the running of the shop at the age of thirteen and doubled turnover within a year.

Interned by the Nazis in 1943 at Garany, Jenö was taken with hundreds of Jews to Auschwitz. He survived this fate and was transferred to a forced-labour concentration camp in Dörnhau. On the day he was liberated, Jenö described it as 'the day I was reborn'.

Resuming the leather shop after the war, Jenö also started a broomstick factory only to have his businesses nationalised, escaping to Austria penniless in 1949.

On a midsummer's day in 1950 he arrived in Sydney with his wife on the cargo ship *El Misr*. Working first as an upholsterer then as a storeman and packer, Jenö opened a sandwich shop at Town Hall Station in Sydney where he met a delivery boy, Frank Lowy. The two were to forge a 30-year partnership. They first opened a delicatessen in Blacktown and later established the Westfield Shopping Centre Group in 1958, which helped to redefine consumer habits in the 1960s and 1970s.

Jenö changed his name to John Saunders, taking out Australian citizenship and vowing to give back to the country that had sheltered him.

Saunders was to become one of our great Australian philanthropists, giving to a wide range of good causes such as the Deaf and Blind Society, Israeli welfare organisations, and heart and diabetes research. John Saunders also opened HopeTown Special School on the NSW central coast to help mildly intellectually disabled children.

Meanwhile the Westfield group grew into one of the world's largest shopping-centre development and management companies. In the mid-1980s Saunders resigned his joint chairmanship of Westfield to pursue his own business interests with his Terrace Tower Group, and subsequently became a significant property owner and developer.

One of the great legacies of John Saunders is the Sydney Jewish Museum, which he established in the hope that the horror of the Holocaust will never be forgotten.

Saunders died in December 1997 aged 75, and is survived by his daughters Betty and Monica and his son Mark.

John Saunders was, in every sense of the word, a metaphor for the remarkable contribution that was made to Australia by the Jewish people of eastern Europe who fled the most appalling manifestation of human evil that the history of the world has seen.

They came to Australia, in almost all cases, without any capacity to speak English and, within a generation, left their mark on commerce and business as well as community and charitable endeavours. From that background they came and, as John Saunders exemplified, went on to become forever Australian.

John Howard

John Howard
Prime Minister

CHAPTER 1

A Second Opinion

Monday, 28 March 1977 was one of those impossible days. I rose at six, visited my patients recovering from surgery in several Melbourne private hospitals, and commenced an operating session at eight o'clock at the Royal Melbourne Hospital. I had two demanding abdominal operations to perform that morning, both on patients who had had several operations elsewhere—what we in the trade call 'salvage surgery'. I finished operating approximately an hour later than planned, at two in the afternoon, and rushed into my office for consultations with patients who were already lined up in the waiting room and were quite obviously unhappy with my lateness.

At about four o'clock that afternoon a phone call came through from Sydney. The caller identified himself as Dr Sanyi Pollack. 'I practised medicine in your home town of Kassa in Hungary. I have also known your parents for many years', he told me.

'How can I help you?', I asked, perhaps a touch curtly.

'There is a very sick woman in hospital here in Sydney who has had surgery', Dr Pollack said. 'She has had her gallbladder removed, and is now extremely ill as a consequence of an unexpected complication of surgery. She possibly has peritonitis, and there is also bile coming to the exterior from the drainage tube. Her brother was wondering if you could come to Sydney today to give a second opinion.'

'Dr Pollack', I said wearily, 'I haven't quite finished my work for the day, and I have really had a most difficult day. However, I would be more than happy to let you have the names of experts in this field in Sydney.'

Dr Pollack would have none of it. 'I'd be grateful if you could come yourself. I have read your textbook on the surgery of the gallbladder and bile ducts, as has my son, who is also a doctor, and I would greatly value your advice. This woman's brother would like to call you shortly.'

About five minutes later, there was a further phone call from Sydney. 'John Saunders is my name', the caller announced. 'I wonder if you would come to Sydney to give a second opinion on my sister?'

'I am afraid it is not so easy for me to do that, because I still have not finished my scheduled work for the day', I said.

For the second time in a few minutes, my objections were ignored. 'I have booked a plane for you for seven o'clock this evening', Mr Saunders said, 'and I will pick you up personally at the airport'. He sounded a very worried, very sympathetic person over the phone, so I agreed to go.

I caught the plane, and was duly picked up by John Saunders. Dr Pollack was there as well. He said that he could remember me from Kassa when I was a child and also, after he had migrated to Melbourne and before he had settled in Sydney, when I had some kind of a rash. I didn't say so, but I couldn't recall him at all. John Saunders immediately drove us to the private hospital where his sister Gita was being treated. As we entered the intensive care department, I regrettably committed a blunder of medical etiquette—I did not wait for the surgeon who had performed the operation before seeing his patient. The surgeon was late, John Saunders and Dr Pollack appeared quite worried and, frankly, I was tired and, just at that stage, not very concerned about the niceties of the situation. I went into the ward and examined this poor woman who was semi-conscious and unable to speak. She had a high temperature, was a little tender in the abdomen, and was draining some bile externally through the drainage tube inserted at the time of her gallbladder operation. She was very ill indeed.

I examined her and looked at all her x-rays, including an x-ray of the bile duct performed during surgery. This was a procedure called an operative cholangiogram. A very careful examination of the cholangiogram revealed something unusual that might have been the explanation for her problems. I thought I could just discern a small duct known as the duct of Luschka. This tiny bile duct, not wider than 1 mm, is present in only a small proportion of people, lies very close to the gallbladder wall, and can be inadvertently damaged while the gallbladder is being removed. If such an accident occurs during surgery it can lead to a dangerous, sometimes fatal, accumulation of bile in the abdominal cavity. This small duct can be damaged inadvertently because it is usually not possible to see it during surgery—particularly so when it runs very close, and actually adheres, to the gallbladder wall. In fact, the possibility that such a tiny bile duct may be cut unknowingly during surgery is one of the reasons that a drainage tube is inserted after gallbladder surgery: if such damage has occurred, the bile can drain out freely and not collect dangerously within the abdominal cavity. I should say, for the record, that such a tiny duct usually cannot be seen during surgery by even the most competent of surgeons, and that damaging it is an acknowledged inherent risk of the operation. It most certainly does not amount to a lack of surgical expertise.

Serendipitously, ten years previously I had conducted detailed research into the precise position of the bile ducts, and why their location is important during operations performed in this part of the body. This work focused particularly on the variability of these ducts in different individuals, and why these anatomical variations can sometimes result in a bile duct injury during surgery of the gallbladder. The research consisted of over 100 anatomical dissections of the bile ducts, as well as the careful examination of several hundred cholangiogram x-rays. As a result of this work, I was invited in 1970 by the Royal College of Surgeons of England to deliver The Arris and Gale Lecture. One of my important findings was the rediscovery of a small bile duct, which I later learnt was first described in Germany by Dr H Luschka in 1863. Through this research, it was also possible to link for the first time an injury of this duct during gallbladder surgery to one of the causes of bile leakage after operation. For these reasons, I was therefore acutely aware not only of the likely position and appearance of this tiny bile duct on the x-ray film of the operative cholangiogram, but I also knew that anatomical knowledge of the existence of this structure and its surgical significance had not yet reached mainstream surgery. Importantly, I strongly suspected, after reviewing Gita Klein's x-rays, that this duct was the cause of her bile leakage.

The surgeon was a well-known and extremely competent surgical specialist, and there was absolutely no doubt in my mind that he had done his best; there was certainly never any suggestion or question of incompetence or negligence. He arrived a little later, and made it quite clear to me that he was upset about my seeing Gita before talking to him. I apologised, explaining the circumstances. He then gave me her clinical history, and told me that he was contemplating re-operation. I had a different view about her treatment. 'This lady is so ill that, in my opinion, she couldn't take further major surgery', I said. 'She couldn't even handle a haircut. Also, I do not believe that an operation is necessary, as she does not have definite signs of bile peritonitis. Furthermore, on the operative cholangiogram I can see this little bile duct, which was inadvertently divided, and which I believe is responsible for the bile leakage.' The important point here was that major bile ducts, when damaged, never heal without further surgical intervention. By contrast, when this little duct is damaged it closes spontaneously and results in no late complications or *sequelae*, provided the bile can be satisfactorily drained out of the body through a drainage tube.

The surgeon and I then had a lengthy discussion about Gita's future management. With the new information I had provided, he agreed that further surgery was not necessary at this stage. As well, because of the special abnormalities of fluid and mineral balance that can occur following such prolonged bile leakage, she needed some changes in her intravenous fluid therapy, which we discussed with the doctor in charge of the intensive care unit. She also needed a change in her antibiotics and regular manipulation of the drainage tube every twelve hours, to make sure that there were no little pockets of bile remaining in her abdomen.

After the consultation, John Saunders and I went off to the Boulevard Hotel, where I was spending the night, and we had a meal and some wine together. I was very hungry and in need of a glass of wine after such a long day. It was here and in these circumstances that my friendship with John Saunders really began. I immediately found him a very interesting and sympathetic person.

The following morning I left Sydney on the first available plane so that I could start operating back in Melbourne at a private hospital by eight o'clock. I stayed in daily telephone contact with the hospital, the surgeon, and John Saunders. Gita became a little worse over the following twenty-four hours because of the twelve-hourly manipulation of her drainage tube. Such manipulation often releases bacteria that have collected near the tube or on the tube itself to pass into the general blood circulation. This results in short periods of blood-borne infection known as bacteraemia or septi-caemia. Happily, two days after my consultation she was a little better, and she improved again the following day. When I visited her the following week-end, it was clear that she had turned the corner. Gradually Gita recovered, and slowly regained her health over a three-month period.

As a postscript, I was so inspired by this case and several others that, with my associates, I wrote a paper which was published in the prestigious *British Journal of Surgery* in 1989, and which may have helped to bring into promi-nence the significance of this small bile duct.

CHAPTER 2

MISCHIEVOUS BOY

Béla and Berta Schwarcz were overjoyed with the birth of their second child and first son in November 1922. He was named Jenö and later nicknamed Jenczi (pronounced Yentsi). Béla had a small leather business in the main street of Sátoraljaujhely, which was the almost unpronounceable name of a small town of 22,000 inhabitants in north-eastern Hungary. Béla was a greatly respected and trustworthy citizen who spent much of his spare time helping the town's poor and needy. This kind man, even in his dreams, could not have imagined that his son, young Jenö, would one day become one of Australia's greatest businessmen.

What sort of a world did this baby boy come into? There was serious trouble brewing in Europe. The Italian Fascist Party, led by Benito Mussolini, 'Il Duce', was granted absolute power by the Italian Chamber of Deputies in the same year that Jenö was born. The German mark continued its rapid fall in value, foreshadowing economic disaster for Germany and much worse for European Jews. The British were strong, exploitative, and uncompromising, ruling almost one-quarter of the world's surface; they sentenced the Indian nationalist Mahatma Gandhi to six years in jail. The United States was rapidly becoming the most important economic force in the world. In Canada, Frederick Banting and Charles Best isolated insulin from the pancreas gland of the dog, and showed that an injection of this hormone cured experimentally created diabetes in dogs. Insulin soon became a lifesaver to millions of diabetics; many years later, insulin was also to be of great benefit to Jenö Schwarcz.

Australia remained blissfully unaware of the world in 1922. Sydney celebrated plans for the construction of its harbour bridge, and a record crowd of 115,000 saw King Ingoda win the Melbourne Cup. A new airline named QANTAS (Queensland and Northern Territory Aerial Services), later to become a global airline giant, and which up to then had only carried mail, commenced a passenger air service in Queensland.

The town of Sátoraljaujhely, situated at the foot of a low mountain range, and adjacent to the renowned Tokaj wine-growing district, was one of Hungary's little gems. Nineteenth-century Italianate houses and public buildings adorned its main streets. It was an important centre for schooling, commerce, and industry, and it was also a busy railway junction. The major employer was a tobacco factory, now owned by the large American company, Reynolds.

The First World War destroyed the Austro-Hungarian Empire. Between them, two post-war treaties—the Treaty of Trianon and the Treaty of St Germain—reduced Hungary to a quarter of its former size. Its territories were ceded to Romania, the newly formed Czechoslovak Republic, Yugoslavia, and Italy. The carving up of Hungary was done in good faith, in order to create states out of national minorities. But the new states also created Hungarian minorities. For example, in 1920 the southern part of the new Slovakia was almost entirely populated by ethnic Hungarians. Trianon turned Sátoraljaujhely into a border town with the Slovakia part of the new Czechoslovak Republic. As a border town, its significance diminished slightly, although it still remained the capital of one of Hungary's counties, the Zemplén county. At the time of Jenö's birth there was a large, well-established Jewish community in the town. Jenö attended the famous Kestenbaum Jewish School.

A family man who lived frugally, Béla Schwarcz had good business sense, got on well with people, and was trusted by his leather suppliers. Young Jenö, a happy child, seems to have sensed these positive human traits in his father early in childhood and made them his own in adolescence and adult life. His mother, Berta, was a quiet, supportive, and caring woman who brought up four children: Lilly, eighteen months older than Jenö; Gita, eighteen months younger than him; and the youngest boy, Ernö, born in 1930. In 1932 when Jenö was just ten years old, Béla Schwarcz became ill, and his illness was eventually diagnosed as leukaemia, a cancer of white blood cells. He consulted doctors in Sátoraljaujhely as well as specialists in Budapest, and was advised to have many forms of treatment including x-rays to his liver and spleen. These were very expensive, creating a major financial burden for the family. In 1932 there was no real cure for leukaemia, and Béla succumbed in September 1933.

The tree-lined main street of
Sátoraljaujhely and the main
square, with the large Roman
Catholic church in the background. The heroic statue of
Kossuth, the 1848 Hungarian
revolutionary and a native of
Zemplén County, is in the fore-
ground. The Schwarcz family
leather shop is directly behind
the woman on the left wearing
a white blouse with a folded
white parasol in her right hand
(All these postcards of
Sátoraljaujhely were taken in
the 1920s, about the time Jenö
Schwarcz was born)

Another part of the main street
with the County Hall and
Library built in 1768, now the
main Administrative Centre

Part of an important shopping street and meeting place, Rákoczy Street, with its nineteenth-century Italianate houses. Note shop owners' family names, such as Klein and Burger—witness to the strong and fully integrated Jewish component of town life at the time

The State-owned tobacco factory was the major employer of the town. This factory remains largely unchanged, and is now owned by the American tobacco company, Reynolds

The illness and death of Béla Schwarcz had a profound effect on young Jenö—an effect that remained with him for the rest of his life. From then on, he hated to go to hospital either as a patient or as a visitor. He disliked medical treatment of any kind, and particularly any intervention such as surgery or even an injection. He suppressed or ignored symptoms. He would never complain, even when he was obviously quite unwell. This attitude, as well as his positive approach to his life when he was unwell, became very useful for his survival during difficult times in his early life. However, in later life, when survival was not an issue, secrecy about his symptoms and non-compliance with suggested treatments was to cause major difficulties for his doctors.

Jenö's instinctive understanding of his father had left him with the legacy of a sharp business mind, and of knowing the importance of being totally trustworthy in business and in life. Just like his father, Jenö devoted a large part of his later life to helping people—not only his family and friends, but also the community he lived in.

He was a mischievous lad who did not greatly enjoy formal learning. He was only interested in learning what his instincts told him were to be important for his future life—reading, writing, arithmetic, and other practical skills. In primary school he got up to many pranks. One of these concerned a bearded teacher who was in the habit of falling asleep during class. Whenever this happened his head would drop, and his beard would brush over the front of the desk. On one of these occasions, Jenczi glued his beard to the desk. The teacher woke with a start and, as he lifted up his head, nearly pulled his beard right off. The teacher knew immediately who the offender was.

Jenczi Schwarcz continued his formal education for two years after his father's death, until his Bar Mitzvah at the age of thirteen, when he decided to start his second life.

CHAPTER 3

MOTHER'S LITTLE HELPER

*He held the lantern while his mother
chopped the wood.*

ANONYMOUS

Jenö Schwarcz stood in front of the Torah at his Bar Mitzvah. On this momentous day when, according to tradition, he took his place in the Jewish community as a man, he made a dramatic decision. Jenö left school, and immediately joined his mother in the family's small leather shop on the main street of Sátoraljaujhely. The shop was part of the fabric of the town: it stood just across from the large Catholic church in the main square of the town, and there was a wine tavern in the basement. His older sister, Lilly, also left school and started to work in the leather shop. Today, the shop is a hair salon, and the only evidence of the wine tavern is a small square window just above footpath level, which no doubt served as the sole form of ventilation for the alcoholic vapour and smoke.

For as long as he could remember, Jenö had wanted to be in business, so his new role was a natural transition. Moreover his father had served as a role model. Jenö soon took over the running of the business, and within a year the turnover of the leather shop doubled. In the evenings, he studied by correspondence to complete his secondary education.

What might have been the reasons behind the rapid business success of this young teenager? Although there were many boot makers in town, the Schwarcz leather shop survived initially because their main leather supplier had great trust in Jenö's father. Then, after Béla's death, they sent one of the directors from Budapest to the leather shop. He told Jenö that the company would still support his mother and, as he was leaving the shop, the director said, 'You can buy as much leather as you need from us, and just pay us when you can.' This was an unbelievable situation in the 1930s, when the Great Depression gripped the world and credit on goods was uncommon.

As we shall see shortly, Jenö was also the beneficiary of a long tradition of Jewish traders in the region. His innate ability to get on with all classes of people—market traders, customers, peasants, leather manufacturers, and even members of the local Hungarian nobility—seems also to have been important in his achieving business success. He started to take leather boots to sell at the spring local markets, which usually commenced in February

A 1920s' postcard of the main street of Sátoraljaujhely, the place of the Sunday promenade known as the 'Corso'. The Schwarcz family residence, which remains largely unchanged today, is the house just to the left of the shop whose owner was named Adolf Lövy. The Schwarcz family occupied the front apartment on the first floor with the balcony. The family leather shop is to the left of the Catholic church, as seen in the photograph at the top of p 10

A recent photograph of the Schwarcz family leather shop, now a hair salon (second shop from the corner). The only external evidence of the wine tavern that was situated in the basement is the small square window just above footpath level, below and to the right of the shop window. It served as ventilation for the alcoholic vapour and smoke in the tavern each year, thereby getting to know many other traders and customers. He became acquainted with the Richter family, who imported and sold spices and groceries in the nearby villages. Jenö travelled with them when they were selling their merchandise, and was able to make deals with the local merchants so that they would sell various leather goods that he supplied, such as soles or heels. He also came to an agreement with them that they could pay for their supplies later.

Young Jenö's gift for getting on with people is fascinating, because this trait remained very important and had many facets. Jenö did not care about class distinctions, nor did he discriminate according to a person's background or education. Yet at the same time he was able to deal with each person at whatever level was appropriate. He was always an excellent observer, a great listener, and someone who did not jump in with his set piece. All of these attributes helped him to understand people. As well, his keen sense of humour and a degree of mischievous behaviour just added to his charm and ability to get on with all sorts of people. Working on a basis of trust established many good and lasting friendships, and there were few defaulters. Added to all this, Jenö had an excellent memory and an amazing facility to do even quite complicated sums in his head. He already possessed the basic qualities needed to become a successful businessman.

Life was hard, yet Jenö still had time for his friends and the simple pleasures they enjoyed together. He loved to walk, particularly in the main street of the town. This was an activity known as 'doing the corso'—talking with his friends, ogling and flirting with the girls. At times he would invite his friends home to the front apartment of the nineteenth-century Italianate building that the family rented. His mother would make tea with real lemon and sugar cubes (things that were hard to get in Hungary at that time), or she would serve real coffee and 'penetzli', slices of bread toasted in the oven with butter and then smeared with a little fresh garlic. Among his friends were two sets of brothers: the Korda boys, Csi Csi (Les) and Imre (Eric) who lived fifty kilometres away in Kassa; and the Pongrácz boys, Sanyi (Alex) and Gyuri

(George) from nearby Sárospatak, who met Jenö while visiting relatives in Sátoraljaujhely.

Today, these men remember Jenö as a happy, slightly overweight, mischievous, and somewhat shy adolescent who was not particularly successful flirting with the young girls of the town. They remember him being accepted by his peers, but certainly not being thought of as one of the leaders. Modern ontological theory would have it that it was then that Jenö made a major decision and said something like this to himself: 'There is something wrong here. I am failing to be enough, failing to belong. I shall correct this and become successful, and not only with women.' This way of being became his trademark for the future.

The dark forces of evil were gathering momentum in Europe while Jenö and the Schwarcz family were enjoying their work and their life. There were warning signs of danger for European Jewry surfacing in Germany, Italy, Austria, and even in Hungary in the 1930s. Yet many Jews did not appreciate the gravity of the situation. To understand this, we need to take a closer look at the history of Jews in the Zemplén region of Hungary.

Legend has it that some Jews had lived and traded in the Zemplén area since Roman times. There is also historical evidence that they became traders in the region from the tenth century onwards when the Magyar tribes, spearheaded by the Kabar-Khazars, who held the Jewish faith, invaded and occupied Hungary from the east. In a fascinating account of one of the origins of European Jewry, Arthur Koestler writes in *The Thirteenth Tribe*: 'There may have been a small number of Jews living in Hungary from Roman days, but there can be little doubt that the majority of this important portion of modern Jewry originated in the migratory waves of Kabar-Khazars, who play such a dominant part in early Hungarian history.'

There is certainly strong, well-documented evidence of intense trading activity among Jews over the past three hundred years, lasting until the middle of the twentieth century when they met their dreadful fate in the Holocaust. The earliest authenticated record of trading is of Jews buying wine in the Tokaj district in the seventeenth century. Jews were the first to be regular wine-buyers and, subsequently, vignerons who initially leased their property. Later, they also leased flour mills and taverns in which alcoholic drinks were sold; they traded in timber, furs, and leather; and they were coach builders. The alcohol connection is interesting, because Jews as a group drink little alcohol and the profession is in marked contrast to the typical Jewish lifestyle.

In the eighteenth century, Jews were generally under feudal patronage, and their lot was probably only a little better than that of vassals. Some became travelling traders in the villages, and others continued to sell wine. Almost all were poor and in the lowest socio-economic strata. Jews were still not accepted as members of craft or merchant guilds. High taxes were also exacted from them, quite apart from them having to pay rent to the local nobility. Gradually, Jews were able to organise themselves into communities in which they had schools, synagogues, and burial grounds. At the end of the century, Sátoraljaujhely assumed a position of importance in the region and became a centre of commercial activity. By this time a middle class had emerged in Hungary, many of whom were Jewish. The Jews maintained their position mainly as middle-class citizens throughout the nineteenth century; in general, their lot continued to improve, although they bore an increasing burden of taxation.

At the beginning of the nineteenth century, Rabbi Moses Teitelbaum arrived in Sátoraljaujhely and became a 'Wonder Rabbi'. Legend has him performing minor miracles—curing illnesses, including an illness of the great leader of the Hungarian Revolution, Lajos Kossuth, who later became most benevolent towards Jews. A statue of Kossuth has pride of place in the central square of Sátoraljaujhely. It happens to be next to the site of the Schwarcz family's leather shop! The tomb of Moses Teitelbaum has been restored within a memorial building to which orthodox Jews from all over the world regularly come to pay homage.

In 1848, under the leadership of Kossuth, the Hungarians embarked with great passion on 'the war of liberation and independence'. Jews also became conscripted, and several of them served valiantly alongside Kossuth, the poet-hero Petöfi, and other Hungarian heroes. One of these was Vilmos Schwarcz, a native of Sátoraljaujhely who was apparently close to Kossuth and gained the rank of captain. He was one of Jenö's ancestors. The war of liberation was unfortunately lost, and the Austrians took reprisals against the Jews because of their role in the war, forcing them to pay an enormous fine. An interesting man of that era was Michael Heilprin, a Jew who was actually born in Poland but migrated to Zemplén, wrote many patriotic Hungarian poems, and enlisted in the National Guard during the 1848 war. He fled to Paris after the collapse of the revolution but returned to Zemplén where he became the administrator of the Kestenbaum School in Sátoraljaujhely in 1853. Kossuth said of him, 'Aside from me, the best Hungarian of all is Heilprin'.

After the 1848 war of independence and for some years after the First World War, Jews were given equal civil rights with non-Jews. The principles and practices of liberalism had been introduced by the great Kossuth, and by revolutionary aristocrats and intellectuals during the independence struggle. Jews now increasingly filled the middle classes of Hungary. There were many Jewish professionals—particularly doctors, lawyers, journalists, jurists, authors, members of parliament, and university professors—who con-tributed enormously to the vitality of the region. This time was a golden age for all the Jews of Hungary, including those in the Zemplén county around Sátoraljaujhely. This golden era of some seventy-five years was referred to by the Jews as the 'time of peace'. History has repeatedly shown that when Jews are given half a chance to function in freedom they will blossom, contribut-ing immensely to the vitality and prosperity of their country. And so they did in Hungary during the 'time of peace'. Jews played an important part in the life of the Sátoraljaujhely and Zemplén district during this time. From the beginning of the twentieth century, there was very little discrimination between Jews and non-Jews in this part of Hungary. Jews lived in all parts of town; there was no Jewish ghetto, as there was in many parts of adjacent Poland and Ukraine. Tolerance and liberalism was the order of the day, and there was no public evidence of anti-Semitism.

At the beginning of the twentieth century, the mayor of Sátoraljaujhely and the superintendent of police were Jews. Jews had small and large businesses, owned furniture and ceramic factories, and were very prominent in both wine production and wine sales in the Tokaj region. Most of the lawyers and doctors in the region were Jewish. The Jewish community had an outstanding school called the Kestenbaum School, established in 1838 from a large bequest of Raphael Kestenbaum, a wealthy tavern owner who died without an heir in 1829. This school continued for 106 years until 1944. The Jews also had an excellent hospital, open to all, which was founded around the time of Jenö's birth.

Although Hungarian Jews enlisted freely during the First World War, and often showed great courage and national pride, the loss of the war in 1918 caused a change in attitudes to them. The press as well as other right-wing elements looked for scapegoats, and found them: they were quick to blame the Jews for the economic ills of the country. A wave of anti-Semitism built up gradually, and from 1919 there were raids on Jews by the military police. Although a degree of liberalism ensued in the mid-1920s, Jenö Schwarcz was born into the beginning of an era of anti-Semitic restrictive laws. The first of these was promulgated in 1920, restricting the participation of Jews in universities, in politics, and in the economy. The Jews, scattered throughout Hungary, did not form a united body, so they became easy targets for right-wing elements. With the advent of economic problems and the Great Depression in the 1930s, the so-called 'Jewish question' became a major issue. Once again, Jews were the scapegoats and the subject of further restrictive laws and anti-Semitic practices.

So Jenö Schwarcz's early life was just one small part of a major struggle for survival that the Jews of Hungary had been engaged in for at least three hundred years, often under very difficult conditions. It was a struggle in which his ancestors usually lived under restrictive laws, often paying enormous taxes and having to use their wits constantly to survive and earn a daily living. It was not just the ability to trade well and to use one's wits, but the very instinct for survival that was already in Jenö's blood. This was to become more evident as events moved relentlessly in Europe during the 1930s.

The Italian fascist Benito Mussolini was given absolute power in 1922, the year of Jenö's birth. In Germany, the National Socialist Party, led by former corporal Adolf Hitler, held its first public congress in Munich in January 1923. Although Hitler's popularity waxed and waned in the 1920s, his domination of German politics gradually increased, and by 1930 Nazi thugs had attacked Jewish traders in Berlin, shouting, 'Down with the Jews'. Hitler took over as chancellor of the German Reich in 1933, and almost immediately increased the harassment of German Jews, and introduced anti-Jewish laws and regulations. He also instituted progressive militarisation throughout Germany, and in 1936 the Nazis entered the Rhineland.

The prime minister of Great Britain, Neville Chamberlain, seemed ignorant, or at least disregarding or disbelieving, of Hitler's plans for the domination of Europe. Chamberlain, who had been a successful businessman in Manchester prior to assuming a political life, naively took Hitler's word that he had limited territorial ambitions, and followed a policy of appeasement with both Hitler and Mussolini. He infamously signed the Munich agreement on 30 September 1938, giving away the Sudeten region of Czechoslovakia to the Nazis and claiming to have found 'peace for our time'.

Winston Churchill, in his passionate quest for the preservation of freedom for the peoples of England and Europe, was the only significant British politician or person of importance to denounce Hitler. Unfortunately, Churchill's voice was not widely heard during Chamberlain's time because he was not allowed to talk on British radio. The BBC, a government media monopoly, regarded Churchill's views as too 'controversial'. Just one year after the Munich agreement, in September 1939, Churchill was vindicated when Germany invaded Poland and took most of western Poland, including Warsaw. Soon after, the Soviets invaded eastern Poland and gained control of the region. War was immediately declared by Britain and France; Australia, New Zealand, and India quickly joined in the declaration. Fortunately for

England and Europe, Chamberlain was relieved of office eight months after the declaration of war, and Winston Churchill became prime minister in May 1940.

The 'Jewish question' became an important issue for the Hungarian government after 1932. As we have seen, Jews were blamed for the economic problems of Hungary—problems that were, in fact, global. A number of 'Jewish laws' were passed, restricting Jews from partaking in the professions, in administration, in industrial and commercial enterprises, and in the economic life of Hungary in general. When the Second World War broke out in September 1939, there was much discrimination against Hungarian Jews. Transit refugee camps were established in Zemplén, initially to intern those Jews who escaped from Poland. One of these camps was set up in Garany, near Sátoraljaujhely, a place which quickly became an 'Administrative Detention Camp for Jews'.

In return for its pro-Nazi sympathies and activities, and its systematic and pervasive discrimination against and assaults on the Jews, Hungary was rewarded by Hitler. In a decision taken in Vienna in November 1938, Hungary received a sizeable portion of what was then Slovakia. The Hungarian government continued to oust Jews from what little was left to them of the country's economy: it confiscated all Jewish-owned properties, vineyards, and other similar enterprises. In 1942 a new government came into power with an indecisive prime minister, Kállay, who was apparently to some extent sympathetic to the Allies, although he still continued to discriminate grossly against Jews. The combination of Kállay's policies and his rumoured sympathy towards the Allies, the approach of the war front from the east, and the failure of Hungary to 'solve the Jewish question' brought about the German occupation of Hungary on 19 March 1944. With this act, the fate of the Hungarian Jews was sealed.

Most Jews did not comprehend or accept the increasingly restrictive laws directed against them, in spite of the obvious outward signs. Jews were proudly Hungarian, firmly believing they were a part of the very fabric of

Hungary. Initially, they were disbelieving of the power of the Hungarian Nazi movement, and were stunned when many of their friends and neighbours turned against them. Meanwhile Nazi Germany increased its levels of military mobilisation as it drew up plans to rule Europe. It also had what it called a 'final solution' to the 'Jewish question'—a brutal and systematic all-out war against the Jews, in the pursuit of which it eventually murdered six million European Jews. At the time, nobody with a sound mind, including the Jews, could believe that there was a master plan for them to be exterminated.

By 1943, Jenö Schwarcz, then twenty-one, was one of the few singled out by the pro-Nazi political police in Sátoraljaujhely as being 'untrustworthy'. It was once alleged that he had listened to BBC broadcasts, and on another occasion that he had over-charged for leather. In fact, he was picked out partly because of his success in business, partly because he was Jewish (and the restrictive laws in place gave the authorities special powers against Jews), and partly because he was thought to hold liberal views directed against the regime. He was interrogated several times at police headquarters, in a building that now serves the town as its main hotel. In April 1943, Jenö was taken to the Garany administrative detention camp for Jews, situated some thirty kilometres from Sátoraljaujhely. It was here that he began his third life, which was to be his ultimate test of survival against all odds.

CHAPTER 4

TWO YEARS IN HELL

He who has a why to live for, can bear with
almost any how of existence.

FRIEDRICH NIETZSCHE (1844–1900)

On a small hill at the edge of the neat village of Garany there stands a large, magnificent nineteenth-century mansion reminiscent of a 'grande maison bourgeoise'. This century it served as the summer residence of a Hungarian aristocrat, Count Almássy, before he sold it to the state in the late 1930s. Just before the outbreak of war the residence became a psychiatric institution; during the war, the inmates were relocated. Today, Garany, although mostly a Hungarian community ethnically, is a part of Slovakia and is called Hran, and the mansion serves as a psychiatric institution for children. A large plaque written in Slovakian states that this was the house in which communist political internees were kept during the war. In fact, the majority of those interned were Jews, and they certainly did not live in the mansion. They were interned at the foot of the hill behind a barbed-wire fence, in buildings that were originally the horse stables of Count Almássy.

Currently the children's psychiatric institution houses about eighty children with a variety of psychiatric problems. The children are free to roam in this magnificent place: it includes a football field, and a huge vegetable garden where some of the children work as part of their therapy. The children know nothing of what went on at the foot of the hill during the last part of the Second World War. Unfortunately, the horse stables were pulled down by the Russians in the late 1950s on the pretext of disuse and dilapidation, but in fact it was done to 'tidy up history'. Flat fields and one building is all that remains of the internment camp.

The men in the Garany camp were kept behind barbed-wire fences, and worked either in the fields or in specially constructed factories, making metal parts for army vehicles. At the beginning of their internment, there was little brutality and ill-treatment. Until the German occupation of Hungary in March 1944, the internees were guarded by local Hungarian policemen, many of whom were sympathetic towards Jews. Some of the interned men were able to craft metal and bone charms, and other pieces of cheap jewellery, which were smuggled out and sold at the local market to buy food from the neighbouring peasants.

Jenö, barely twenty-one, was one of the youngest men in Garany. Using his wits, he was able to obtain a relatively good assignment as a helper, cleaner, and general factotum at the medical clinic which had been created in one of the stables of the camp. The doctor who visited daily was also Jewish and came from Sátoraljaujhely, but he was not an internee. He worked under what was called 'work duty'. Jenö persuaded him to bring the local newspaper and to leave it in the medical clinic. This provided welcome news and information for the prisoners.

Current photograph of part of the nineteenth-century mansion of the Hungarian aristocrat, Count Almássy, in Garany. Thousands of Jews, including Jenö Schwarcz, were interned by Hungarian Nazis in the stables of the mansion (now demolished), before being moved in May 1944 to concentration camps such as Auschwitz

After a short time, Jenö was able to persuade a young Jewish lawyer friend of the Schwarcz family, Pali Lichtenstein, to send a message to the camp that Jenö was required to be a witness at a court case in Sátoraljaujhely. This was merely a subterfuge for Jenö to go to Sátoraljaujhely with a police guard to visit his family and friends. The policeman was also glad to get out for the day, and his sympathies were no doubt helped by a good meal from the Schwarcz family and a little 'pocket money'. With the help of Pali Lichtenstein, Jenö made several of these phoney trips to appear as a witness on various bogus charges. On his return trip he always brought newspapers, as well as current information, which he shared with the others in the camp.

It is easy to forget that we are talking about virile young men, such as Jenö Schwarcz and Pali Lichtenstein, who were full of vitality and a zest for life. I was reminded of this, delightfully, in 1997 when I was visiting Sátoraljaujhely, seeking out people who might have recalled Jenö. I met a handsome and charming old lady who could not recall Jenö but remembered the lawyer. She looked up towards heaven and said with a wistful smile, 'Oh, Pali Lichtenstein! What a man he was!' Discretion stopped me from asking any further questions.

The exploits of Jenö Schwarcz in Garany did not go unobserved. In particular, his survival skills caught the attention of Feri Vadász, then aged twenty-eight, but already the leader of a socialist and communist group within the Garany internment camp. Feri had already spent two years in jail because of his socialist activities. He was a steady, stable man, mature for his years—a man who was a natural choice as leader of the group. Initially there was opposition by some members of the group to Feri's acceptance of Jenö. 'You shouldn't invite him into our group', he was told. 'He is a rich young man, and not really one of us.' In response, Feri said, 'Look, he is not rich. They just have a small leather shop in Sátoraljaujhely, and he is just an ordinary citizen.' These words from their leader were enough for them to accept Jenö. The future was to reveal the wisdom of Feri Vadász.

By the beginning of 1944, it was becoming clear that the fronts had turned around, and that Germany was losing the war. The Germans were on the run, particularly from the Russian front, with Russian troops attacking and winning back Leningrad which had been under siege for two years. The front was advancing south and west towards Hungary, and the Red Army was also rapidly sweeping the Germans out of the Crimea. In March 1944, because of the advancing front, because the Hungarian government was suspected to have sympathies towards the Allies, and because of what the Germans regarded as weakness in solving 'the Jewish question', Germany took total control of Hungary. This action sealed the fate of 800,000 Hungarian Jews. Up to then, most Jews were comparatively safe—except for 50,000 of them, such as Jenö Schwarcz, who had been incarcerated in various internment and labour camps throughout Hungary.

A few days after the arrival of the Germans, a curfew was placed on all Jews in Sátoraljaujhely. A few days later, a large ghetto was established in the poorest part of town, where many of the Jewish poor already lived. The ghetto was fenced off with barbed wire, all non-Jews previously living there were placed elsewhere in town, and the police herded all 8,000 Jews in Sátoraljaujhely into the ghetto with a minimum of personal belongings. Every house had a yellow cross painted on it, and each person had to wear a yellow cross as well. Moreover, some 7,000 Jews from neighbouring villages and small towns were also rounded up, removed, and enclosed in the newly created ghetto. This meant that there were about 15,000 men, women, and children in the town ghetto, all at immediate risk of illness from gross overcrowding, little food, and poor hygiene. Fortunately, the bakery, owned by a Jew, was within the ghetto precinct; as the baker had a good supply of flour, at least bread was baked every day.

Talking to non-Jews in Sátoraljaujhely who were old enough to live through and remember the German occupation, I learned that there were many who went along with this assault on Jews. However, there were also many other decent men and women who found this a very distressing and sad

A drawing of the Hungarian special police, Csendörs, searching the belongings of Jews in the Sátoraljaújhely ghetto as they were being rounded up for deportation (the four drawings in this chapter were done by Dr Imre Holló, a dentist from Sátoraljaújhely, who was with Jenö Schwarcz in both Auschwitz and Dörnhau)

period of their lives. Many of them, particularly those who knew Jews prior to the Nazi occupation, frequently took fresh food over to the people in the ghetto, racing in and out before they were caught.

The somewhat lax discipline and relatively tolerable conditions in the internment camp of Garany rapidly changed with the Nazi occupation of Hungary. The police were replaced by a special branch of criminal police known as the 'Csendörs', which means 'guardians of peace and quiet'. In fact, many of these guardians were a specially selected group of young Hungarian Nazis and thugs. They were quite vicious and brutal, particularly to Jews, but also to other minority groups such as the gypsies. With the arrival of the guardians, all the men in Garany were forced to remain within the camp. There were no more fraudulent trips to Sátoraljaujhely for Jenö, and there was no extra money from the sale of cheap imitation jewellery with which to buy food.

Jenö quickly sized up the new situation in Garany, and made a careful plan to escape. One evening, he cut through the barbed wire and escaped into the adjacent fields. His escape route was over a river that had only one bridge in the area. As he was getting close to the road and to the bridge, it was clear that he had forgotten one factor. The bridge crossing was a strategic point for the Germans, and was guarded by the SS. The only way to get across was to swim; but, like so many others in Hungary at that time, Jenö could not swim. If he tried to cross the bridge he knew he would be quickly discovered and

Jews being herded to the Sátoraljaujhely railway station by special police (by Dr Imre Holló)

summarily executed. He went back to the camp with some difficulty, found the spot in the fence where he had cut the barbed wire, and snuck himself into the camp, unnoticed, to await events. Jenö and the others in Garany did not have long to wait.

Some six weeks after the Germans occupied Hungary, the local police returned as guards of the Garany camp. One morning in mid-May 1944, the several hundred men in Garany were assembled and marched about thirty kilometres to the railway station of Sátoraljaujhely. They were lined up alongside a wagon train, whereupon about seventy men were herded into each boxcar. Feri Vadász wanted everyone to stay together, so most of the seventy-or-so men in his group, including Jenö, managed to get into a single box-car. As they were lined up alongside the train, Jenö's oldest sister Lilly, who had run away from the ghetto that day and had disguised herself by wearing

A photograph of the Sátoraljaujhely railway station taken in 1997 by the author. During 1944, 15,000–18,000 souls were deported to concentration camps from this railway station. Jenö Schwarcz and his family were all deported from here

a Red Cross armband, searched him out and told him that their family was in the ghetto. (Only after the war ended did it become known that most of the 15,000 Jews deported from the Sátoraljaujhely ghetto had been taken to Auschwitz or Dachau—and that most of them, including Jenö's mother and younger brother, had died of disease or malnutrition, or had been murdered.) Lilly also told Jenö that she was going on another train with her younger sister Gita.

Each boxcar was guarded by an SS guard as it departed for an unknown destination. They were told that they were going to do some agricultural work in the fields. One of the men in the wagon was apparently from Budapest, where more information about such matters was available. He said that he had heard about these trains: they were being taken to places such as Auschwitz, and those who could not work were likely to be murdered by the Nazis. The horror of all this is unimaginable. The men who were in the wagon with Feri and Jenö did not speak out loud about any of this. Many years later, Feri Vadász told me there was a feeling that their being together would be important, because the next step would likely be a question of life or death. 'We didn't know what would happen to us and whether the Nazis would just beat us to death when we arrived', Feri Vadász recalled. 'But at least we knew we could count on support, in whatever form, from the others in the group.' Feri and his men couldn't quite believe that they could all be murdered—it was hard for a sane person to imagine that such a thing could be done to them by other human beings.

The wagons rolled on through North Hungary and through the large railway centre of Kassa, taking two or three days, and finishing up in the hell camp of Auschwitz. And yet even here, on the way from Kassa, Jenö's powerful instinct for survival was ever present: he was able to pick one of the locks of a wagon door, and made plans to escape. However, he was forcibly persuaded against this by a large and loud man who told him that, if he escaped, all the others in the wagon would be murdered by the Nazis on arrival.

A 'transport' of Hungarian Jews arriving at Auschwitz in 1944. Jenö Schwarcz was in Auschwitz for a few days before being selected, along with others, by Dr Mengele, 'The Angel of Death', to go to a work concentration camp at Dörnhau. Mengele is shown here, with his back to the camera, meeting the transport with other German officers. The entrance and tower of the Auschwitz camp is in the background (courtesy of Yad Vashem)

The train arrived in Auschwitz. Over the gates was the sign, 'Arbeit Macht Frei'—'Work Makes One Free'. Everyone was marched into the concentration camp. By this time, most of them knew that their life was hanging by a thread. After about five days in Auschwitz, the men were lined up again. This time, Dr Josef Mengele, 'The Angel of Death', picked out those who were to go to a work camp. Amongst those selected, everyone in Feri Vadász's group, including Jenö, were picked to leave Auschwitz. It was as simple and as mysterious as that: whether you lived or died depended on a nod from Dr Mengele. Feri Vadász recalled later, as Primo Levi did so graphically, that, instead of finding an apocalyptic situation in Auschwitz, they

observed Mengele and the SS quietly and efficiently going about their daily
job of condemning or reprieving inmates. (Mengele was believed to be
responsible for over 400,000 deaths. He escaped to Brazil after the war, and
a forty-year hunt for him ended in 1985 when it was discovered that he had
died in a swimming accident in Brazil in 1979. His remains were exhumed
in 1985).

The men selected to leave Auschwitz were packed into wagons, given a
piece of sausage and some bread, and despatched to their new destination. In
Jenö's wagon, two SS guards, both armed with machine guns, sat at one of
the slightly ajar wagon doors in order to get a little air as the train trundled
along. At this point, Jenö did something simple that was to have extraordinary consequences: he treated the guards as fellow human beings. He said to
them, 'At least we got out of hell'. As a Jewish saying goes, 'The rest is pure
profit'. One of the prisoners suggested they all sing a song: Jenö had a good
voice, so he sang a Hungarian folk song whose title would translate as something like 'The girl from the village of Szabadka is my dove'. When he finished the song, one of the two SS guards said, in Hungarian, 'Please sing it
again, it was so nice.' This guard was a 'Schwáb', a German migrant living in
north-western Hungary, able to speak both German and Hungarian. After
Jenö sang the song again, the guard gave him a pinch of his own tobacco and
some cigarette paper. Jenö rolled the smoke and, with his usual generosity,
had only a couple of puffs of the cigarette before passing it around to some
of the other prisoners in the wagon.

The train journey took all day, and eventually they arrived in Dörnhau in
southern Silesia near Germany's border with Czechoslovakia and Poland; it
is now a part of Poland, and is called Kolce. It was raining as they were
marched by the SS guards to a large, disused, three-storey factory building
encircled by a barbed-wire fence. In the past, the carpet factory had
belonged to Jews. The signs outside said, 'M Kragen & Co'. Their first job
was to remove rotting old carpets, broken-down, rusted-up machines, and
leather transmission belts to an adjacent field in order to make room for the

The inmates of the Dörnhau prison, who included Jenö Schwarcz, shown cleaning up the premises of what was previously a carpet factory owned by Jews. Dörnhau was then part of Germany; it is now part of Poland, and is called Kolce (by Dr Imre Holló)

men. Behind the factory was a stone building where the SS guards and officers had their quarters.

The commanding officer, Franz Wolf, was known for his brutality. He directed the clean-up operation with a large wooden stick, mercilessly and viciously beating the men as they went past him. This was to become a daily event as he maimed and killed many men for no special reason. Jenö, Feri, and the other men from Garany understood very quickly that this was going to be hell for them. Wolf, in his thirties, had previously been a primary-school teacher in Germany. Suddenly being elevated to the powerful position of commanding officer, he realised that he was the final arbiter of who lived or died among the 1,500 or 2,000 men in Dörnhau. In the concentration camp, it seems that both guards and prisoners lost their veneer of civilisation and reverted to type: an honest man behaved honestly; a brutal man, brutally.

It was rapidly becoming clear after two escape attempts that Jenö Schwarcz was fearless. This fearlessness was to some extent tempered by his feeling for reality, as he used his intelligence in a practical way to survive in the face of almost unimaginable adversity. Now came another example of this ability. Whilst helping to remove the old machines, the rotting carpets, and the leather belts, Jenö found several jars of wax and grease which in the past had been used for the cleaning and maintenance of the carpet-factory equipment. Knowing something about leather, Jenö hid the wax and grease. This find was to play an important part in his survival.

The men were assigned to heavy work—some of them in a quarry, others digging trenches to lay thick oil-pipes. Jenö also started to do this arduous work. He was not used to heavy physical labour, but did it for about three days. Then, quite by accident, he met in the yard the Schwáb SS guard who had asked Jenö to sing in the wagon.

The Dörnhau inmates shown digging trenches as one part of their work, which was done under extremely difficult conditions (by Dr Imre Holló)

'What are you doing?', he asked Jenö.

'I am doing the same as the other men—heavy work', Jenö answered.

'Why don't you become my putzer?'

'It would be a pleasure', replied Jenö.

A 'putzer' is a German slang word, also used in Hungarian (which literally means 'polisher'), for an officer's valet. He does all his boss's cleaning, brings him his coffee and meals, and in general looks after his quarters. Suddenly the wax, the grease, and the cleaning fluids that Jenö had found and kept became very useful: he was able to polish the officer's belt and brass so that they looked sparkling clean, like a billiard ball.

The household situation of the interned men was supervised by a tall, heavily built Jew of Hungarian extraction from Bratislava called Muki Klein. An excellent and delicate violinist, Klein was at times tougher in his treatment of his fellow Jews than they felt he needed to be. It was a delicate balancing act for him to perform the dirty work of the Germans, because if he was too lax they probably would have killed him.

Muki Klein now announced that the dreaded Franz Wolf wanted a putzer. At about the same time, Wolf saw the Schwáb SS guard's shiny belt and brass, and asked him for the name of his putzer. A day later, Wolf called for Jenö. In the meantime, nobody had dared to take the job that Muki Klein had advertised, because Wolf was known to be such a beast of a man. Before being called, Jenö had asked Klein what the job involved. 'Cleaning and other similar jobs', he was told. 'He likes to have his boots cleaned so that they are like a mirror.'

Years later, Jenö recalled, 'I more or less decided to take on the job overnight, and the next morning I was called to see Wolf. I was shitting myself when I got this message. You have no idea how scared I was when that man called for me. However, I went to see him, clicking my heels together as I arrived.'

'Are you the Schwáb's putzer?', Wolf asked Jenö.

'Yes.'

'From tomorrow morning you will be my putzer.'

Jenö was told to get Wolf's shoes and belt shiny by five o'clock every morning. He was also to get his clothes ready and to give him coffee at that time. 'On the first morning, I got in there very early. He was in bed when I knocked on his door, and when I entered he got his revolver out from under the pillow and pointed it at me while I was serving him coffee. This scary performance fortunately stopped after a week when he got to know me and trusted me.'

Becoming Wolf's putzer gave Jenö a little freedom and many advantages, because he could walk anywhere in the camp, including the kitchens. It allowed him to steal food, particularly items such as potato peelings that were being thrown out, which he could throw together into a pot. At his peril, and using various ploys, he was able to take this food to the prisoners' building and to give it to some of the weaker men in the camp as well as to his friends from Garany. Jenö's prestige grew in the camp, among the prisoners and even with the tough Muki Klein, for taking on the job with Franz Wolf.

Jenö understood the usefulness of observation. 'I noticed that on many afternoons Wolf had a shave and put some perfume—which to me smelt like urine—on his face, and I guessed that he had a girlfriend he was visiting outside the camp. So I went and stole some tomatoes and artificial honey made from coal by the Germans, wrapped it up, and gave it to Franz Wolf. When he asked how I got the stuff, I replied, "I organised it and you deserve it."'

Jenö knew that, according to the officers' Germanic rules, stealing was *verboten*, but 'organising' was something else again. In this very subtle way, Jenö was able to bribe his man. He knew the correct way to talk to a person, and had the ability to see what they might need. I suspect all this was done instinctively. Many years later, that very creative teacher of self-actualisation, Werner Erhard, told future managers that the greatest asset of a manager is not simply to predict what is likely to happen in the future, but to create what is lacking and needed. 'Create what there is not', he said. Jenö Schwarcz preceded Werner Erhard in management theory by a whole generation.

One evening, about four months after their life in Dörnhau commenced, the men returned from their day's work to find a group of Jews who, although too weak to work, were praying and singing, and clearly in a celebratory mood. For one thing, it was Rosh Hashana, the Jewish New Year, and they were celebrating the Jewish year 5705. But, more importantly, they had learned that day that Wolf was to be transferred from their camp, probably to the Russian front. Although nobody knew who the new commander was to be, he could not be worse than Wolf—and so they prayed for that, too. The Allied troops had stormed ashore in Normandy in June 1944, and were advancing not only on the Western front but also through Italy, and the Red Army was rapidly advancing towards Germany on the Eastern front. As an able-bodied soldier, Wolf was needed elsewhere.

He was replaced by Hans Mucke, an older man who had been a barber in Düsseldorf. Mucke was a conscript, not an SS volunteer. He was a family man with a teenage son, and had served many Jews in his barber shop in the past. After the arrival of Mucke, the condition of the men improved a little; at least they had a commandant who was not brutal, not even to the weaker men. They believed that, if Wolf had remained, none of them would have survived. Even with the slightly improved conditions under Mucke, about thirty or forty men died every week from exhaustion, malnutrition, and illness.

Very early during Mucke's time, something remarkable occurred to a man by the name of Simon Paszternák and to his fourteen-year-old son Fredi. This event was almost symbolic of better things to come. The Schwarcz family knew Simon as Uncle Simi. A well-known vigneron in the renowned Tokaj district, he was almost twenty years older than the others in Dörnhau. He held himself well, had pink cheeks, and looked youthful. He had instinctively lowered his age in Auschwitz when the selection took place.

His son Fredi, although thin, was very tall for his age, and would have passed for a seventeen or eighteen year old. Even though he was not strongly built, he still had to do the hard manual work of the fully grown men. Fredi figured out early that if he continued to do this work, and continued to get such meagre rations, he would die very quickly. So he asked for a less demanding job from the Jewish 'housekeeper', Muki Klein. As it happened, there was an extra job available as a putzer for the officers and, fortunately, Fredi got the job. This is where he first met Jenö Schwarcz. Fredi recalled later, 'It was clear to me then that Jenö was not only eight years older, but also much more experienced and wiser than I was.'

Jenö taught all the finer points of the putzer work to young Fredi. He also told him that the job was not only useful for them, but also for many others— because he and Fredi could help them to survive this ordeal. Jenö explained that it was possible to steal food, particularly of the type that was not counted, but that it was a dangerous assignment. Jenö had a brilliant idea for transporting these food remnants, because it was absolutely forbidden to bring them into the camp. He devised a method whereby a string was threaded around the bottom of their trouser legs, and a hole was cut in their pockets, so that any food they put in their pockets would slip down their legs and stay there. The food sometimes needed to stay and slosh around above their ankles for a few hours before they returned to the camp in the evening. Night after night Jenö and Fredi went through the camp gates, were checked, saluted the guards, and were allowed to pass. They always ran the risk of being caught and punished. Punishment consisted of lashings. They never got caught.

During November 1944, there was an announcement that those who were under sixteen would not be going out to their usual work the following day. For the sake of their health, they were to be transported elsewhere before the coming winter so they could work in a heated factory. There were two hundred such young men, and virtually everyone knew what this meant. In fact, all the teenagers who left were never seen again.

Fredi stayed up all night discussing the announcement with his father Simon and Jenö, who also strongly supported Fredi's decision to speak to the commanding officer, Mucke. The next morning, Jenö foreshadowed this sit-uation to Mucke and suggested to Fredi that, on this day, *he* take the break-fast tray into him. After Fredi entered Mucke's room, he put down the plate and said, 'I know I am to be removed from here today, and I know that it is for my benefit. However, I have my father here and I don't wish to be part-ed from him. I know that you have a son my age, and it would be wonderful if you could understand what it means for me to be with my father.'

Mucke apparently thought for a minute or two, and then told Fredi to stay in his room and to hide under the bed. He was to lock the door of the room, and if anyone knocked he was to say nothing and to stay there until Mucke returned. Fredi saw what happened next. Through the window in his room, Fredi saw all the young men lined up at the central roll-call area, put into the back of several trucks, and taken away. After this, Mucke came back and said, 'Look, from now on, if you see any inspections going on, or any-thing suspicious, you hide anywhere you can.' It seems that on one such occa-sion, when there was the possibility of an inspection, Jenö helped Fredi as well as another young man to hide in a boiler room.

Life remained hard for the interned men. In particular, the older and weaker found it increasingly difficult to do the hard quarry work, digging trenches and laying pipes. The special squad carted away the dead more and more often.

There were some better moments which helped to sustain even the old and weak. Jenö, along with his lawyer friend from Sátoraljaujhely, Pali Lichtenstein, who was also an amateur radio operator, somehow got the bits and pieces together to make a radio set with short-wave reception, so that they could hear the BBC foreign service in Hungarian. Instead of hiding the radio set, they wired it under a watering can, and placed it directly outside the main entrance of the building where the prisoners were located. Every evening at the right time, the set was turned on and Jenö went to the front entrance to listen to the news. He would then relay all the information about the war to the men inside. The older men, like uncle Simi Paszternák, were much relieved to hear Jenö say, 'The Germans have lost the war and the Russians will be here tomorrow or the day after.' Even when there was a lot of static or noise during the broadcast from Allied planes flying overhead, Jenö still went into the barracks after the news and lied to the older and weaker men, saying, 'Yes, I heard the news. The Russians will be here in a few days.' Jenö instinctively understood what these weak and disheartened men needed most at that time—an aim for life, a hope for a future.

As the Eastern war front approached Dörnhau, the enterprising Jenö and Fredi, with the help of another young man who worked in the workshop, were able to make false keys to the storeroom where the German officers kept their food and rations. Using the false keys, they were able to steal provisions, in part to supplement their meagre rations, and in part for use after liberation. They stored the food in a landing under the stairs of their building.

By early 1945, it was clear that the Allies would win the war and that the war would soon end. The Allies were making rapid advances on both the Eastern and Western fronts. At the end of January, the horrors of Auschwitz were discovered by Marshall Zhukov's Red Army during its relentless advance towards Germany. Moreover, the Allies on the Western front were bombing and marching into Germany.

As the gas chambers and ovens in Auschwitz were no longer in operation, many fatigued and sick men weighing about thirty kilograms and called 'Muselmänner' (literally, 'Moslems') were moved by the Germans to Dörnhau to die in the last few weeks of the war. At this time, Jenö brought commandant Mucke to see Feri Vadász. He told Mucke, 'This man will be important after the liberation and, if you protect us from now on, we will protect you when the Russians arrive.' Mucke agreed and, after liberation, the group protected Mucke as well as a small number of officers sympathetic to Jews whilst in Dörnhau.

During the last month in Dörnhau, in April 1945, a typhus epidemic broke out among the prisoners. Typhus in the past has been called 'jail fever' or 'camp fever'. It is an infectious disease caused by a small organism and is spread by body lice: the infection enters through broken skin, a pathway that is made more effective by scratching. Epidemics of typhus are particularly common in an environment of overcrowding and close contact, poor hygiene, verminous clothes, lack of ventilation and, above all, a state of starvation that results in poor immunity against infection. Every one of these dreadful conditions that was necessary for the onset of a typhus epidemic was present in Dörnhau, and was becoming more and more prominent. Typhus infection is characterised by a fever, a skin eruption, sweats, distressing headaches, shivering, pains in the limbs, and severe muscle prostration. These symptoms lead to semi-consciousness or even unconsciousness at times. In the young, and in sufferers up to the age of thirty, the infection usually resolves after about two weeks, leaving the person weak for several more weeks. However, deaths can occur in older people. Men died from typhus in the last few weeks in Dörnhau, particularly the older and weaker men who had been brought there from other concentration camps.

When the typhus epidemic broke out in Dörnhau, the campsite was totally isolated so as not to transfer the infection to the officers. All those concerned with food preparation who did not have typhus were placed in a separate building outside the camp, and continued to serve the officers. Thus Jenö Schwarcz and Fredi Paszternák did not see the others in the month before their liberation.

Whilst the typhus epidemic was raging in Dörnhau in April 1945, events moved very quickly on the European war front. By the middle of the month the Allies entered Nuremberg, advanced on Hamburg, and liberated the concentration camps at Bergen-Belsen and Buchenwald; soon after, the camp of Dachau was freed. Winston Churchill said of the camps, 'No words can express our horror.' On 28 April, Italian partisans shot and then hanged Mussolini by his feet with his girlfriend; two days later, Hitler shot himself in his bunker, where Eva Braun and Goebbels also died.

By early May most German troops had surrendered, and at about this time the SS guards left quietly, with the exception of commander Mucke and a few others who had been sympathetic to the Jews in Dörnhau. The three hundred men who remained alive waited for the Russians to arrive. The Germans signed an unconditional surrender on 7 May, and total victory appeared on 9 and 10 May. Prague was the last European capital to be liberated.

In those concentration camps liberated by the Allied forces, the Americans had an excellent plan with regard to medicine, food, and other aid, as well as procedures for the repatriation or transportation of former prisoners. However, the Russians were in complete chaos when they arrived at Dörnhau, had no plans, and merely said, 'You are all free; you can go now.' In fact, the typhus epidemic was still raging. During this time, Feri Vadász and his group of men, who had all survived, became a vital force in the rehabilitation and repatriation of the Dörnhau inmates. They were able to protect Mucke and a few other guards, give them Red Cross armbands, and help them work in the store. Vadász told the Russians, 'These were some of our guards, but they were decent people.' The Russians did not harm them, and eventually they were all able to return to their homes in Germany.

The Vadász group created eleven emergency hospitals from converted schools and public buildings, in which they housed the typhus sufferers as well as those who were sick and terminally malnourished. Doctor Adler, a Dörnhau inmate who was in charge of the medical aspects of treatment, commandeered about one hundred German women from the village to look after them, and gradually almost all of them recovered. Feeding these undernourished men was difficult. The starved men broke into stores and overfed themselves with heavy food, gobbling down salami, sausages, and other foods they had not seen for at least a year. A number of them died simply as a result of this overeating. In fact, one man died while he still had a stick of salami hanging out of his mouth! Those who initially ate very light gruel and other nutritious food did in fact survive.

Just around the time of liberation, Jenö also developed typhus and had to be put into hospital. With his characteristic strength of will and macho suppression of symptoms, Jenö was in bed only for a few days, said that he felt a little weak but fine, and joined the Vadász group to help revive and repatriate the remaining men in Dörnhau. They obtained clothes and food from the village, since many of the residents had fled before the Russians arrived. Feri Vadász obtained papers from the Russians with official stamps, and his group also made their own stamps to indicate that these men had been recently liberated from concentration camps and were returning home.

By this time Jenö and Feri had become very close friends, and had a deep though unspoken understanding of each other. When I interviewed him many years later, Feri told me what a valuable friend Jenö had been in Dörnhau—not only because of his generosity in providing food, sustenance, and moral support for the men, but also because he always had hope for the future and was able to see the 'big picture'. This was something, Feri admitted, which in the depths of darkness he could not always see. At the same time, Jenö was very much comforted by being such a close friend of Feri and a member of a group which in the end rehabilitated the three hundred-or-so men who survived out of the 1,500 or 2,000 men who had been taken there from Auschwitz. The rehabilitation process took three or four weeks after the arrival of the Russians. Feri Vadász and Jenö Schwarcz were the last two to leave Dörnhau for home. At the age of twenty-two, Jenö was about to begin his fourth life.

CHAPTER 5

A New Life,
A New Tyranny

Jenö had been liberated after surviving two years in hell. Did he himself understand how and why he had survived, or was he still numbed by the grossness and brutality of the previous two years? Much has been written about the spirit of human survival. Here I offer a few thoughts about Jenö Schwarcz's survival.

There are many reasons that humans are able to survive under impossible and apparently hopeless conditions. Miracles and good fortune are rare, and Jenö benefited from neither. We can say that he had an instinct for survival, perhaps related to the two-thousand-year history of struggle by Jews in Europe and in the north of Hungary. Perhaps, in years to come, with developments in molecular genetics, researchers will discover a 'survival gene'. Whatever happens in this area, there is no doubt that Jenö had the knack of talking to people, observing what they needed and, as he put it to the commandant, 'organising' it. He engaged instinctively in observation, talk, action. He also had the support of Feri Vadász and his group, and he in turn provided support for them as well as for the older and weaker men, especially in Dörnhau. Jenö Schwarcz was able to spot an opportunity for survival when it arose and seize it, even though it may have involved personal risk. When the right moment arrived, he was prepared to act. Taking risks when an opportunity arose remained an outstanding characteristic of Jenö Schwarcz for the rest of his life.

This rational and logical description of survival in the face of adversity does not, of course, explain everything. We must also examine the spiritual and psychological aspects of survival. Jenö had a stubborn belief in himself. Nietzsche's aphorism, 'that [insult] which does not kill me, makes me stronger', might have applied to Jenö's capacity for survival. Jenö Schwarcz also had hope in the midst of despair. He had faith in the future, as well as a large measure of optimism in the face of desolation and depravity. He was able to maintain his own belief in a better tomorrow, and he was also able to inspire others to retain their faith that survival and liberation were close and certain. Viktor Frankl, one of this century's most important psychiatrists, and himself an Auschwitz survivor, expressed these spiritual and psycholog-ical aspects of survival in his book, *Man's Search for Meaning*. It was almost as if he had known Jenö Schwarcz, even though the two men never met.

As had Nietzsche a century before him, Frankl came to believe—from his concentration-camp experiences—that staying alive depends significantly on a sense of purpose and a belief in the future. He ascribed his own survival to his ability to find hope and purpose in the midst of despair and depravity. Helping others to survive, he did as Jenö Schwarcz did: 'Whenever there was an opportunity for it, one had to give them [the prisoners] a *why*—an aim—for their lives, in order to strengthen them to bear the terrible *how* of their existence. Woe to him who saw no more sense in his life, no aim, no pur-pose, and therefore no point in carrying on. He was soon lost.'

By early June 1945, the typhus epidemic at Dörnhau was over, all the men had been despatched home, and Feri Vadász and Jenö Schwarcz had started their long trek home. Feri went to Komárom with Jenö but stayed there for only a short time as, not wanting to be deemed a Czechoslovakian national when the territory became part of Slovakia, he went to Hungary in July 1945 to become a Communist Party secretary. He also recommenced his life as a journalist and writer. From Komárom, Jenö continued on, riding on freight-train wagons and hitching rides on trucks being driven by Russian soldiers. He was back home in Sátoraljaujhely by July 1945.

As Jenö and other Holocaust survivors were making their way home, they did not know that, following the historic meeting of Churchill, Roosevelt, and Stalin in Yalta in February 1945, Europe had already been carved up. Before the war was even over, these men—particularly Roosevelt and Stalin—acted with supreme arrogance, and without consultation or discus-sion, to redistribute power over a significant part of the world. Churchill, as prophetic as ever, and with great wisdom and sanity, did not hide his distrust of Stalin nor his unhappiness with Roosevelt (whom he regarded as naive in world politics) for giving away too much to Stalin without attention to the rights and interests of different European peoples.

Roosevelt died in April 1945. Harry Truman, up to that time virtually unknown internationally, was sworn in as the next president. In the event, Truman turned out to be much tougher, shrewder, and wiser than predicted; unfortunately, much harm had been done by then. The war in the Pacific was turning against the Japanese: the Australians were fighting to liberate Borneo; and the Americans, after a long and bloody fight, took the strategic island of Okinawa by the end of June 1945. Not long after Jenö Schwarcz reached home, the British Labour Party came into power with an absolute majority for the first time in Britain's history, in an election shock that dumped the Tories and Winston Churchill. The election brought Clement Attlee to power, and commenced England's long slide into austerity. By the end of July 1945, the Western Allies fell out with Stalin, and were angered that Russia would occupy half of Germany. The American assault on Japan continued. Then came dramatic news: on 6 August 1945, Hiroshima was destroyed by an atomic blast; three days later, Nagasaki was destroyed by another atom bomb. Emperor Hirohito surrendered unconditionally to the Allies on 15 August, nine days after the destruction of Hiroshima. In total, fifty-five million people, including six million European Jews, died in the Second World War. By August 1945 there were signs that even this immense human sacrifice was not going to stop wars and human misery in the future.

Jenö reached Sátoraljaujhely in early July 1945. His two sisters, Lilly and Gita, had also survived and were already home. In fact, they had also been taken to Auschwitz, from where they had been sent to work in a Krupp steel factory. Jenö learned that his mother, younger brother Ernö, and his mother's uncles and aunts had not survived Auschwitz. Of about eight thousand Jews who had lived in Sátoraljaujhely before the war, only about 400 (5 per cent), returned from the ravages of the Holocaust. Many of these subsequently emigrated or escaped from Hungary to evade the oncoming Soviet tyranny, while many others died prematurely. When I visited Sátoraljaujhely in 1997, the main synagogue had been converted to a furniture store, the baths had been pulled down to make way for a clothing factory, and the

Jewish cemetery was largely neglected. The handful of Jews who still lived in the town worshipped in a small room.

So the bitter irony is that Hitler was quite successful in his plan to eradicate many Jewish communities in Europe, as exemplified by what happened in Sátoraljaujhely. This was Europe's loss in more senses than one. The Jews, as we know from history, had been making an immense contribution—financially, spiritually, and intellectually—to the welfare and vitality of these communities.

Jenö was, of course, distraught that his mother, brother, uncles, aunts, friends, and acquaintances had been killed by the Nazis. At the same time, he decided that he had to start yet another life, and that he couldn't make a living out of being sad and sorry. He and his two sisters were able to return to their old apartment on the main street of town shortly after its occupants moved out. Within two or three months, Jenö had started up the leather business with Lilly's help. It was almost impossible at that time to obtain treated leather. But, having survived two years of deprivation, brutality, and depravity, the little issue of not having treated leather at hand was not going to stop Jenö Schwarcz from reopening the family's leather business.

A few days after he arrived home, he started nosing around the railway station, and thereby got to know Major Carnikoff, who was in charge of requisitioning and the distribution of food and essential rations in the town. The major, who was a tall, large-boned man, asked Jenö, in German, if he was Jewish. When Jenö told him that he was, the major told one of his sergeants to give Jenö a tin of lard, flour, dried beans, and some other food to take home with him. Soon after, Major Carnikoff came to Jenö and asked if he could get him a large leather coat—a luxury item in those days. Getting a large leather coat for such a big man was not going to be easy, but Jenö said, 'Yes, of course I could, but we need some leather.' He asked the major to give him a truck with some guards. As he knew the leather manufacturers in Budapest from before the war, Jenö took a truck full of raw hides from the Zemplén region to Budapest, and brought back a truck full of treated leather

Izr. templom.   Sátoralja-Ujhely.

A 1920s' postcard of the Jewish synagogue in Sátoraljaujhely, now a furniture store, as seen in the photograph taken in 1997

The neglected state of the Jewish cemetery in Sátoraljaujhely in 1997

A tombstone erected post-war in the Jewish cemetery by Jenö Schwarcz for his father who died in 1933, and for his mother and younger brother Ernö, who both died in the Holocaust in 1944

A portrait photograph of the handsome Jenö Schwarcz taken in Sátoraljaujhely in 1947

in exchange. This was an enormous amount of leather, and it allowed him to re-start his business. There were many leather tailors in town, but of course they had had nothing to work with until Jenö arrived with the leather. And not only did the major get his large leather coat. Eventually, the major's wife arrived from Odessa; she was a very large lady, too, and she also wanted a leather coat. Assisted by Major Carnikoff, Jenö went to Budapest several times with a truck, a driver, and two guards to exchange more raw hides for manufactured leather. So the leather business prospered.

A restless person, Jenö always looked for further challenges once he had conquered his existing problems. One day, he met an engineer and handyman who told him that he knew how to put some machines together in order to start a wood-working factory. Jenö left his two sisters in charge of the leather business, got all sorts of old equipment together with the handyman, managed to get leather belts to run the wheels of the wood-working machines, and started to manufacture wooden broom handles, as well as large boxes which were used for the transportation of apples and other goods by train and truck.

The broom handles were made from beech, a hardwood. In 1997, I talked to one of Jenö's old employees, Laci Mizsák, and he confirmed how difficult it was to push the beech through the machine manually to make just one of these handles. Of course, nobody would now dream of making broom handles from beech, a luxury timber even for furniture. Jenö, striving for improvement and expansion, went to a trade fair in Prague in early 1948 and bought an automated machine by means of which several broom handles could be made simultaneously, with the wood being fed in at one end and the broom handles coming out at the other. The wood-working business expanded, and Jenö finished up with forty employees. Men who worked for Jenö told me what a good-hearted person he was. He was the only employer in town who would regularly give every employee a Christmas present. One year he gave each employee a pair of pyjamas for Christmas; his thoughtfulness was much appreciated, as everyone knew that he himself did not observe Christmas.

The characteristics of Jenö Schwarcz as a successful businessman were already emerging. When we look back, we can see clearly his restlessness, his need to create and respond to challenges, and his search for constant improvement by visiting trade fairs or seeking other sources of information, and by purchasing modern, efficient, and automated machines and equipment. His ability to relate to all manner of men, such as Major Carnikoff, the engineer-handyman and others, is very evident. As well, it must be said that being warm-hearted and generous to his employees engendered a sense of enthusiasm and high spiritedness, which was a boon for productivity.

Life for Jenö consisted of hard work in expanding his two businesses, but also in having time for fun with his friends, including the ever-present Pali Lichtenstein (Pali had also survived Auschwitz and Dörnhau). Jenö loved dancing and singing, and was partial to pretty girls who had a sense of fun, round bottoms, and big breasts. Not even

Jenö Schwarcz pushing his low-capacity motor cycle on the streets of Sátoraljaujhely in 1948

Nazi terror had managed to damage the young man's normal sexuality or his sense of fun. On one occasion, he visited his Dörnhau confrere, Simon Paszternák, uncle Simi, whom he had helped so much in Dörnhau, and whose son's life he had helped to save. Uncle Simi entertained young Jenö in his wine cellars and got him drunk, although Jenö was unaware of this until he went out in the fresh air and staggered around the main street of the village of Tállya where the Paszternáks lived. He did not meet Fredi at that time, because Fredi was finishing his secondary schooling in a private school in Budapest. They were to meet many years later in a most unusual way.

Jenö was a highly uncommitted member of the Hungarian Communist Party. At no stage of his life was he even vaguely interested in politics— especially communism or socialism. He had joined the party out of necessity. In Hungary after the war it was very difficult to get on in a small town without being a member of the Communist Party. Jenö's main interest was in attending social functions such as dances, which were periodically organised by the party. At one of these events, he met a charming young woman called Rósza (Rose) Lukács. Both of them told me later that they had had a platonic relationship. She was a charming and intelligent woman, a homely person rather than a beauty. A Jewish girl born in Budapest in 1929, she and her mother had escaped the Nazis—each in a way that could be the subject of another book. However, just before the end of the war she had gone to Sátoraljaujhely, where she stayed until 1947. Immediately after the war she became a fervent member of the Communist Party, selling books in the party bookshop and organising social events.

She found Jenö an interesting man; but, most importantly, she remembers him as being a jovial person who would be up to tomfoolery at every opportunity. She loved dancing, as did Jenö, and they spent time together at Communist Party balls. On one occasion, when they had a big ball around the festive season of Christmas 1946, there was a lottery, and the lottery tickets also served as a popular election for the ball's beauty queen. Those buying lottery tickets wrote the name of the girl who, in their opinion, was the most beautiful at the ball; after the lottery was drawn, everyone returned their tickets with the name of the beauty of their choice. Jenö, who enjoyed a practical joke, bought 500 tickets and put Rósza's name on all of them, so that she had no difficulty in winning the beauty contest.

Life is full of surprises and ironies. Jenö told Rósza, in one of his many discussions with her, that she should meet a good friend of his named Feri Vadász. They would get on very well, he told her, because they were both such ardent communists, and because both were such nice people. Rósza returned to Budapest in 1947 and, as fate would have it, Feri Vadász became her boss in the Communist Party secretariat in Budapest. After their respective spouses died, Feri and Rózsa started living together. They have remained partners ever since.

Feri Vadász left his native town. He became an active member of the Hungarian Communist Party, serving on the executive in the country town of Kecskemét where the renowned apricot brandy is made. Jenö visited Feri three or four times during visits he had to make to Kecskemét to pick up treated leather, and he also went to his wedding in 1947. Feri and Jenö had many discussions and friendly arguments, in the course of which Jenö told him that he hated the communist system, and that communists were anti-Semitic. Feri replied that they weren't anti-Semitic; they merely disliked people who had made money and had become members of the bourgeoisie.

Jenö put some of the money that he made from his businesses into a savings-bank account. Shrewdly, as he was scared that the police would search his place, he gave the bank book to Feri to hide. The police would not go to Feri because he was a well-known, high-ranking Communist Party official. Feri played a game with Jenö, saying that he didn't want to know anything about his friend's anti-communist sentiments and that he didn't want to know anything about Jenö's hints that he would have to leave Hungary and escape. Feri Vadász, knowing Jenö well, suspected that he was seriously thinking about escaping from Hungary. But he pretended not to hear it, and instead engaged in mock arguments with him. The law was that statements and sentiments such as those expressed by Jenö regarding communism had to be reported to the authorities. Dissidents, if caught, were dealt with severely by the communist regime.

In the meantime, life for the Eastern European nations who were under Soviet domination was becoming bleaker. The danger signals were there well before the end of the war: the Soviets would dominate Eastern Europe ruthlessly. In April 1943, when Jenö Schwarcz was being taken to the Garany internment camp, the German army accidentally uncovered a mass grave of some 4,000 Polish officers in the Katyn Forest. These officers had been murdered by Stalin for opposing the Soviet occupation of sovereign Poland. In February 1945, at the historic Yalta meeting attended by Churchill, Roosevelt, and Stalin, and their advisers, Stalin's toughness, intransigence, and absolute determination to rule Eastern Europe was very evident to Winston Churchill. Only three months after the end of the war, the Allies realised the danger posed by Stalin. In a historic lecture delivered in March 1946 at an American university, Churchill stated prophetically: 'From Stettin in the Baltic to Trieste in the Adriatic an iron curtain has descended across the continent. The dark ages may return. Beware, I say. Behind this curtain across Europe, Russia might even now be preparing for spreading communist tyranny.'

In September 1947, the communists won a rigged general election in Hungary, and the powerful Soviet forces also began to dominate Czechoslovakia and Poland. While Princess Elizabeth and the Duke of Edinburgh married in November 1947, the Soviet onslaught on Eastern Europe continued. Opposition parties were dissolved in Hungary and Poland, leaving the Communist Party as the only political force in these countries. In Czechoslovakia, many had been arrested in September 1947 for plotting the unsuccessful assassination attempt of the democratically elected president, Edouard Benes, and on 21 February 1948 Benes declared that there could be no totalitarian communist regime in his country. However, just a week later a communist coup succeeded, with prime minister Klement

Gottwald seizing power and silencing Benes. A fortnight later, the communists pushed foreign minister Jan Masaryk through the window of his flat to his death. Masaryk, the son of the first Czechoslovakian president, had been the last hope of opponents of the communist takeover of Czechoslovakia. In June 1948, president Benes resigned, and Klement Gottwald took his place.

The only voice in Eastern Europe raised against Stalin was that of Yugoslavia's leader, Marshall Tito, who broke his previous agreements with Moscow in June 1948, and then severed relationships completely in September 1949. Russia denounced him, and this was followed by similar statements from Soviet-dominated eastern states such as Hungary, Romania and Czechoslovakia. The Russian domination of Czechoslovakia, Poland, Romania, and Hungary moved relentlessly forward in 1948. In August 1948, a pro-Soviet figure, Arpád Szakasits, was sworn in as president of Hungary. By the end of 1948 the Catholic primate, Cardinal Jozsef Mindszenty, was charged with treason and held for 'plotting against the government'. A bogus trial was held in February 1949 in which the cardinal was sentenced to life imprisonment. Eventually, he was granted asylum in the American embassy in Budapest in 1956, and was allowed to leave Hungary in 1971.

By the beginning of 1949, there was a trickle of so-called 'political refugees' fleeing Hungary through the borders of Yugoslavia, Austria, and Czechoslovakia. Medium-sized and large businesses, including those of Jenö Schwarcz, were being 'nationalised' without compensation by the Hungarian communist regime. Jenö had made another major decision—to escape from Hungary and to start yet another new life.

CHAPTER 6

FROM AUSTRIA TO AUSTRALIA

In mid-1949, carrying just one briefcase, Jenö fled across the border to Czechoslovakia. In his briefcase he had two shirts, a singlet, underpants, and socks. He was smart enough to carry a few condoms, also, so that if he were caught he could say that he was visiting his girlfriend across the border. Jenö was to find out later that during 1949 about one thousand Hungarian refugees fled their homeland. He was in good company: the Czech tennis player, Jaroslav Drobny, a Wimbledon finalist and later Wimbledon winner, defected at exactly the same time.

Jenö first went to a small town, Král-Chlmec, in Slovakia, just across the border from his home town, and where Dr Adler, a member of Feri Vadász's group, had set up a medical practice after his return from Dörnhau. The doctor was a little worried about hiding Jenö, because at that time the Czechoslovak secret police were making unannounced visits to houses that were suspected of harbouring Hungarian refugees. So he passed Jenö on to a taxi driver who put him up for the night. When Jenö arrived he was completely exhausted and, as his room was in darkness, he took his clothes off and went to sleep on the bed. When he awoke, he found that he was on an L-shaped bed, and that on the other limb of the 'L' there was a large brutish-looking man asleep. When the man woke up, he said in a loud voice, 'I am breuges!' In Yiddish, to be 'breuges' is to be annoyed or angry, so Jenö meekly asked him why he was angry. The man replied, 'I am not angry. My name is Breuges!' This turned out to be a great joke, but it was an even greater relief for Jenö.

The following day, Jenö went to the larger town of Kosice, a town of about 60,000 inhabitants that had previously been called Kassa (and was my home town). Jenö had already been there in 1944, albeit inside a wagon on his way to Auschwitz. He had also visited the town several times after the war because of friends and business, and also because he followed the soccer matches between his home-town team and Kosice's. He knew two brothers who lived there, Les (Csi Csi) and Imre Korda, and with their help he was able to escape by train to Bratislava, the capital of Slovakia, and then on to

Vienna in the company of other Jews. In the late-1940s, Les Korda was the leader of an organisation called BRICHA whose principal aim was to smuggle Jews out of Czechoslovakia and Hungary, and into Vienna. This was done essentially by bribing railway and border officials. Jenö initially helped several friends, including Alex and George Pongrácz, to get into Vienna this way, and eventually used the same means himself to escape. Like the others, Jenö had false papers with which to cross into free Vienna. On reaching Vienna, the refugees were declared 'displaced persons'.

Jenö's youngest sister, Gita, who had married Pista Klein, escaped at the same time. They were re-united in Vienna, together with other friends, including members of the Pongrácz family. (Jenö's older sister, Lilly, and her husband, Miklos Somogyi, who moved to the nearby town of Miskolc in 1949, eventually left Hungary in 1956.) Jenö, Gita, her husband, and some other friends from around Zemplén and Slovakia lived in what before the war had been the Rothschild Hospital—the only Jewish hospital in Vienna before the Nazi occupation of Austria. Amazingly, the great Viktor Frankl had been in charge of the hospital's neurological department from 1938 right up to his deportation to a concentration camp in 1942. The post-war Rothschild Hospital retained its name, but it had become a hostel for Jews who had once again been displaced and alienated, this time by Russian communism.

Jenö's life as a young bachelor took a new and happy turn not long after his arrival in Austria when he met Eta Schwarcz. A distant relative, Eta had been born in Slovakia near Stropko, and for over eighteen months during the war had hidden from the Nazis in an old disused quarry. After the war, she and her family migrated to Belgium, and she was merely visiting Salzburg when she met Jenö. Eta was not only beautiful, with a serene face, but she was also a well-educated and cultured person who spoke several languages, including English. She also had a wonderful, childlike sense of fun. Jenö liked Eta's looks and cultured ways, while she enjoyed his sense of fun, vitality, and his ambition. It is no wonder that they fell in love and were married within three or four months of meeting. They had a Jewish wedding, a *chupe*, in the

Salzburg synagogue. The wedding turned out to be a scream in more ways than one. For a start, the rabbi and the cantor was the same person, but added to that the rabbi kept turkeys and chickens in the backyard. When he started to sing during the ceremony, the chickens started to sing and scream with him, and the entire wedding party dissolved into laughter.

Jenö and Eta were determined to leave Europe and to migrate to the new world. Their first choice was the United States; their second, Canada; and their third, Australia. However, while the waiting time for migration was three years to the United States and two years to Canada, there was no waiting time for Australia. Jenö was a restless soul, as we have already seen, and the possibility of immediate departure was the main reason that he and Eta decided to migrate 'downunder'. Jenö was also encouraged to move to Australia because of his great love of freedom without oppression or discrimination, and the promise Australia held out of life in a true democracy. He was not to be disappointed in this.

With the help of friends and the Jewish welfare organisation JOINT, Jenö was able to get a landing permit to Australia for both of them. With some difficulty, Jenö was also able to get two berths on a migrant ship called *El Misr*. When they arrived in Marseille to board the ship they discovered that, for some reason, their names had been crossed off the list. Jenö found the offices of JOINT in Marseille and, being able to talk in Yiddish—a language he had picked up in Dörnhau from Polish Jews—was able to converse with the executives.

'Why were our names crossed off?' he asked.

'Because we had a telegram just yesterday to say that we should not give you places on this ship, as you are a rich man.'

'I am not rich', Jenö protested. 'In fact, I have no money at all.'

'Well, here is the telegram.'

The telegram had been sent by a secretary from JOINT in Vienna. Why she sent this telegram nobody, even up to the present time, knows. (By an extraordinary turn of events, the woman in question migrated to Australia

herself, and some years later applied for a job with Jenö. When he confronted her about the telegram, she denied having sent it. But having been shown
the telegram in Marseille, Jenö said to her, 'You would be the last person I
would give a job to.' If Jenö had been a Buddhist as well, he might have said
that this was a bit of Jewish karma.)

Jenö was able to talk his way back onto the list, and he and Eta boarded
the ship about two days before sailing. In keeping with its name, the living
conditions on this ship were indescribably miserable. There were several
hundred people in the hold of the ship, men and women separated, two to
three hundred sleeping in each hold in hammocks. Once again, Jenö wasn't
to be outdone by this little challenge. The day before departure he went
ashore, bought two folding army beds, and put them up next to each other
on the deck. He and Eta slept there throughout the journey. There were a
few others who decided to sleep on the deck rather than in the hold of the
ship, but they didn't have beds and had to sleep on the deck itself—although
it was still better than in a hammock below. Also on board was Michael
Deutsch, a Hungarian with a wonderful singing voice whom Jenö had first
met at the Rothschild Hospital in Vienna, and who was a witness at his wedding. (Michael was to become the cantor at Sydney's Temple Emanuel, and
he was to remain a good friend of Jenö's to the end.) The trip took about four
weeks. *El Misr* sailed into Melbourne first, and then went on to Sydney. It
arrived in mid-January 1950.

As the migrant ship was pulling out of Marseille on its way to Australia in
early December 1949, the Aussies were getting ready for a general election
about whose outcome there was great excitement and anticipation. As it
turned out, the pipe-smoking, ex-train driver Ben Chifley and his Labor
Party were thrown out. Bob Menzies became the new prime minister, heading the newly formed Liberal-Country Party coalition. It was ironic that, just
as Eta and Jenö Schwarcz were migrating to escape communism, Bob
Menzies won an election on the twin platforms of anti-communism and, for
the first time in Australia's history, the promotion of mass migration.

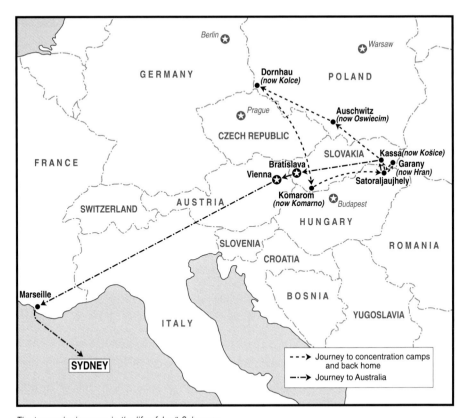

The two major journeys in the life of Jenö Schwarcz

CHAPTER 7

THE HOLE-IN-THE-WALL SHOP

El Misr sailed into Sydney Harbour in January 1950. Jenö and Eta couldn't leave the dreadful ship quickly enough. They arrived in Sydney Harbour on a warm midsummer's day with high hopes, but with not more than a few pounds in their pockets and a few personal belongings. They were not to know, of course, that Australia was about to enter a long period of prosperity. They were greeted on the wharf by Jenö's younger sister, Gita, and her husband, Pista Klein, who had arrived a few weeks earlier; and by some of Jenö's old friends from Hungary, the Kordas, who were also recent arrivals. Les Korda and his wife Klara, a concert violinist, were renting a house in Gladesville, and for three weeks Eta and Jenö stayed with them. They had little money, but a lot of hope, energy, enthusiasm, and ambition as they heard about their newly adopted country. It was a free land, had food in abundance and plentiful employment, and its people were generous and easy-going, with a wonderful, light-hearted sense of humour. Jenö spoke very little English, and arrived with a Hungarian-English dictionary in which he had already crossed out the word 'impossible'.

Australia was certainly on a roll, beckoning migrants with open arms. They came in large numbers from the United Kingdom and Europe: over 80,000 arrived in 1950 alone, representing about 1 per cent of the total population of Australia. Industry and agriculture were expanding rapidly. In the sporting arena, Frank Sedgman, Ken McGregor, and John Bromwich regained the Davis Cup, thereby ushering in a long period of Australian tennis supremacy.

When it first became clear that Jenö was going to migrate to Australia, one of his old friends from Hungary who had just arrived in Sydney had written to Jenö in Austria to tell him earnestly that, whatever else he did, he must learn two things: the first was the upholstery trade, because upholsterers in Australia were in short supply; the second was the manufacture of toothpaste, because his friend saw so many people with teeth falling out and so many others with full sets of false teeth that he figured out that the toothpaste in Australia couldn't be much good. Jenö took this advice seriously, and learned both of these skills whilst in Austria. Soon after his arrival, however, he discovered that there was plenty of good-quality toothpaste around, but there was certainly a shortage of upholsterers. He learned later that many young women in Australia had all their teeth removed just before they got married, even when their teeth were completely normal. The reasons for these mass tooth-extractions remain a mystery. It is perhaps a good subject for a Ph D thesis.

Soon after arriving, Jenö did in fact get a job as an upholsterer, and Eta worked in a shirt factory making shirt collars. They lived in a boarding house in Bondi, and both enjoyed Bondi and Bondi beach. Jenö remained loyal to Bondi beach to the end, walking there almost daily and soaking in the sea water in summer. They enjoyed the beauty of Sydney Harbour, the company of their few friends, and the abundance of fresh food. This was a culture that to them seemed classless, and they quickly got to love the good-natured and friendly people of Australia. They were supremely content and happy in their new country.

After a few months of upholstery work, Jenö got another job as a packer and storeman at the Anthony Hordern department store, which he held for eighteen months. During this time he worked in the carpet department where, with overtime, he earned about ten pounds a week. Apart from his job, he also sold carpet ends, called 'flock', to a man who made pillows from them, and each week he would earn as much doing this as from his regular job. These carpet ends were thrown away at Anthony Hordern's before Jenö arrived, so they were quite happy to let him have them. Just as Jenö had two jobs, so did Eta. During the day she was employed by the department store Mark and Foys to repair stockings, and at night at home she did the same job for David Jones. Being happy and content, working hard, and enjoying life was wonderful for Jenö. But very soon it was not quite enough. He could see business opportunities waiting for him—opportunities that appeared to be inviting him with open arms.

During the early 1950s, the Soviet communist oppression of Eastern Europe and East Germany created reactionary anti-communism and anti-Russian sentiment around the world. Julius and Ethel Rosenberg were sentenced to death and executed for spying against the United States, whilst there was a grossly misdirected anti-communist purge in that country by Senator Eugene McCarthy. Also in response to the rise of communism, atom bombs were being tested by the great powers, and the United States also developed and tested the horrific hydrogen bomb. By contrast, Australia in the early 1950s was a land of bliss and peace. There was full employment, and the country had virtually no economic problems. In spite of the conservative Menzies government, the country developed good social services for pensioners, the sick, and those with young families. The country was gaining not only wealth and prosperity, but confidence as well, as it embraced the influence of several migrant cultures such as those of Holland, Italy, and Greece. An energetic, ambitious young entrepreneur like Jenö Schwarcz could not, at that time, have chosen a better country in the world in which to carve out for himself a good career in business. He was certainly the right man in the right place at the right time.

One Saturday midday after work in 1952, while still working as a packer and storeman at Anthony Hordern, Jenö met Eta to buy some weekend provisions. While they were 'window shopping' at David Jones, a downtown Sydney department store, Jenö heard a familiar voice behind him call out, 'Hello, Jenczi.'. A cold shiver ran down Jenö's spine—for while he recognised the voice, he didn't think that the man now speaking to him, George Zimmermann, was alive. An old friend of Jenö's who had been a prisoner of war, George's whole family in Sátoraljaujhely had been killed by the Nazis. By the time George had returned to Hungary at the end of 1949, Jenö had already escaped from Hungary. George had migrated to Australia in 1952 and was working as a gardener for the Public Works Department in Sydney. He had also just finished work for the day. They reminisced about old times, and then George Zimmermann suggested that they grow mushrooms as a business venture.

Jenö and Eta now had a house in the Sydney suburb of Lakemba. The house had a large garden at the rear where Jenö grew tomatoes and peppers as well as other vegetables. George Zimmermann told him how to grow the mushrooms. So, first of all, Jenö decided to experiment in his own garden to see if the mushrooms would grow—and they did. The two of them found a suitable place in Glebe in an old house that was occupied by nuns. In the basement, which had not been opened up for some twenty years, there were several dark rooms that were perfect for growing mushrooms. They rented it from the nuns, put up shelving made from old boxes, and managed to bring in some cheap horse manure that was delivered to the house from a stud nearby. After the two men finished their jobs at 5.30 pm, they went to their mushroom hide-out. Here they worked until eleven o'clock at night before returning home for a good night's sleep. It was hard work, as the mushroom venture was by now Jenö's third job.

They sold the mushrooms directly to greengrocers, and were able to sell as many as they could produce. The nuns moved out and let the floor above the mushroomery to a Hungarian by the name of Kovács (a name that translates to 'Smith'), who started to manufacture Hungarian mixed pickles, called 'csalamádé'. One day, the down-pipes burst in the basement, flooding the whole area and destroying all the mushrooms. With his usual optimism, Jenö wanted to start the mushroom business again. But Zimmermann became very downhearted and depressed. He didn't want to continue, and soon after the disaster he migrated again, eventually settling in California.

Jenö Schwarcz, however, was not put off. In early 1953, he talked a railways official into giving him space in the underpass of the Sydney Town Hall railway station. He was given a 'hole in the wall' in the underpass. With the help of a builder he put up a ceiling and some walls, obtained cabinets, shelves, and a refrigerator and, with the help of Eta, started to sell smallgoods and sandwiches. Jenö became acquainted with a Hungarian migrant, Bill Szabolcs, who was a ticket collector at the railway station, and they often spent time together swapping jokes. Szabolcs left the railways to study architecture but, curiously, his and Jenö's lives were to become entwined again in the mid-1960s.

Jenö's friend Sam Moss, also an expatriate Hungarian, had a delicatessen in downtown Sydney, and he couldn't understand why Jenö would want to go underground. 'Well, that's where the people are', Jenö explained. Jenö had not heard of the notorious Willie Sutton, infamous for committing daring bank robberies in the United States during the Depression. When finally apprehended by the gendarmes after one of his daring robberies, he was asked by the chief of police why he only robbed banks. Willie Sutton replied with simplicity and logic, 'Well, that's where the money is.'

It was hard work but satisfying for Jenö to have his own business once again. Eta was of immense help to him. Not only did she support him morally when he took a risk in establishing a shop in an underground hole in the wall; after the shop opened, she made the sandwiches and, by being her charming self, looked after their customers who were often in a hurry to get to work or have their lunchtime sandwich.

Jenö and Eta were becoming busier and busier in their little shop. Jenö was ordering increasing amounts of smallgoods, ham, sausages, and salami, and some of his Australian suppliers at times failed to turn up as promised. But there was a young man who delivered smallgoods to Jenö who was different. Always prompt, courteous, and reliable, he was also of Hungarian (and Slovak) background, born in 1930 near a town called Losoncz, then and now part of Slovakia. At the age of fifteen, he had left his family in Slovakia and had gone to Israel, then called Palestine, and had later served in the Israeli army. He came to Australia in 1952, and was reunited with his family—his mother, brothers, and a sister—who had migrated to Sydney from Slovakia. This prompt, reliable young man, then 23 years old, was Frank Lowy.

Although Jenö was eight years older, both men came from the same part of the world, had a similar background, were full of energy and enthusiasm, were not daunted by hard work, were not afraid of taking risks and, importantly, shared a roguish sense of humour. Both men were personable and direct in their approach to life and to each other. Within a short period of time they got to know each other quite well. Jenö's gut feelings once more led him to make a shrewd assessment. Without referring the matter to the logical side of his brain, he knew that in Frank Lowy he had found a good business partner for the future. Not long after recognising this gut feeling, Jenö was talking to Frank.

'Look', he said to him. 'If I find a good shop, I would like to make you my partner.'

'I would like to be your partner, but I have no money', Frank said.

'That's OK. I have no money either', Jenö replied.

And so their partnership was born. Jenö had committed himself to move forward once again. He had Eta's full support, he had found an energetic and ambitious partner and, being a man of action, his next move was to find and open a shop 'where all the people were'. Their partnership was based on trust entirely. Amazingly, at no stage did they have a partnership contract, nor did they sign any formal agreements. However, right from the beginning they made two stipulations. The first was that the wives would have no part or say in the running of the business; the second was that if a project went sour, and it had been promoted by only one member of the team, the other who initially had had doubts about its success was not allowed to say, 'I told you so!'

The western suburbs of Sydney were expanding, bursting at the seams with newly arrived migrants. Right in the middle of this amazing and exciting expansion of Sydney's west, Jenö found an empty shop in Blacktown in early 1954. He thereby started a partnership with Frank Lowy that was to flourish for 33 years.

CHAPTER 8

BLACKADATOWN

During 1953, just when Jenö was contemplating business expansion and a partnership with his new friend, Frank Lowy, it was becoming clear that Australia was about to become one of the most successful countries in the Western world. Its economy was fuelled by high wool prices, large profits from agriculture, and the promise of great mineral wealth. Then, in December 1953, oil was discovered off the coast of Western Australia. The find sent Ampol Exploration shares sky high, causing newspapers to report with calculated understatement that, as a result, 'Many brokers are said to have made tidy sums'. Migrants continued to flock to Australia, bringing with them much that was new and exciting in culture, customs, and food. About this time there was just a hint of inflation, and newspapers reported with some criticism that the Melbourne-to-Sydney airfare had increased by four shillings and sixpence to eight pounds eleven shillings and sixpence.

Not long after Jenö and Frank opened their food store and delicatessen in Blacktown, Australia was visited by Queen Elizabeth II and Prince Philip. They received an enthusiastic and genuinely open-hearted welcome from Australians. Their schedule was just a little too full to visit the Blacktown delicatessen, so Jenö's first meeting with royalty had to be put off for a few years.

Blacktown was expanding rapidly as it received an influx of migrants: many came from the Mediterranean countries of Italy and Greece, and others came from Hungary, Yugoslavia, and England. They were mostly hard-working people who earned a reasonable wage, especially with overtime included, and spent generously on food for their families. Jenö was delighted to see Italians coming in to buy a whole salami in Blacktown, compared to the 'hole-in-the-wall' shop where women would ask for 'three slices of salami, thinly sliced, and please not the first slice'. Jenö and Frank were good friends with Sam Moss (later to be the joint founder of the popular Katies chain of women's fashion shops with Joseph Brender). Sam already had a delicatessen in downtown Sydney, and another near Kings Cross. The two men boasted to Sam about their Italian and Greek customers taking home whole salamis, dozens of sausages, and slabs of cheese, as well as large quantities of toilet paper and other goods. Sam couldn't quite believe this. One day he drove to Blacktown, quite some distance from central Sydney, and found hectic activity going on in the Blacktown delicatessen.

The three men, Jenö, Frank, and Sam, figured out that if they went to a wholesale butcher together and ordered a large quantity of goods they would get a discount, and would finish up with a much cheaper price. They found, also, that if they bought more than one hundred loaves of bread they would get a halfpenny off each loaf. It's wonderful what three Hungarian business-men can achieve if they put their heads together.

Many years later, Sam Moss recalled how Jenö and Frank, although work-ing very hard, always had time to joke, laugh, sing, and clown and, as Sam put it (imitating an Italian accent), 'They always make ah de funny.' There is

The famous 'Blacktown Deli' van recreated for the Saunders valedictory celebration in 1987. From left to right: John Saunders, Frank Lowy, and Sam Moss

no doubt that this was a very happy time for Jenö, seeing their business build-ing up, becoming familiar with the delicatessen trade, and enjoying life in spite of the long hours. He got to know many of his regular customers. In an affectionate way, without any malice, he imitated these warm-hearted Italians who were full of vitality but often had poor English—as, for exam-ple, when they referred to the suburb they lived in as 'Blackadatown'. Jenö had a similar sense of fun to them: he was warm hearted, down to earth and, with his olive skin, even looked a little Mediterranean. In turn, his cus-tomers, particularly the Italians and Greeks, got to know Jenö and to trust him. They frequently asked him for business advice—a state of affairs which was to become important later.

In mid-1954, looking out from the microcosm of Blacktown, Jenö knew that it was time for further expansion and for a new venture. He flew to Melbourne and visited Pellegrini's, a coffee lounge in Bourke Street, to see their espresso machine in operation. Soon after, Jenö and Frank opened a coffee shop just a few doors up from their Blacktown grocery store. At first, they installed a one-arm espresso machine. Their espresso coffee proved to be extremely popular, particularly among Mediterranean migrants—so much so, that within one month the partners had bought a machine with three arms in order to cope with the demand. They quickly got the services of Leo, an Austrian migrant, to run the coffee shop. The quest to get the lat-est and most efficient equipment was ever present in Jenö.

The two men recalled later how many Italian road workers, among oth-ers, came to the coffee shop during their 'smoko'. Italians tend not to enun-ciate the last syllable of many words, so when a few of these men came in together for coffee, a popular question Jenö and Frank would ask was, 'You for coff? You for coff? You for coff?' Nowadays, with our sterile political cor-rectness, this might be considered racist or crude, but no offence was ever intended or taken. In fact, Jenö's and Frank's sense of humour was much appreciated and enjoyed by their fun-loving, Italian road-worker customers.

In 1955, Jenö experienced some chest pain. He saw a doctor in

Blacktown, who told Jenö he had a heart problem and asked him what he did for a living. When Jenö replied that he had a grocery store and delicatessen, the doctor said, 'Sell it, retire, and rest up from now on.' Jenö was only 33 at the time, and had no intention of retiring. Nevertheless he and Frank did sell the coffee shop in late 1955, making a tidy profit on the goodwill.

The Hungarian-born architect, Ervin Graf, who had settled in Sydney in 1950, first met Jenö Schwarcz and Frank Lowy at their delicatessen when he came in to buy his lunches during a period when he was building houses in the area. 'One day', he told me, 'I suggested to Jenö that, instead of selling salami in Blacktown, they might do better building a few shops or subdividing some land.' The next phase in the successful business careers of Jenö Schwarcz and Frank Lowy was about to begin, and it was to reveal that they possessed two crucial entrepreneurial characteristics that were enormously important yet almost impossible to quantify in money terms. First, a new idea, such as that of Ervin Graf's, was quickly taken up, researched, and acted upon at the first opportunity. Second, Jenö and Frank displayed total integrity and trustworthiness—a subject on which theories of business success, even today, are largely silent. In essence, they were trusted because they consistently demonstrated that their word was their bond: they paid interest and bills on time, delivered promptly, and did not charge excessively.

As Jenö was getting to know the neighbourhood, and as his customers were getting to know and trust him, he was apparently told one day that some old shops on a corner near their delicatessen were up for sale—shops that were owned by a local resident. He and Frank had no money, but they figured out that the existing shops could be pulled down and several more could be built on the site. The two partners scrounged around for money, and bought an option to buy the property. They already knew Les Irwin, the manager of the Blacktown branch of the Bank of New South Wales (and sub-sequently a federal parliamentarian). Irwin came to trust Jenö and Frank, and approved a bank loan that enabled them to buy the property and build the shops. Irwin backed his judgement the way bank managers used to do; he would also have been shrewd enough to predict that the two men were going places, and would very likely become good clients of the bank. The shops were built on a shoestring budget and, for everybody concerned, on a basis of trust—a bank loan without much security, and a bit of local knowledge that the shops could be bought. It was also the spark, the catalyst, which propelled Jenö and Frank into their next business venture. With the comradeship and enthusiasm of Frank, and the moral support of Eta, there was no doubt in Jenö's mind that he was doing the right thing.

Timing is important in business, and it was certainly the right time in the 1950s for Jenö and Frank to make their next move into land subdivision and development. Australia's population was expanding rapidly, and the country was enjoying increasing prosperity and affluence. Nevertheless the partners were entering a completely new world of business, a field in which they had no previous experience. A stone's throw from the grocery and delicatessen in Blacktown were small farms and fields which were beginning to be rezoned for residential purposes to accommodate a fast-growing population in the west of Sydney. By 1957, entrepreneurial builders were getting involved in land subdivision and building.

Jenö and Frank decided to buy some of the rezoned land from local owners. They had the basic ingredients needed for success, but no more: a sympathetic bank manager who trusted them and would lend them money, access to contractors to build the roads, and agents to sell the subdivided land. Jenö and Frank didn't know anything about subdividing land; but they were both young, enthusiastic, and entrepreneurial people who were prepared to take some risks. They knew that more money should come in than go out, and that was about the limit of their specialised knowledge. Their careers in building and development had begun.

As it happened, the subdivision business was not all cakes and ale. There were frequent problems with local councils. However, Frank and Jenö decided very early on to do the job properly: there was to be no corruption, and they would try to avoid lawyers in any dispute. Instead of confrontation and litigation, they were always ready to compromise. As Jenö put it, 'You can always come to a mutually suitable arrangement.' These business characteristics remained a hallmark of their partnership, and held them in very good stead. Their principles eventually gained them support, trust, and respect from many quarters of the business world in Australia.

Without undertaking any special business planning, the two men instinctively saw the other's strengths. They worked closely together on a day-to-day basis, each complementing the other in a quite natural way. Jenö was usually the one with new ideas, which he pursued relentlessly, whilst Frank had a leaning towards the practicalities of finance and organisation, and the legalities of business. From very early on in the partnership it was clear that Jenö was more the 'ideas man' and Frank more the administrator and 'money manager'.

At the end of 1957, Jenö and Frank sold their grocery and delicatessen in Blacktown. They had become totally immersed in subdividing land in the western suburbs of Sydney. Importantly, they were also contemplating their next move, which was to radically change their business interests once again. The pattern seemed to be that when a business venture became successful, and the challenges had been met, Jenö looked for new challenges.

Having become interested in subdivisions and building, Jenö and his wife visited the United States in early 1958. They experienced for the first time the thrill of what were called 'shopping centres', in which everything and anything could be bought in one area. Most excited about this, Jenö apparently proposed to Frank that they build just such a shopping centre in Blacktown. Frank was extremely receptive to this new project. The two men borrowed more money, and proceeded to build their first shopping centre. It comprised a department store, fifteen shops, a supermarket, and parking for fifty cars. This shopping centre, which they called Westfield Place (see below) caused a minor sensation in the western suburbs of Sydney, and was an immediate success. Jenö and Frank sold it some time later and, although

The first shopping centre built by Jenö Schwarcz and Frank Lowy in Blacktown, named 'Westfield Place' and opened in 1958—
by which time Jenö had become an Australian citizen and had anglicised his name to John Saunders

it has since been enlarged, it is still there—a reminder of their beginnings in
shopping-centre development.

One evening, when Jenö and Frank were returning home in their van
from Blacktown, and when the building business looked very much a success, they started to discuss a name for their new enterprise. They both felt
that 'Schwarcz and Lowy' was not exactly the sort of name to put on a cop-
per plate in Australia. So they started to throw around some ideas. As they
were working in the western suburbs, they thought of names such as
'Westland' and 'West Gardens'. Finally, the word 'Westfield' stuck. Very
soon after, they named their new shopping-centre enterprise 'Westfield
Place' and their company 'Westfield'. They did not even dream then that
Westfield would eventually become a household name in Australia, just like
Woolworths or Coles.

Whilst Jenö and Frank were building the exciting Westfield Place in 1958, and continuing with successful subdivisions in Sydney's west, Australia also continued its economic, cultural, and educational expansion. Historically, the year 1959 was most interesting for the two men. In that year Robert Hawke entered the political and industrial-relations stage as the leading advocate of the Australian Council of Trade Unions, arguing at a hearing before the Commonwealth Conciliation and Arbitration Tribunal for a twenty-two shilling increase in the basic wage, with quarterly cost-of-living adjustments. Hawke would later become a long-serving and successful Labor prime minister of Australia, but well before that he also became a great friend of Jenö and then of Frank. Historically, 1959 was also to become memorable for Frank Lowy, because in that year the Reserve Bank of Australia was formed to take over the central-banking functions of the Commonwealth Bank. Subsequently, the Reserve Bank became Australia's money regulator, and some years later Frank Lowy was elected to its board of governors.

I suspect that Jenö Schwarcz had an inkling that some of his ambitions would be realised, particularly after building Westfield Place and founding Westfield with Frank Lowy. But what was to follow was unimaginable, even for a man who believed that nothing is impossible. In his new country, a country that he came to love and believe in, he took out Australian citizenship in 1957, and in 1958 anglicised his name to John Saunders. By the end of 1959, Saunders and Lowy were at the helm of a new ship called Westfield, and the vessel was very much on the move forward.

CHAPTER 9

SAUNDERS AND LOWY GO PUBLIC

The two men decided to float Westfield as a public company in March 1960. One of the main reasons for doing so was that it was becoming increasingly difficult for non-listed firms, especially in the building industry, to obtain substantial loans from banks. Although Australia at that time produced one-third of the world's wool, other areas of the economy were incurring an increasing current-account deficit. The Australian treasurer and later prime minister, Harold Holt, on advice from the Reserve Bank, instituted a 'credit squeeze' not long after the public float of Westfield was announced. The Australian banks were directed by the government to stringently limit business loans. The credit squeeze affected the building industry first, and then the textile industry; finally, motor-car manufacturers General Motors Holden and Ford cut production and dismissed workers. For the first time since the Depression, there was serious unemployment in Australia.

By the 1960s, John Saunders knew instinctively that he and Frank Lowy would be a success in business. The two men had already made overseas trips looking at building and development. John Saunders had found new ideas, and had studied how best they could be introduced into Australia. He had less time but more energy to develop his friendships, not only with his business partner but also with others: mainly expatriate Hungarians such as Sam Moss who was heading into the clothing and textile business; Andrew (Bandi) Lederer, who later became a prominent smallgoods manufacturer; the Korda brothers; and the Pongrass (Pongrácz) family. All of his friends were working equally hard, and in burgeoning Australia they could see wonderful progress.

John remained close to his two sisters, Lilly and Gita; their husbands, Manczi and Pista; and his nieces, Judy and Suzie. John also retained his connection with the Jewish community of Sydney. John and Eta adopted Betty in 1960, and this added great joy to their lives. So every hour of the day was taken care of. John was literally thrilled with the work he was doing, and he was once again the patriarch of his family. He loved Sydney—its cosmopolitan feel, the beauty of its harbour, its bays and coves, Circular Quay, The

Rocks, Bondi, Manly. John knew he was living in one of the most beautiful cities of the world. As a citizen of Australia he was proud and grateful to be accepted on an equal footing to others. In fact, he remained forever passionate about Sydney and Australia.

The Westfield float of debentures for £A150,000 was substantially undersubscribed because of the economic downturn and because of the government-induced credit squeeze. At the time, John and Frank were quite close to finishing their first major shopping-centre development at Hornsby. The float was on the verge of failing when, at the eleventh hour, what seemed like a miracle occurred. The principal of the brokerage firm underwriting the float simply wrote a cheque for the under-subscribed amount—about £70,000—and presented it to John and Frank. Using that wonderful tool, hindsight, this was no miracle: the brokerage-firm principal displayed shrewd judgement about the bright prospects of Westfield and about the integrity of its two owners. The float was saved, the company went public, and it was possible to complete building the Hornsby shopping centre in 1961.

Hornsby was a great success. It had thirty shops, a supermarket, and ample car parking. Having the large department store McDowells as an anchor tenant was a major coup. Right from the start, Westfield won the trust and support of major retailers such as McDowells. This was essential in regional shopping centres, as we will see shortly. Hornsby has been enlarged and renovated since, and remains very successful. It was the first of the substantial centres to be built by Westfield under one roof as a one-stop shopping centre. This concept had been introduced in the United States just four years previously, in 1956, by the Viennese immigrant town-planner Victor Gruen. His utopian vision of creating the milieu of a central European city centre had been given shape by the construction of Southdale Center in Minneapolis, with its seventy enclosed stores and parking for over 5,000 cars; this made it at the time the biggest shopping centre in the world. In Australia, John Saunders' and Frank Lowy's dream of becoming investors and developers was rapidly taking shape. The end of the credit squeeze was announced

The first major shopping-centre development of Westfield Development Corporation was the Hornsby Plaza, north of Sydney, completed in 1961. Rebuilt, enlarged, and renovated several times, it remains very successful

by the Reserve Bank, and there was a feeling in the air that it would be 'roses, roses all the way' for Westfield, John Saunders, and Frank Lowy.

Australia yet again entered a period of prosperity and development. In the early 1960s, with its population reaching eleven million, the key economic sectors of primary production, manufacturing, and building were once more on the rise. The image of Australia as an important economic force in the world of wool and wheat production was confirmed, with large sales to the West as well as to Russia, China, and Japan. Rupert Murdoch confidently published the first national newspaper, *The Australian*, in mid-1964. In the same year, Donald Horne described Australia in his book *The Lucky Country* as a prosperous, fair-minded, fun-loving, tolerant, genuine nation in the making. It is not difficult to understand why John Saunders was so happy and grateful to be living in Australia, having escaped both the Cold War and the suppression of his freedoms just a decade earlier.

By the early 1960s, John and Frank had realised the importance of large department stores coming into their shopping centres as tenants. They also realised that chain stores such as G J Coles didn't have the know-how to buy and build stores to their requirements, so they undertook to build stores for Coles, Myers, McDowells, and others.

In 1959, after a trip to an international shopping-centre convention in Las Vegas, John and Eta had hired a car and taken a leisurely drive along the coast from San Francisco to Los Angeles, staying at American motels on the way. These were all modern and well equipped, with television, up-to-date bathrooms, refrigerators, restaurants, and good service. Of course, there were motels in Australia at the time, but many of them—particularly along main highways—were somewhat shabby, with meagre facilities and poor service. John had come back to Australia with the idea of building a high-quality motel outside central Sydney. Imbued with the American principle of what was important in real estate—position, position, position—he went looking for a piece of land. He found it just north of the Harbour Bridge on the Pacific Highway, a major thoroughfare that connected Sydney with Brisbane.

In 1962 they contracted it out to a builder who was to build a fifty-room motel to be named 'The Shore Inn'. Unfortunately, the building group went broke halfway through the construction, and Westfield had to take over its completion. The Shore Inn had a wonderful Spanish-style façade with a tower, and it quickly became a well-known local landmark.

The first manager chose himself when the building was in its finishing stages, responding to a sign outside which said, 'A motel is being built here'. One afternoon, when John was checking on progress, a man came in from the street. He told John that he was Swiss and a diplomate of one of the famous hotelier schools, and that he would do an excellent job as manager. His name was Emile Fehr, and John engaged him on the spot. He did indeed do an excellent job, building up the motel so that it developed a very good name and prospered for many years after it was first opened early in 1963. John and Frank developed the premises with the changing times: they enlarged the motel, added new facilities, such as a high-class restaurant, a good bar, and a swimming pool, and later on built function rooms for meetings and conferences. Between 1965 and 1972 The Shore Inn was run by John Bock, and became a profitable venture.

Right from the beginning, John took on The Shore Inn as his special project; in fact, he visited it almost every day for many years. After a trip to Hungary in the early 1980s, he met an excellent chef at the Forum Hotel, Imre Halász, and invited him to come to The Shore Inn. Imre accepted, and he and his family have since settled in Australia. He turned out to be not only a first-class chef but also a delightful man who, in recent times, opened a very successful Hungarian restaurant in Sydney's fashionable Double Bay. Keeping it all in the family, his wife Ili was John's faithful housekeeper up to his final illness.

Sydney's population was expanding at an incredible speed. For cheaper living coupled with a rural ambience, many of its residents were enticed to satellite towns that had good commuting facilities. One of these satellite towns was Wollongong, and its spectacular growth did not escape the attention of John Saunders and Frank Lowy. As a result, Westfield Figtree opened in 1964.

The Shore Inn, opened in 1963, was the first hotel-motel venture of John Saunders and Frank Lowy. The hotel had an exotic Spanish-style façade with a tower, and it rapidly became a local landmark

John and Frank were always growing and adapting to life and business changes in Australia. An illustration of their sensitivity to change was provided in 1964 when they were about to embark on another shopping-centre development in Burwood, a western suburb of Sydney. Westfield had bought almost fifty houses, all of which had to be pulled down in order to build the centre. As there was a rising community consciousness about the environment, John, Frank, and Westfield's senior management all pitched in to assure the council and the residents that the shopping centre would be a responsible development, with due regard to the environment and locality. John was always able to summon everyone's help to work together as a team when a major problem arose. On this occasion, they were able to persuade council and the residents that the Burwood shopping centre would not cause pollution of the neighbourhood. They were able to bring in the department stores Farmers and Grace Brothers, a variety of other shops, and a large supermarket, and provided undercover car parking on five acres of land. As the shopping centre was on three levels, they were able to utilise fifteen acres worth of space. Utilising vertical space was always on John's mind. As he said, 'It doesn't cost anything to buy the sky'. Burwood was opened in 1966 by Sir Robert Askin, the premier of New South Wales, and remains an important part of Westfield.

The Burwood shopping-centre development was an interesting turning point for Westfield for several other reasons, as recalled by John Biro. Biro, an expatriate Hungarian, was one of Westfield's first executives. He joined the company in 1959, and was involved with searching out land for development, and later also with Westfield public relations. In the 1960s, he apparently suggested using and registering the name 'Westfield Shoppingtown', which has since become an excellent symbolic term for one-stop shopping. Biro was apparently also the first to think of turning a shopping-centre opening into a 'special event' that was newsworthy in itself. For the Burwood Shoppingtown opening, for example, Westfield invited Sir Norman Hartnell, the Queen's couturière, as its special guest, and combined his appearance at the shopping centre with a fashion parade featuring top models. This event was widely reported by the media, and lifted the company's profile. John's instincts and Frank's commercial logic would both have approved this type of promotion. Indeed, Westfield openings have remained something of a phenomenon ever since.

Nineteen sixty-seven was the year that John Saunders and Frank Lowy began thinking about building shopping centres in Queensland. They chose

Brisbane, the fast-developing capital. Frank Lowy recalled later that his brother John spotted a piece of land in Toombul. When John Saunders was being driven there by an agent, Donald Petrie, to be shown the site for the first time, Petrie cautioned him about it. The agent described the land as 'big—about forty-five acres—and there is also a canal going through it, so it could be on a flood plain.'

'Can we buy it?' Saunders asked.

'It could have a lot of problems', Petrie replied.

'I like problems', Saunders said.

And so John and Frank got an option on the land. They saw the huge population around it, and realised that the place itself was in an excellent position for one-stop shoppers. Westfield apparently engaged experts from Brisbane University to make a model of the flood plains. Then they bought the land, filled it in, and built a successful shopping centre which opened in 1967. John recalled with a chuckle that when they had all the approvals and had filled in the area, the Queensland education department said they would like to buy ten acres of the land. In fact, the department paid nearly as much for the ten acres of land as the whole area had cost to buy and fill.

John's idea of a market survey was to hop into a taxi or hire a car, and to travel about the neighbourhood talking to the taxi driver or the locals to find out from them what was needed in the area. He would then repeat the process two or three times. That was often the sum total of his market research. In 1966, John and Frank were looking to expand to Melbourne, their first venture outside New South Wales. Frank Lowy recalled that a site owned by G J Coles had been offered to them for development in Doncaster, then an outer suburb of Melbourne. The two men soon discovered that the area around the suburb was being developed at a staggering rate. Numerous orchards and small farms were being rezoned for residential and commercial development; at the same time, major through-roads had been built, such as Doncaster Road, to help commuters.

John and Frank did not need to think long before accepting the offer. John Saunders told me years later that he made an appointment to see Sir Henry Bolte, who at that stage had been the premier of Victoria for fifteen years. He told the premier that Westfield planned to invest significantly in Melbourne and build a major shopping centre in Doncaster. Sir Henry was, according to John, very pleased, as he was with any project that enhanced the prosperity of Melbourne and Victoria, as well as the prestige of his government. Bill Szabolcs, Westfield's chief architect of the time, designed the centre, and Sir Henry Bolte opened Doncaster Shoppingtown in 1969. It was a spectacular success instantly, and has remained one ever since. It will be recalled that Bill Szabolcs, who was Westfield's architect between 1964 and 1983, first met John Saunders when Bill was a ticket collector at the Sydney Town Hall railway station in the 1950s.

We have now reached 1969, the year that Neil Armstrong became the first man to walk on the moon. In its first ten years as a public company, Westfield had built or had under its control nine shopping centres: in Hornsby, Eastwood, Dee Why, Yagoona, Burwood, Figtree, and Miranda (to be redeveloped) in New South Wales; Toombul in Queensland; and Doncaster in Victoria. It controlled about 150,000 square metres of lettable space leased to over 500 tenants, including the major retailers of the time as anchor tenants—McDowells, G J Coles, Winns, Sydney Snow, Mark Foys, and Farmers. After a decade, its total assets were worth in the vicinity of fifty million dollars.

In 1961, Westfield paid a healthy 10 per cent dividend on its shares; by 1969, the dividend had risen to 13 per cent and the share price had risen correspondingly, reflecting the sustained success of the company. John Saunders and Frank Lowy, with their hard work, good business sense, imagination, and creativity had become established as shopping-centre developers in Australia. By the end of the first decade of Westfield's existence as a public company, its two founders, who had arrived from Europe as migrants, possessing not much more than hope and ability, were on their way to joining the select list of Australia's all-time business greats.

CHAPTER 10

BLUEMETAL

In January 1994 I spent two weeks with John Saunders in his beloved Queenstown, in the south of the south island of New Zealand. Queenstown was originally established as a small gold-mining town during the gold rush of the last century. Situated in the heart of New Zealand's Southern Lakes, it is now a major winter and summer tourist resort. It has about 6,000 full-time residents, and the population swells to about 25,000 at Christmas time and during the ski season. John's house was on Panorama Hill, and the balcony had a breathtaking view of Lake Wakatipu and of the mountain range, the Remarkables (so named because their appearance changes dramatically as the sun moves from east to west). From 1974, this house was John's haven and summer retreat. This was the place, the secret precinct, where only his

An aerial view of Queenstown on the south island of New Zealand, with the township situated on Lake Wakatipu. John Saunders' house was high on Panorama Hill, opposite the tip of the expanded peninsula seen in the middle of the picture, which is now the Queenstown golf course. With a million-dollar view, it was John's summer retreat. A few years ago, on one of these summer holidays, the story of the bluemetal quarry came out one evening, and triggered this biography

closest friends and soul mates gained entry. This was the place where he 'recharged his batteries' to prepare for the next year's challenges and battles.

John first went to Queenstown for a holiday in 1972. He loved Queenstown as soon as he arrived there. The place felt familiar to him. (Some years later he talked about this to a pilot acquaintance, who figured out that it was about the same latitude as Sátoraljaujhely in Hungary; also, there were as many pine trees in Queenstown as there were surrounding his home town.) John, a man of action, immediately decided to buy a house or a property in Queenstown. After being shown 'a lot of rubbish', the agent showed him some vacant land on Panorama Hill the day before he was to leave Queenstown. There were four adjacent lots, each with a million-dollar view, and the agent said that he had a choice: he could buy all four at $7,000 each, or nothing. John bought them immediately, built a house on one lot, planted pine trees on the next lot, and let the other two lots lie fallow. Although $28,000 was a lot of money to pay for vacant land in the sleepy little resort of Queenstown in the 1970s, John loved the place. Somehow, with one eye closed, he had already predicted that it would soon become a boom town—which it did within the next decade. He subsequently sold the other two blocks for about $70,000 each.

Early one evening, during one of our holidays together in Queenstown, the two of us were sitting outside on the long balcony admiring the lake, the sailing boats, and the old tourist boat *SS Earnslaw*, known as *The Lady of the Lake*, sailing past, with the shadowy Remarkables in the background. We were both relaxed and mellow. Only an occasional consumer of alcohol, John was sipping a small Scotch, while I was drinking some aromatic New Zealand white wine. Suddenly, the thought of writing his biography came into my consciousness. Very bravely, I asked John to tell me a story—any story—which had set him a challenge as well as given him pleasure in business. Just that year I had bought a little gadget for recording conversations. The contraption had a very sensitive microphone, so we could speak in a normal way without pushing buttons or having to change cassettes more often than every hour.

The story he told me is reproduced below. Although it was recorded in 1994, the events it deals with took place in the 1960s. It is a true record of our conversation on that magical evening in Queenstown:

I went overseas in 1959 to an international building materials exhibition, and I left the exhibition realising that the building materials of the future were aluminium, fibreglass and concrete. When I got home to Sydney, I got all the books I could find on these materials and studied them very carefully, and I discovered many interesting things—for example, that there is plenty of bauxite in Australia, often exposed, and that American planes during the Second World War were landing on makeshift airports on a bauxite base because it was very hard. However, to mine it would need a capital of at least fifty million dollars. As we were short of $49,999,999 at that time, I decided that bauxite wasn't for us!

So what happened after that?

Well, after studying fibreglass, I realised that all you need for that is a mould, and you can manufacture just about anything. So fibreglass wasn't for us, either. Then I turned to concrete. I realised that to make concrete one needed river gravel and rock stone, and after reading several books I discovered that Sydney was surrounded by sandstone as its base, and in certain spots under the sandstone there was coal, and at other places the hard rock that I was after. However, the rock stone or bluemetal was already being mined by large companies. I was advised against mining bluemetal, but I don't like to take no for an answer, and when everyone thinks it can't be done that's often the time when I go for it, if I think my idea is right. In 1964 I was referred to Professor Rankin and, through him, I was introduced to Dennis Bell, an English geologist. He came to my office one day.

'Mr Bell, I want to find bluemetal.'

'That's impossible, because all the bluemetal that's around has been taken up by the big companies.'

'Mr Bell, I have a Hungarian-English dictionary, and if in that dictionary you find that word which you just mentioned, then I'll give up this project. If you don't find the word in my dictionary, you'll just have to help me.'

So what did Dennis Bell say to you?

I brought him my dictionary in which the word 'impossible' was crossed out with a red pen. He looked at it and said, 'You are a funny man. So what's the deal?'

'The deal is that I give you a retainer, all expenses paid for hiring or buying a jeep, we get the relevant maps, you get the equipment, and we go to look for bluemetal around Sydney.'

Well, we looked around everywhere—in Campbelltown, Picton, Camden, in a thirty-mile radius around Sydney, and we just couldn't find it. Then we found one spot in the Blue Mountains, but it was far too inaccessible for it to be commercial. We didn't take up that spot. In fact, later on someone else also discovered the area, wanted to open a mine, and they went broke. Well, yes, I knew about access from building and from common sense, so we were smart in not taking up the bluemetal place in the Blue Mountains.

We then went up to Gosford, and about fifteen miles out of town there is a bluemetal quarry they call Peat Ridge which at that time supplied the central coast of New South Wales with bluemetal. Every fortnight Dennis Bell and I would go out for the weekend, and often we camped outdoors. I enjoyed this very much because of the conversations I had with him about geology, and because I was out in the fresh air, not to mention the challenge of it all. On one of these occasions when we were near Peat Ridge, Dennis Bell would use his instruments, knocking on the rocks to test them, when this large Finnish man came along as we were by the roadside.

'What you are you looking for?'

'We are looking for hard rock.'

Dennis by this time more or less told the man to piss off, but I just had the gut feeling that he might know something because he told us he had lived in the district for many years.

'I know where it is, I'll show it to you.'

He took us to a dairy, and he said that at the back we would find harder rock than at Peat Ridge. There was nobody there at the time, so we went in, and sure enough there was the exposed bluemetal washed away. There were also lots of leeches there, crawling on our legs, and Dennis showed me how to burn the leeches off using a lit cigarette.

'Well, that's the stuff we are looking for.'

Frank and I took out an option on the property over eighteen months, and we had the rights during these eighteen months to explore the land. If we exercised the option we would pay for it over five years, and the owners could still keep the dairy up front. We put down ten test drill-holes: in three places we got nothing, and in seven we got very good rock. We exercised the option well ahead of time, and bought the place.

What happened after that?

About two years after it all started, the New South Wales government had decided to build the Sydney to Newcastle Freeway, and our proposed mine was about seven miles from it. This was very fortunate. Timing is everything, and I decided to open the quarry then and there. We were looking around for engineers, quarry managers, as well as other workers, and the opposition got wind of this and offered us £80,000 for the site. Frank was trying to convince me over three days that we should sell out, and I told him, 'No Frank, it was my idea. I found the bluemetal with Dennis Bell, I did all the preliminary research, and the timing is perfect because of the proposed freeway construction. Eta was completely behind me and said, 'If you sell now, you will never forgive yourself'. I told her that I would be away frequently and it would be a lot of work, and she said, 'It doesn't matter. Just go ahead with it.'

She gave me the courage to do this, and I went ahead. At the time I was having tennis lessons with Les Korda from a coach, Jack Musgrave. I got to know him, and one day I invited him to be the quarry manager. He accepted, and did an excellent job. We got the equipment and the machinery, and it wasn't easy. The Australian rock-crusher manufacturers could not provide us with the rock crushers we needed in time. In fact, they did us a big favour because we had to go overseas and buy special crushers, and these were of a very high quality and produced a nice cubical-shaped stone. After a lot of hardship, we opened the quarry. You have to imagine that we started from scratch: there was no water, no road, no electricity. On one occasion, for example, it was raining for so many days that the ready-mix concrete truck was stuck in the mud for a month, and we couldn't get it out.

Tenders were called to supply the road base for the new freeway. We put in a tender for one pound sixteen shillings per ton, whilst the opposition apparently put in a tender for three pounds per ton. After tenders closed, ours just wasn't in. It wasn't there! Curiously, the bank manager who loaned us the money told us that he personally put our tender into the tender box. He apparently went to the commissioner, and they called for tenders again. On this occasion, the other tender was apparently for one pound ten shillings per ton, thereby undercutting us. Nevertheless we still got to supply the Department of Roads more than 50 per cent for this freeway.

You won't believe this, but soon after this, some steel pieces that were even harder than the steel of the hammers were found in the crusher, and we were out of business for ten days. The engineers from the Department of Main Roads came to have a look at this, and said, 'You'll never find out who did it, you'll just have to get new hammers and get on with the job!' Again, they did us a favour, as we got more sympathy and more of the order from the Department, finishing up supplying three-quarters of the total amount.

Our morale improved, making us much more determined than before, so all of this worked to our advantage. We got new hammers air freighted out from the US, and this cost a fortune in those days. We were working three shifts per day, twenty-four hours per day, seven days per week, in order to catch up. Just to be sure we also engaged two security men with two vicious dogs, so that nobody risked getting in and sabotaging our quarry after that.

How long did you work the mine?
About two-and-a-half years. We really only exhausted a small part of it. There is enough bluemetal there for another hundred years. We had geologists come to study the path of the lava, but they couldn't get it right. Then I heard of a retired man in Melbourne, whom I visited, who used to be a quarry manager. After my personal visit he was delighted to be asked to come to the quarry and give us an opinion. All of a sudden he felt that he was back in demand. We paid him a consultancy fee initially, but later on he came just for his own interest to study the place.

What was his conclusion?
He said, 'Look I don't know where the lava started, but if you look at it as four or five open fingers—and he superimposed his hand on the map—that's the flow of the lava, and in between you have the other dead stuff that's no good to you.'

What happened to the quarry?
Well, it's going strong. It's huge now, and it will be going for a long, long time.

So what did you do with the quarry?
We sold it to a man who had owned quarries in the 1940s and 1950s with his brothers, and sold out in 1956. He invested his money and decided to live the good life, buying some boats and cars, but all this good living apparently didn't agree with his health! He went to Honolulu to live for a few months, and when he came back he saw his doctor who apparently said to him, 'For the sake of your health, you'd better go back to work and back to your old business'. Well, we got wind of him being interested, and after talking to him we discovered that he had a nervous habit of lifting up his hook-on tie whenever he was about to make a better offer. So Frank and I had him figured out. We finally sold it well, and we made money on the sale.

We had huge losses when we first started, and then we broke even in the middle, and in the last year we made money—so that, together with a good sale price, we finished up on top. My challenge was met, I proved the critics wrong, and we were getting very advanced in our various shopping-centre plans anyway, so it was time to get out.

By then the sun had set behind the highest peak in the region, Ben Lomond; the Remarkables were just barely visible; and *SS Earnslaw* was on its night run with another lot of tourists. We went in—me to cook a Hungarian goulash, and John to do his famous pancakes.

CHAPTER 11

ETA

Men and women, women and men.

It will never work.

ERICA JONG (1942–   )

It did work for Eta and John Saunders. She was a beautiful, loyal wife, and played a large role in John's important business decisions. The ideas were John's, but it was Eta's support and encouragement to put his ideas into practice that gave him the courage to go into action. Undoubtedly, Frank was integral to all new initiatives, but Eta's enthusiasm gave John an extra strength and determination. To reword the saying, 'Behind every man's great decisions stands a woman'. Like John, Eta was a hard worker and frugal in her habits. Right from the beginning she took on two jobs, and then she worked hard at the Sydney Town Hall enterprise. When that was closed, she took over the home and the job of looking after John. Eta very much appreciated the simple pleasures of life in Australia. She retained her childlike innocence and enthusiasm, and enjoyed sewing, walking, cooking, seeing their friends, and standing behind John's business ventures.

It must have been a romantic trip on the *El Misr* sleeping on the folding army camp beds out on the deck, because when Eta and John arrived in Australia she was pregnant. Unfortunately, the pregnancy was lost, and this event very likely marks the beginning of Eta's subsequently tragic life, because it probably resulted in the development of pelvic inflammatory disease, followed by pelvic scarring and, subsequently, an inability to have children. Eta remained mostly happy and enthusiastic even after this sad event, although at times she had periods when she felt low. After seeing several specialists, it became increasingly clear that Eta would be unable to have her own children, and their doctors advised Eta and John to consider adopting children.

In mid-1959 the opportunity arose to adopt, and the couple went to the appointed hospital. It seems that as they went into the babies' room, John heard laughter in the background and was drawn to see the laughing child. She was irresistible to John and Eta, and she really chose herself to be their daughter. So Betty adopted herself into the Saunders family. She was a happy child, and the couple took her to their heart as their own.

About five years later, in mid-1964, the couple adopted a second child. This was Mark, who for Betty came unannounced and unexpected. Betty tells me that initially she was jealous of this second child, but she soon understood that the baby was to be her brother and a part of the family. Mark was also a happy baby and a happy child.

Eta's health was becoming a problem in the early 1960s. She had a painful hip condition, and John took her to many specialists in Australia. They also went to Switzerland, where Eta was eventually referred to Professor Bernhard Weber in St Gallen. Professor Weber was the head of orthopaedic surgery in the St Gallen Canton Hospital, and was one of the first to use a new method developed in Switzerland, called the 'compression technique', in which

Photographic portrait of Eta Saunders (née Schwarcz).

arthritic joints were fused, and fractures were set and healed much faster than by conventional methods. Professor Weber performed major surgery on Eta in 1969, from which she took much longer to recover than was expected. On her return to Australia she was still in pain, and needed to take painkillers regularly. John remained a very caring husband. He had no more than a few hours' sleep each night for several years during this difficult time—which was also a period when Westfield was expanding at a fantastic rate.

In March 1970, when Eta's hip pain was beginning to improve, she apparently developed viral bronchitis. One evening she went out to a function organised by the Sydney Jewish Community to listen to an ex-Israeli general giving a speech. It was a wonderful night for Eta, despite her feeling unwell. Her bronchitis and coughing became a little worse overnight, and she took some anti-cough mixture. The next morning she got up and took the children to school. John was still at home when she returned. She told him, 'It's so funny, but the top of my body above the neck is so hot, and the rest of me is so cold'. She said she would lie down for an hour or two and then go to the department store, Grace Brothers, to buy some materials to sew a dress for Betty.

Years later, John told me:

> I called her at 11.30 in the morning and there was no answer, so I was sure that she had gone to Grace Brothers for the material. But just after three o'clock in the afternoon the schools called to say that nobody had picked up the children, so I went to pick up one of the children and the company secretary picked up the other. I raced home and there was Eta in her clothes on the sofa, dead.

The doctor concluded that Eta had died from a heart attack. Although she had been chronically unwell, her death was quite unexpected. Eta was forty-two when she died; John was forty-seven; Betty was ten; and Mark was five. John was devastated. He had lost his wife, the mother of their two children, and his best friend.

CHAPTER 12

GO WESTFIELD, YOUNG MAN

If you have no family or friends to aid you
and no prospect open to you there,
turn your face to the great West,
and there build up a home
and fortune.

HORACE GREELEY (1811–1872)

'Go West, Young Man', wrote John Soule in 1851, promoting the burgeoning North American West. John Saunders and Frank Lowy acted as though
they had taken this advice to heart. They started in the west of Sydney, but
then went much further. They went 'Westfield'—not only west, but also
north, south, and east.

Neil Armstrong stepped on to the moon in July 1969 at about the same
time as the long-serving premier of Victoria, Sir Henry Bolte, opened
Westfield's Doncaster Shoppingtown in Melbourne. While the world was
rightly pre-occupied with the former event, the fact that the Victorian premier had opened the enterprise was momentous for the company. It was the
first signal that Westfield and its two joint chairmen had 'arrived' and had
been accepted into the ranks of Australia's business elite.

When Westfield was building Toonbul in Brisbane, a director of the Myer
department-store chain came along to look at progress. When John Saunders
started to talk to him, he said that Myer wanted to open a department store
in Indooroopilly. John and Frank needed no further encouragement: they
found vacant land in Indooroopilly. Designed by Bill Szabolcs, Indooroopilly
was built quickly, and in 1970 it was opened by the premier of Queensland,
Sir Joh Bjelke-Petersen.

In 1970 John Saunders was still grieving after the death of his beloved Eta.
He was in an emotional wilderness, and felt very much alone. His close
friends and family tried to console him, but it seems that no one can really
influence one's passage through such grief. Psychologists tell us that grieving
is normal for about one year after the death of a loved one; if it continues for
much longer, emotional disturbance as well as physical illness can come to
the surface. John threw himself into work whilst grieving for Eta. He worked
day and night, seven days a week, with the children being looked after by a
succession of nannies. Eventually, he realised that he also had to be a mother
and a father to the two children—that, in effect, he had two full-time jobs.
He had to call on all his physical and mental powers simply to exist from day
to day, as well as to cope with looking after two children and running a rap-

idly expanding organisation with Frank Lowy. Looking back, it is clear that John Saunders was in profound grief for almost a year.

Everything happened at Westfield during 1970. Not only was Indooroopilly Shoppingtown being built, but John and Frank bought real estate in William Street, on the edge of Sydney's central business district, in order to build a high-rise office building. The resulting structure, Westfield Towers, houses the central Westfield administration to this day. It has magnificent views of Sydney Harbour, the harbour bridge, and the opera house from its north side. The offices of John and Frank faced each other on the top level. It took only eleven months for Westfield Towers to be built, from the time they started pouring concrete to the time the head office was moved there from Caltex House. This was a construction record for Sydney, and probably also for Australia. Next to Westfield Towers, John and Frank built a magnificent hotel, The Boulevard, which was opened in 1972.

Some light is shed on John's approach to business and development by examining his involvement with the building of the Boulevard Hotel. He took it on as a personal responsibility, just as he had previously with The Shore Inn. Bernie O'Hara, an executive who worked with John for almost thirty years, remembers vividly a meeting during the latter part of 1970 with the architect, the builders, and those who were going to fit out the hotel. When John was presented with some drawings, he took one good look at them and tore them up, calling them rubbish and telling those present that he would go somewhere else if they didn't come up with a better proposition.

Although John's emotional state was somewhat labile because Eta had died that year, this type of approach with the architects and designers was not an isolated incident. Whenever he acted this way it resulted in a degree of confusion, and was for a while counterproductive to progress. There was an apparent contradiction here—between John Saunders relying on his intuition, apparently knowing the right way to go and wanting things done his way, but simultaneously finding it difficult to articulate the details clearly—which I will dissect in more detail in the next chapter. In the event, not long

The Westfield Towers complex, which remains the corporate headquarters of Westfield, was completed in 1973. The adjacent Boulevard Hotel was completed in 1972. The picture shows the two buildings during a New Year's Eve fireworks display. Both buildings have spectacular views of Sydney Harbour after John tore up the early plans, the architects and designers apparently did come up with an alternative for the hotel which was acceptable to him.

John was involved on a daily basis with the building's progress. He even went to Czechoslovakia to buy Bohemian crystal chandeliers and lights, which were to become one of the features of the new hotel. One of the key reasons behind Westfield's successes as builders was demonstrated during the hotel's construction. They used what is now known as 'fast-track construction'—that is, design work went on while construction was in progress, in order for the managers to meet practical needs and deal with obstacles as they were encountered. Using this method, they were able to make major changes to the building, sometimes at the last minute. At one stage, the Westfield building team called it the 'Swiss cheese hotel': the layouts to the rooms had been changed so often, and so many holes had been drilled, that it looked more like a piece of Gruyère cheese than a hotel.

By early 1971 John had emerged from his grief. That year Miranda opened, to become Australia's largest shopping centre of the day. The next year, the Boulevard Hotel and subsequently Westfield Towers became operative, and Westfield made plans to build two new Shoppingtowns, both in outer-Sydney suburbs—one in Liverpool, and the other in Parramatta.

John and Frank bought the land for the Liverpool Shoppingtown in the south-west of Sydney from the Catholic Church. It had previously been a Catholic school as well as a seminary. The development had the support of the mayor of Liverpool, and it was in a part of Sydney which needed more employment as well as more shopping facilities. The 'broker' for the deal was one of the priests who, according to John Saunders, came back asking for further sums of money after the price of the land had been agreed upon. The priest's approach for more money was simply irresistible to John Saunders: 'Things are costing so much nowadays, and God bless you m'boys for your generosity', he would say. He reassured John that he and the other priests in the seminary were saying many, many prayers for the future success of Liverpool Shoppingtown. The prayers must have done the job, because the shopping centre was and has remained extremely successful.

*Westfield Liverpool
Shoppingtown being opened in
August 1972 by the then pre-
mier of New South Wales, Sir
Robert Askin (centre), with
John Saunders (right) and a
Westfield executive, John Biro,
on the left*

In the early 1970s the population of Sydney was expanding at an enormous rate, much of it towards the west where thousands of newly arrived
migrants settled. The centre of this expansion was the suburb of
Parramatta—an area that has remained densely populated and is now, in fact,
the demographic and geographic centre of Sydney. It made sense for John
Saunders and Frank Lowy to want to build a large Shoppingtown there. As it
happened, the opportunity for Westfield to build in Parramatta was provided by Grace Brothers, who owned a suitable piece of land, and already had a
store there. Unfortunately, the timing of this particular project coincided
with the emergence of national financial problems. Not long before, Arab oil
sheikhs had increased oil prices by 70 per cent, and cut back oil production,
in protest at United States' support for Israel in the Yom Kippur War. At the
same time, the reform-oriented Whitlam government was beginning to
incur national debt.

It is self-evident that the realisation of large projects, such as Parramatta, needs firmly secured long-term financial backing. This may be the right place to go behind the buildings, as it were, and to observe the ways in which Westfield financed its projects.

For many years, John Saunders had a wonderful saying that he often reiterated. Westfield had what he called a 'chronical problem'. In his heavy Hungarian accent he would say, 'We never did, never do, and never will have enough money!' Early in the life of the Westfield Development Corporation, Saunders and Lowy made a vital decision and commitment: it was absolutely essential for Westfield's future to find reliable long-term sources of finance. They each put their special skills into operation to secure financial backing. Saunders used his personal, human touch, and people-relationship skills, Lowy used his strategic thinking and financial know-how, and both men benefited from their reputation for reliability, integrity, and trustworthiness.

As William Murray wrote in *The Scottish Himalayan Expedition* (1951):

> Until one is committed there is hesitancy, the chance to draw back, always inef-fectiveness. Concerning all acts of initiative (and creation), there is one ele-mentary truth, the ignorance of which kills countless ideas and splendid plans: that the moment one definitely commits oneself, then Providence moves too. All sorts of things occur to help one that would never otherwise have occurred. A whole stream of events issues from the decision, raising in one's favour all manner of unforeseen incidents and meetings and material assistance, which no man could have dreamt would have come his way.

Providence moved for the two men, soon after they committed them-selves to finding long-term funds, in four main ways. First, they established an excellent relationship with the National Bank (now National Australia Bank) in 1960, the year that Westfield was listed, and retained strong ties with this banking institution. Second, mutual life insurance companies became early long-term investors in Westfield. Thus Temperance & General Life (T & G Life), which is now part of National Mutual, helped to fund the

Hornsby project in 1961 and, subsequently, other shopping-centre projects. Similarly, the Australian Mutual Provident Society (AMP) association with Westfield commenced in 1963, when it funded the Eastwood shopping centre, and the AMP has remained a long-term investor. The third avenue of financing their needs came from public servants' superannuation funds—institutions that looked for long-term, secure growth. It was for this reason that the Commonwealth Superannuation Board, the New South Wales State Superannuation Board, and the Commonwealth Bank Officers' Superannuation Board all invested in Westfield. The fourth means of raising capital was by declaring bonus share issues. Thus a one-for-five bonus issue was declared in 1970 and again in 1972; a one-for-three bonus issue was declared in 1973; and a one-for-four bonus issue was declared in 1976. Furthermore, Westfield Holdings Limited and Westfield Property Trust were formed and listed on the Stock Exchange in 1979. A one-for-one preference share issue was announced in the mid-1980s on favourable terms to the shareholders.

The financial problems posed by the timing of the large Parramatta project in the early 1970s stimulated not only the providence which follows the commitment that William Murray described, but also the complementary skills which John Saunders and Frank Lowy were able to bring to bear in securing financial backing. Providence emerged in the form of Walter Pisterman, a Swiss man living in Melbourne who was the Australian representative of Credit Suisse. Pisterman came to see the two men, and told them that Credit Suisse had heard of Westfield and would like to invest money in it. Frank Lowy, with his great talent for finance, quickly came to the conclusion that Credit Suisse could be a wonderful source of funds.

Walter Pisterman came back two weeks later to confirm that Credit Suisse was indeed interested, and that he would like to see copies of plans of their future ventures. He went away with the plans for the Parramatta Shoppingtown, and took these with him on his next trip to Switzerland. One of the top bankers from Credit Suisse then came out from Zürich, had a look at Parramatta (which was then being built), and asked to see Westfield's other developments. John Saunders apparently took the man to Burwood and Liverpool.

The financier could not believe the number of cars in the car park, and said to Saunders, 'How much are you paying these people to have their cars there whilst I am visiting?'

'Five dollars per car!' John riposted. 'But joking aside, sir, these are genuine customers.'

The Credit Suisse man was very impressed and, after several months of negotiations, his company signed a financial agreement with Westfield. Parramatta, then Australia's largest shopping centre, was opened in 1975. Subsequently, Credit Suisse also invested in other Shoppingtowns. The Swiss connection turned out to be a most successful association for both parties. John became good friends not only with Walter Pisterman but also with the Swiss banker and his whole family.

In the early 1970s Australia was entering an exciting, turbulent era. The Labor government, with Gough Whitlam as prime minister, had a progressive and innovative social agenda. It established a family law court, for example, and legislated to make twelve months separation the sole grounds for divorce. With the establishment of a Commonwealth Administrative Appeals Tribunal, Australia enabled its citizens to appeal federal and state administrative decisions without recourse to common law and to regular courts. This was a world first, and remains a system that is the envy of other developed countries. The government also began to reduce industry protection, and introduced tariff cuts.

However, with the increasing globalisation of trade and the Middle East's doubling of the price of its crude oil, the West's long, post-war economic boom—including Australia's—came to an end. The Whitlam government experienced serious economic difficulties, some of its own making. It was involved, for example, in highly unorthodox means of raising a loan: Mr Tirath Khemlani, a London-based Pakistani money broker, was apparently

*Australia's then largest
shopping centre, Westfield
Parramatta, was opened
in 1975*

given authorisation by an Australian government minister to raise a loan from
the Middle East for two billion dollars. This was followed by the sacking of
several ministers, including Dr Jim Cairns, the deputy prime minister. When
the opposition parties blocked the Budget Supply Bills in the Senate,
Malcolm Fraser, the leader of the opposition, had by mid-October 1975 created a constitutional crisis unprecedented in Australia's history. As a result,
the Governor-General—apparently acting on advice from a previous
Commonwealth solicitor-general, Robert Ellicott QC and from the Chief
Justice of the High Court of Australia, Sir Garfield Barwick—sacked the
prime minister on 11 November 1975. The former opposition leader,

Malcolm Fraser, was sworn in to form an interim government until elections could be held, and was swept into power at the elections held a month later. This sent the Labor Party to the political wilderness for eight years, during which time the country experienced a degree of economic recovery.

This potted chronicle of Australia during the 1970s serves as a backdrop to the political and economic environment in which the two principals of Westfield found themselves. In spite of both global and economic hardships during different periods in the 1970s, Westfield grew rapidly. During this time it built or acquired control of eight further shopping centres in Australia, built extensions or undertook major renovations in four, and built the Westfield Towers office complex as well as the Boulevard Hotel. Thus, after twenty years, over and above its two hotels and one office-block com-

Prime Minister Bob Hawke making a Commonwealth Games plaque presentation to John Saunders in 1986

plex, it had 17 shopping centres under its control. This involved over 500,000 square metres of lettable space (a figure which had more than trebled in the course of its second decade), and over 1,500 tenants (which was also three times the number of its tenants at the end of its first ten years). Its total assets were worth in the vicinity of $100 million. It was also during the 1970s that Westfield entered the United States shopping-centre scene for the first time (see below).

The successes of Westfield, particularly those of John Saunders and Frank Lowy, in becoming a major force in Australia as shopping-centre builders and major employers did not escape the attention of the key players in politics—particularly those politicians who were in the ascendency.

Bob Hawke met John Saunders soon after he became president of the Australian

Council of Trade Unions in January 1970, when he took over from the long-serving Albert Monk. Their friendship became close in the 1970s, well before Bob Hawke entered parliament, let alone before he became Labor leader and prime minister in 1983. John Saunders knew instinctively that Hawke was a natural leader and would some day become the head of the Labor Party and possibly the prime minister of the country. Hawke went to Israel and also to Russia in the early 1970s and, among other achievements, helped to facilitate the emigration of Jews from Russia to Israel. John Saunders admired men of action, so he found Bob Hawke's style very impressive. For his part, Bob Hawke saw very clearly John's deep love for his children, as well as his overwhelming commitment to his extended family— Jewry in Australia and elsewhere. He was greatly impressed by John's skills, and regarded Westfield as one of the greatest success stories in Australia's business history. Quite shrewdly, he identified two vital elements in John's life: a river of positive energy, that flowed with love of his family and carried him along to business success, and a well of despondency in which lay his personal tragedies and sadnesses. Bob Hawke described John's latter condition as 'a state of sad bitterness'. This was a remarkably accurate observation. The two men respected each other subtly and quietly.

Neville Wran, who was a successful barrister in Sydney, became the Labor Party's leader of the opposition in New South Wales at the end of 1973, in what was to become the 'new look' Labor Party for that state. He met John Saunders soon after this (as he did Frank Lowy), and the two men respected each other's qualities and became close friends. More of their friendship is discussed in chapter 15, which deals with the 'bosom friends' of John Saunders.

The political friends of John Saunders came from both sides of politics. Sir Phillip Lynch, who became federal treasurer in the Fraser government of 1975, became a good friend. In fact, he used to visit John every four or six weeks, and have dinner with him. Lynch was always keen to find out what was happening in business, and he used John as a sounding board. Phillip

Sir Phillip Lynch, treasurer in the first Fraser government, introduced John Saunders to Henry Kissinger. Saunders and Kissinger were amazingly similar in their facial appearance and gestures—something John Saunders realised and which amused him

Lynch introduced John Saunders to Henry Kissinger when Kissinger visited Australia. As the photograph shows, the two men were uncannily similar in their facial appearance, posture, and gestures—something that they both realised. Saunders found Kissinger a very serious man in all his subsequent meetings, so he did not indulge in too many jokes. However, he admired Kissinger in his proactive role of attempting to achieve peace, or at least détente, with his 'shuttle diplomacy' in Vietnam, China, the Soviet Union, and the Middle East.

John Howard met John Saunders in 1977 when he was treasurer in the Fraser government. Their acquaintance became closer through Bevan Bradbury, who was chairman of G J Coles and then of Coles Myer, and a staunch Liberal Party supporter and senior office-holder—finance director and then president of its New South Wales branch. John Howard always found John Saunders to be a happy soul, optimistic about the future, loyal to his friends, and charitable, and he could not recall anyone speaking ill of him.

John Saunders met John Howard in 1977 when Howard was treasurer in the Fraser government. The two men are seen here at a public function some years later

In business, he was impressed by John's hard-working, entrepreneurial spirit, his pragmatic approach, and his expectation of a decent return for his investment. John Howard had no doubts about the probity of John Saunders. 'He was honest, and successful', he said. He felt that John Saunders was a 'European liberal' politically—that is, he was not a conservative, and had true liberal views. These two men, with such vastly different backgrounds, were in some ways soul mates. When John Howard became prime minister of Australia in 1996, John Saunders sent him his congratulations and a gift of a small desk clock. The clock still sits on John Howard's desk in his parliamentary office in Sydney.

Westfield's entry into the USA is interesting because once again we see the complementary skills of Saunders and Lowy in operation. John Saunders had visited the United States once or twice every year since 1958, and in that time he had attended international shopping-centre conventions and looked at shopping centres throughout the country. He was fascinated by the thought that Westfield might begin building shopping centres in the United States; apparently, quite independently, Lowy thought this as well. Saunders' instincts and gut feelings told him that the United States was not only a bastion of world economic stability, but also that investment in America would be a good move for Westfield—a conclusion Lowy probably reached on the basis of figures rather than gut feelings. Saunders apparently proposed to Lowy that they should expand into the USA and, as Frank was more than agreeable, John started to look for a shopping centre that was already in existence. After a year's search he found one in Trumbull, Connecticut. It belonged to an American Italian family, and was somewhat neglected when

The now refurbished Trumbull Shopping Park was a somewhat run-down shopping centre when it was purchased by Saunders and Lowy in 1977 as Westfield's first venture in the United States

Westfield bought it in March 1977. Both parties felt that they had done a good deal: the Italians were happy with the relatively high price they received for a run-down shopping centre; Saunders and Lowy, with Westfield's experience and excellent track record in refurbishing shopping centres behind them, saw the potential of their purchase and felt that they had paid a comparatively low price for it. In the United States, it was usual for such a centre to be bulldozed and a new one built to replace it. Westfield, however, proceeded to refurbish it. Moreover, John Saunders was apparently instrumental in sending a small team from Westfield to Connecticut in order to assess what needed to be done. The somewhat neglected shopping centre was refurbished over a few months. Sending the team over from Australia was a great morale booster, not only for those who went but also for the rest of the Westfield staff. In fact, their endeavours got them a mention in *The New York Times*.

Further shopping centres followed—in Connecticut, California, and Michigan in 1980, all using the same plan of refurbishing rather than bulldozing. This was followed in 1984 by the construction of a beautiful and large shopping centre, 'Westside Pavilion', in a busy part of Los Angeles near UCLA, in which Australian construction design and know-how from the Westfield team was very prominent. Westside Pavilion opened in 1985, and put Westfield on the map in the United States. This was a major achievement for an Australian company.

By the mid-1980s there were twenty Westfield shopping centres in Australia (with 150 million shoppers going through its doors every year), and there were also seven shopping centres in the USA. Its 2,200 tenants now occupied about 630,000 square metres of floor space. Westfield's total assets were worth in the vicinity of a staggering $800 million, and profits after tax and share dividends were increasing. Progress after 1985 was almost exponential. So it is evident that Westfield, John Saunders, and Frank Lowy moved from strength to strength in the 1960s, 1970s, and 1980s. The only blemish in an otherwise spotless Westfield report card of achievements over a period of thirty years was the major investment in television by Westfield Capital Corporation (listed in 1987) through Northern Star Holdings. This was later sold at a substantial loss. John Saunders told me that he was opposed to the television investment when it was first mooted, but it was carried by the majority of the board. Although Westfield Capital Corporation did make other relatively successful investments, it was delisted two years later in 1989.

Saunders and Lowy came to be surrounded by experts in management, marketing, finance, promotion, architecture, and design. Starting in 1960 with a handful of associates, the Westfield team grew to about 800 after thirty years. Many of them were long-term employees, their loyalty indicating that morale was high among the staff. Shareholders were also satisfied: shareholder funds increased from $1.5 million in 1965 to $400 million twenty-five years later. The Australian Stock Exchange statistician, Mr D M Peacock, calculated in 1990 that an initial investment in 1960 of $1,000 (then £500), when Westfield shares were first listed, would have been worth over $3.5 million thirty years later (if all dividends, capital repayments, and proceeds from the sale of rights and property-trust units had been reinvested into additional Westfield shares). He calculated that the average compound growth-rate of the shares since 1960 was over 30 per cent per year, compared to an average 12 per cent increase in the shares which made up the Australian All Ordinaries Index, and a 7 per cent average annual inflation rate over the period. The Stock Exchange statistician also concluded that Westfield shares had almost certainly out-performed any other Australian listed share that was available to the public in 1960.

Throughout Westfield's quite spectacular rise, John Saunders and Frank Lowy remained very close; they met on a daily basis, both as friends and as business partners. Frank Lowy compares the relationship to that of a marriage. The two men must have known precisely how the other thought and would act in any given situation. Two examples out of many that could be cited involved one of Westfield's senior executives, Jim Doe. The first occurred when Doe went up one day to talk to John Saunders about a project. When they were halfway through the discussion, Saunders became involved in a personal telephone conversation, and Doe stepped out of the office into the intermediate area to wait until he had finished. But Frank Lowy's door, which was directly opposite, was open. Lowy called Doe in, and he finished off the conversation about the project with Lowy while Saunders was still on the phone! Nowadays this would be called a great example of 'synchronicity', but the two partners just put it down to experience and a very close association.

On another occasion, Doe was called up to see Saunders after going through a particularly difficult and busy time completing a project. When Doe went in, Saunders thanked him for what he had done, reached under his desk blotter, and gave him a plane ticket for an overseas trip. Jim Doe thanked him profusely and left. As he did so, Frank Lowy called him in through his ever-open door. Lowy also thanked Doe for his good work, and reached under his blotter to give him a plane ticket. Doe said, 'I already have one from John'. Then Frank said, 'No, this isn't for you. It's for your wife'. Obviously, the two men had decided to play a practical joke on Jim Doe. Even after so many years of being together, they had not lost their belief in the virtue of a little mischief-making. This was a partnership of many years, made in heaven, and cemented in such a way that it could never be undone. Or could it?

CHAPTER 13

SECRETS OF THE SAUNDERS SUCCESS

Success is a science

OSCAR WILDE (1855–1900)

Success is flair, vision and drive, and
John Saunders had all three

BRIAN WOOLSTONE (1931–)
FIRST CHIEF ARCHITECT OF WESTFIELD

Wherever you'd 'ave dropped him, he would have made it

BEN NATHAN (1914–)
PAST WESTFIELD EXECUTIVE, ON JOHN SAUNDERS

When asked, 'What else does one need to have to succeed
apart from being Hungarian?',
Sir Alexander Korda (1893–1956) replied, 'Talent'

'John had a good nose for business', were the exact words that John Saunders' friends, Andrew Lederer and Sam Moss, as well as a past leasing expert, Ben Nathan, all used when I talked to them about John Saunders. Andrew Lederer also suggested that, unfortunately, Saunders would take his good business sense to the grave with him—unrecorded and unsung—so others would not be able to profit from his experience.

However, I take the view that it might be possible to tease out, albeit only partially and in a somewhat artificial way, some of the characteristics of John Saunders which made him so immensely successful in business. Although incomplete and fragmented, what follows may be of some benefit to an ambitious young person wanting to succeed similarly. I am aware, of course, that there may be other or additional explanations for Saunders' success. This chapter makes no pretence at being part of a business or management manual; it is, rather, a personal account. Some may think that what follows is naïve; others, that it is opinionated. But a description, and at least one view, of this man's extraordinary business skills should be attempted.

A Trader's Heritage

John Saunders was born into a family of traders that went back for at least four generations. From the day of his birth he absorbed business acumen, almost by osmosis. He also had behind him the legacy of 300-or-more years of trading among the Jews of north-eastern Hungary. Moreover the Jews in that part of the world had been exploited over the centuries—paying heavy taxes, and conducting their trading under difficult and often unfriendly circumstances. This struggle for survival in the face of much hardship toughened them up, giving them an edge and special skills when faced with changing circumstances. Interestingly, modern theory on success suggests that, at a pivotal and difficult time in early life, the successful individual overcomes adversity by making a virtue of necessity. He or she often makes a decision which goes something like: 'If I am no good at sport, I'll be clever'; or, 'If I am exploited by taxation, I'll find a way to increase my wealth'. Thus is born triumph in adversity.

In spite of the adversity and struggle, or perhaps because of it, these traders learnt to focus on the business at hand, and to ignore or repress the dross. This is something that I observed in John Saunders on many occasions. His capacity to adapt to change and to grow through it was an important characteristic, as it was for Frank Lowy. Although Hungarians are not noted for learning other languages easily, both men learnt over the years to speak in public—initially a difficult task for them. Another example of their capacity to change their thinking was shown by their realisation that shopping centres were not static structures. Each had a life of its own, and each needed expansion and regular upgrading, as well as changes to what was sold there and how it was sold, in harmony with the changing needs of shoppers.

We cannot choose our parents, nor can we elect to be born into a 300-year-old trading heritage. So should an ambitious young person discount the role of heritage? Some of this heritage can be acquired from reading. There is, for example, a wonderful biography of the Rothschild family by Derek Wilson, *Rothschild: a story of wealth and power*, which may be a good start for 'acquiring' a slice of heritage. The Rothschild family banking business, which started in Frankfurt in the sixteenth century, also achieved success in the face of adversity by continually learning, applying their trading skills to new situations, and handing power readily from one generation to the next. Apart from reading books, it is also possible to seek out and talk to men or women who were born into a family of traders, just as John Saunders was, and learn from them some of the techniques of adaptation and the skills involved in focusing on the project at hand.

An Entrepreneur

A trading heritage seems to produce a genuine entrepreneurial spirit in a person running a business, whereby he or she is quite open to the possibilities of producing or selling a wide variety of products, and taking a reasonable profit from the investment. It also involves taking a risk—a part of the process that critics of successful entrepreneurs often forget. Unfortunately, in recent years the word 'entrepreneur' has to some extent been tarnished by the actions of some high-flying businessmen who took unacceptable risks, often with other people's money. There was, however, nothing shady or sleazy about the entrepreneurial enterprises of John Saunders—quite the contrary. Right from the age of thirteen he showed great trading skill when he was in the leather business in Sátoraljaujhely. He showed the same ability after the war when he opened a wood-working factory. After escaping from Russian oppression in 1949, he learnt how to make toothpaste. This turned out to be a false lead, but we know that many drill holes have to be sunk to find one oil well. On the other hand, at that time he also learnt upholsterery, how to grow mushrooms, and how to sell food—first in a sandwich bar and then in the Blacktown delicatessen and grocery. He built on this experience by later establishing with Frank Lowy a coffee shop that used an espresso machine, equipment that was then new to Australia.

Ervin Graf, the Sydney architect, observed, 'I admired John's entrepreneurial spirit, because it seemed to me that all he needed was just a hint of a new idea. He studied it and ran with it to develop a new enterprise if he thought it was right.' This is how John Saunders and Frank Lowy started to build shops and then undertook subdivisions in the very part of Sydney which had the greatest population growth. The story of the bluemetal quarry is an outstanding example of the depth and breadth of John Saunders' creative talent for establishing a new and entirely different enterprise.

The creation of Westfield and the development of Westfield Shopping-towns was, of course, John Saunders and Frank Lowy's major entrepreneurial success and triumph. But what led to a shopping-centre empire started with shoes and leather heels, broom handles and wooden boxes, mushrooms, groceries, subdivisions, bluemetal quarries, and hotels. Clearly, it is not what one manufactures or sells that matters; it is, rather, a state of mind or an ethos of openness to new enterprises, however diverse they may be. It seems to require a way of thinking which firstly and most importantly can recognise a new opportunity, an ability to follow up with research on the feasibility of a new project, and the capacity to make an informed decision about whether to go ahead or not.

An Informed Man

When he signed himself out of school at the age of thirteen, informal education in the 'university of life' began for John Saunders and continued for the rest of his life. Ben Nathan, with his cockney wit, claims a university degree for John Saunders—that of 'QFL … qualified for life'. John's native intelligence and common sense told him that to be successful one had to be aware and informed. He had a very inquisitive mind, and was a voracious reader of fiction and non-fiction alike. He loved to read biographies, particularly biographies of successful men. He also greatly enjoyed reading economic theory, and comparing each version to his own homespun views on the economy.

John Saunders was an admirer of the writings of Milton Friedman, the American economist and Nobel laureate—perhaps because Friedman's economic philosophies corresponded with some of his own. Friedman argued, for example, that a nation's economy can best be controlled through its supply of money, with a minimum of government control; on another level, he argued that bilateral voluntary and informed transactions which were beneficial to both parties formed the basis of a sound economic model of 'competitive capitalism'. He also believed that this economic model could only work in the free marketplace of a nation that also provided political freedom. Friedman's ideas have since been expanded to take in the concept of a global market economy—although, admittedly, its utility is yet to be proven.

Friedman believed that economic and political freedoms were closely and inextricably intertwined. Both Friedman and Saunders would have subscribed to the view of Baron James de Rothschild that 'finance cannot exist without liberty', and also of the anonymous philosopher who told us that 'democracy is the handmaiden of economic prosperity'. John Saunders knew well from his post-war experience in Russian-dominated Hungary that if there is no political freedom there are no individual rights and no economic freedom. That was why he escaped from Soviet tyranny. John Saunders frequently made jokes about Westfield's 'chronical' lack of money, yet he knew that an assured money supply was an essential part of business success. He repeatedly impressed on me (as he would have on others): 'Gabi, credit is everything in life.' Of course, he meant not only bank credit but, in a much broader sense, the credit created by the trust placed in one by one's business associates.

Being aware and informed extended to listening to news broadcasts each day, reading business reviews in financial papers, listening to the radio, and watching television. He was also in the habit of reading newspapers from front to back every day. In the 1950s, whilst running the Blacktown delicatessen with Frank Lowy, he read on one occasion that there was going to be a shortage of European olive oil because of a poor harvest. The two men bought up all the olive oil available from wholesalers, and made a tidy profit when it was subsequently in short supply.

A Creative Right Brain

Right from the beginning, it seems that most of the ideas for new projects in the Saunders-Lowy partnership came from John Saunders, and that the new financial and organisational ideas came from Frank Lowy. Saunders remained forever observant and informed, both in Australia and whilst on overseas business trips. Overseas, he would quietly observe and focus on new developments, which he often adapted for Australia. Once he had a new idea he studied it thoroughly by extensive reading, by seeing the concept work in practice and, if there was a chance, by testing it out personally. He was forever interested in new technology and in ways of making things work more cost-efficiently. We have already seen this trait in his wood-working factory in Hungary, in his purchase of an espresso machine for his Blacktown coffee shop, and on several other occasions during his career with Westfield.

John would chuckle, and his pink cheeks would light up with his happy little smile, when people talked about the need for market research in developing a new project. He usually told them that, when Westfield was contemplating a new shopping centre, his 'market research'—as we have seen—consisted of hopping into a taxi and finding out from the taxi drivers and from the ordinary people in the neighbourhood whether a new shopping centre was needed, and if so, what focus the shops should have.

John Bock, who was with Westfield from 1963, and was the company's Queensland state manager between 1977 and 1986, recalled an anecdote about John conducting such 'market research' whilst in a taxi. On one occasion when Saunders was visiting Westfield's Indooroopilly shopping centre, he was still asking the cab driver questions when they reached their destination—so he asked the cabbie to drive around for half-an-hour until the conversation was finished. Being observant and informed, doing his market research, and using his gut feelings (which we will discuss shortly), John Saunders was able to predict what would be successful in the future. This street-level research was in itself invaluable for Westfield. Brian Woolstone, the company's first chief architect said, 'With John's market research, he decided where the battlefield would be, declared war, and Frank was the one to put it into action in the best possible way commercially.'

One of the 'new age' gurus of self-actualisation and life management, Werner Erhard, suggested that a good manager could predict what would be profitable in the future; but that a great manager, over and above this prediction, also knew what was lacking. Not knowing Werner Erhard's theories, John looked around and realised 'what there was not', sensed what was lacking and was needed, and then went ahead and created it. The Viennese architect and urban planner, Victor Gruen, who migrated to the United States in 1938 with eight dollars in his pocket, was a visionary: he was the man responsible for the modern shopping centre, which he called a shopping town. John Saunders and Frank Lowy followed Gruen's lead, and were one of the first in Australia to understand that, with the expansion of large cities into suburbs and satellite towns, swelling population centres badly wanted local and complete shopping areas so that they would no longer be obliged to do their shopping in central business districts.

When John Saunders visited the United States in the late 1950s, he saw that downtown department stores had been detrimentally affected by the proliferation of suburban shopping centres; indeed, by the late 1970s many had closed. This major change in the United States took place in the face of a general economic boom at that time. After several visits to the USA, Saunders understood that this change in the pattern of shopping was also bound to occur in Australia. With Lowy's business and organisational support, the two men decided to create US-style shopping centres in Australia—and apparently took up John Biro's suggestion to use and register the name 'Shoppingtown', which had first been used by Victor Gruen in his 1960s book, *Shopping Town USA*. Gruen developed the idea of an important store (an 'anchor store') at each end or at each important angle of the shopping centre, in order to persuade people to walk from one end to the other. Apart from the economic aspects of these centres, Gruen also had the utopian idea of creating central open spaces with seats, fountains, and sculptures, which would encourage some social interchange and a sense of the shopping centre being a community-oriented place.

The real creativity that John Saunders displayed in developing an idea which was new to Australia required switching from the logical left brain and employing the intuitive and creative right brain. I remember once, when Saunders was asked about some important business decisions which did not seem to be based on logic, that he did not even attempt to explain them rationally. He merely said, 'That's just how I felt about it'. Not only that, but he smiled and pointed to his not inconsiderable abdomen and said, 'I just had a gut feeling about it'.

We have known for a long time that the brain can influence the gut; for instance, a student may experience nervousness-induced diarrhoea before an exam. But only recently have we learnt that signals flow in the other direction as well: there is a complex and hidden 'brain' in the gut which can influence the brain, too. It seems that emotional states and feelings can be present in this 'gut-brain', and are felt by those who pay attention to them. I have little doubt that the gut-brain of John Saunders was alive and well, that he perceived its workings quite acutely, and that he used it to help him make important commercial decisions.

There is, of course, a downside to all this. The problem with a person who has a highly developed and sensitive, intuitive, and creative right brain, and a logical left brain that is not well exercised—as appears to have been the case with John Saunders—is that they have serious problems defending or explaining rationally the details of their concepts and creations. This can lead to confusion, frustration, and delay. We have already seen this at work when John tore up the first plans for the Boulevard Hotel, even though he was unable to explain what was needed. It apparently occurred on other occasions as well, when Saunders wanted something done his way but was unable to articulate it precisely to Westfield staff. John Saunders was highly creative, but he was no logical interpreter of his own ideas. He was no strategist. Frank Lowy was the rational strategist and, fortunately, the two men understood that.

At times, John Saunders even relied on the talents of those who drew their conclusions from the supernatural. After the war, John's sister Lilly visited a graphologist who would tell one's fortune from a sample of handwriting. She took some of John's handwriting to her. The fortune-teller was told only that it belonged to a man, but she did not know whose handwriting she was examining. She predicted that the man would become a successful, rich businessman, and that he would migrate from Europe, but that if he was not careful his fortune would be taken away from him by the Chinese. The first two predictions came true. Then John Saunders and Frank Lowy apparently were invited to build a large hotel in China, in the days when Australian business was first engaging in collaboration with the then developing nation. John Saunders told me that, remembering the prophecy which the graphologist had made some thirty-five years previously, and relying on his gut feeling that the United States was a better option for investment than Asia, he talked Frank Lowy out of accepting the proposal. For whatever reason, Saunders was right. It seems that those who took it up instead did not do too well commercially.

Value for Money, Always

John Saunders always made it abundantly clear—on occasions, brutally so—that he was a tough businessman: in any business transaction, whether it involved buying toothpaste or a coat or a shirt, or getting the job done by an employee, or building a shopping centre, he wanted value for money. It didn't matter to him how large or how small the amount. It was a matter of principle that he got the best deal and, even more, that he was not cheated. Although he was a frugal person by nature, he didn't mind spending money on anything, provided there was a need for it. For example, he was quite happy to bargain for a shirt in an exclusive menswear store, even though this was something that most people would not even dream of doing. This approach of Saunders often embarrassed his family, his friends, and his business associates. But it was never an embarrassment for him to ask for the best possible deal. As his friend Neville Wran put it, 'John had no qualms about asking for the sun, the moon and the stars, and he could do this without batting an eyelid.'

In order to teach his family his business ethos of always getting value for money, John Saunders very much controlled the money supply. Every item had to be accounted for. This controlling behaviour was often regarded as excessive; it caused upsets and, at times, serious resentment. And yet, in contrast to his frugality with his family, he always generously extended a helping hand to those friends who were in financial difficulties. Over the years he lent large sums of money to business friends who unexpectedly struck serious problems. The loan was made quietly, and always without fuss and publicity. This apparent paradox at the heart of John Saunders may have an archetypal origin, as evoked by Shakespeare's hot-headed Hotspur in *Henry IV*:

> I'll give thrice so much land,
> to any well-deserving friend.
> But in the way of bargain, mark ye me,
> I'll cavil on the ninth part of a hair.

Decisions, Decisions

Often an excruciatingly long time would pass whilst John Saunders was making up his mind about whether or not to proceed with a new major project. He would collect all possible information on the project, seek advice from several quarters and the opinion of many, and in his brain and gut would constantly evaluate the pros and cons. During this time also he was working out—almost always in his head—what the deal had to be in order for Westfield to make a reasonable profit, and how not to spend a cent more. Brian Woolstone recalled, 'John was always bargaining with himself regarding the price.' His ability to make calculations in his head was almost legendary. Neville Wran recalls: 'John Saunders could spot a piece of property, for example, that was likely to increase in value, and after a brief inspection he could say how much the property was worth at the time and how much it could be sold for later on, and he was rarely wrong.' Apparently most of the properties bought by Westfield were acquired on Saunders' advice. Whilst a building was in progress, he could assess precisely how far it had advanced, and his assessment was often more accurate than that of the quality surveyor who was employed for this purpose. All this was done in his head, without pencil and paper. Never once did he use a calculator.

However, John Saunders' elongated, apparently meandering decision-making process—his collecting of information, talking to people and asking their advice, making calculations, and talking out loud about the good and bad points of a new proposal—created, quite understandably, a degree of confusion among his work associates. As Brian Woolstone put it, 'John often suffered from the pressures of his own creativity.' It was not appreciated by most around him that this long gestation period of indecision, assessment, using the right brain, then the left brain, then the right brain again, is often the way of most creative people, and that often this is a painful process for them. Frank Lowy told me, 'I am the sort of person who likes to make a decision fairly quickly after considering the facts, and John at times seemed to me so slow and indecisive in making up his mind regarding a new project.'

One often heard the statement that John Saunders and Frank Lowy were always on a good investment. What most did not know was that the majority of the proposals they looked at were not acceptable to them, and that their skill in selecting commercially profitable projects was once again due to the complementary talents of John Saunders' creative mind and Frank Lowy's excellent commercial and organisational sense. It was not a coincidence that almost all of their ventures succeeded, since many projects were eliminated long before Australia's business world even knew that Westfield had considered them.

John Saunders utilised his skill of making calculations in his head and his determination not to get carried away by the apparent gloss and excitement surrounding a new project. He and Frank Lowy were never greedy for new acquisitions; they knew that over-bidding could lead to disaster. If senior executives showed disappointment when a decision was made not to go ahead with a project into which many people had put a lot of time and enthusiasm, Saunders would say, 'There will always be another deal and another opportunity.'

When Do You Want It?

Once the decision was made to go ahead with a new project, the apparent 'fog' lifted completely and one saw another side of John Saunders. His unbelievable, almost superhuman, persistent drive to get a project completed on time was revealed in many ways. This was yet another of the secrets of his business success. He enjoyed challenges—such as when establishing the bluemetal quarry, and the many obstacles he needed to overcome to obtain difficult building permissions, or to get construction finished on time. He often set unrealistic deadlines, and then cajoled, urged, humoured, and repeatedly confronted his staff during the production phase of a new project. His stock answer when asked for the deadline on a job to be done was, 'Yesterday'.

At times, progress with John seemed to move at a snail's pace. But he was almost always successful in achieving the end result. His drive was subtle, measured and, therefore, quite deceptive. It was never a blustering approach; it was the purposeful movement of a tortoise, getting slowly but surely to its destination. Once, when one of his executives asked why he worked seven days a week, he replied, 'Because the week hasn't got eight days.' On the debit side, his incredible drive to succeed and the long hours he put in at work inevitably took their toll on his home life. He was totally committed to his work, and never balanced this with a life at home which satisfied his family. His children would mainly see him during weekends, and even then he would often drag them along for one of his unannounced shopping-centre visits.

Marketing and Promotion

John Saunders was an excellent marketer. He was always thinking about promotion or listening to new ideas about how to promote Westfield Shoppingtowns. In 1958 he attended the International Shopping Centre Convention in New Orleans, and whilst in town was struck by a magnificent cake display in a shop which was run by woman called Judy Hall. Saunders invited her, on the spur of the moment, to come halfway across the world to Australia, to advise on food display in Westfield Shoppingtowns. Hall accepted, and her contribution has turned out to be remarkable. Interestingly, after a short time, she went on to have an outstanding career with Westfield, leasing mainly food-related shops. Judy Hall now recalls:

> I had a sixth sense that the invitation to Australia was an opportunity for me to grow, as I have always liked new challenges, and John Saunders must have had a sixth sense also that I would contribute to Westfield. I have never regretted this decision. Not only did John Saunders and Frank Lowy make me feel good about my work, the entire spirit in the Westfield organisation was such that it actually encouraged me to develop further.

After renovating Miranda, one of the Sydney shopping centres, Saunders suggested that a pound of sugar and a packet of butter be given free to all those who came on the first two days to view the renovated centre. However, before they got this 'freebie' they were obliged to go through the entire shopping centre.

John Saunders was associated with some quite spectacular ways of promoting Westfield Shoppingtowns. For example, he brought to Australia a group of Hungarian gypsies who sang and danced and played authentic Hungarian gypsy music in Westfield shopping centres. On another occasion, whilst taking a walk around the Kings Cross district, he noticed that a well-known troupe of female impersonators, Les Girls, were performing in a theatre, and got the idea to engage them to perform at Miranda Shoppingtown during lunchtimes. This turned out to be an extremely popular promotion. Another spectacular promotion was that of the Royal Coaches Exhibition in Westfield's Indooroopilly Shoppingtown, which was opened by Prince Charles.

On another occasion, Westfield brought out the Apollo astronauts. They proved to be extremely popular in the shopping centres, especially with children. They also brought with them some artefacts, such as displays of NASA and displays of space shuttles. This event also included a ticker-tape parade from Westfield Towers in William Street, with the astronauts sitting in the back of an open car, down George Street to the Sydney Town Hall, where the

The Hungarian Music and Dance Troupe performed in fifteen Westfield Centres in Sydney, Wollongong, Melbourne, Brisbane and Adelaide. This was a promotional idea of John Saunders. Here we see them outside Westfield Towers in Sydney

HUNGARIAN GYPSIES AND FOLK DANCERS DIRECT FROM BUDAPEST.

The Hungar Music and Dance Troupe won the hearts of Sydney all last week with their unique folk dances and songs. Your last chance to see them this week at these Westfield Shoppingtowns.

Burwood — Monday 24th September   Liverpool — Wednesday 26th September
Parramatta — Tuesday 25th September   Show Times: 11 a.m. and 1 p.m. each day.

The Hungar Music and Dance Troupe fly interstate with ▲ **ANSETT**
AIRLINES OF AUSTRALIA

mayor of Sydney, John Saunders, and Frank Lowy presented them with the keys to the city.

Neville Wran, whilst premier of New South Wales, started the Gala Concert held each year in Sydney which featured famous artists and orchestras. The major sponsor for this event was Westfield. Up to 18,000 senior citizens came from many parts of New South Wales to listen to this concert at the Sydney Entertainment Centre.

John Saunders was very much behind a track-and-field and swimming event for disabled children which was called The Westfield Challenge. The Honourable Charlie Lynn, MLC, now a parliamentarian in the New South Wales upper house, was the organiser of this event, which Westfield sponsored, and to which John Saunders had a strong attachment. The event went on for two years, and Westfield flew many children to Sydney's Homebush Stadium from all over Australia,

The annual Gala Concert for Senior Citizens hosted by the New South Wales premier, featuring well-known artists and orchestras, was held under the longstanding sponsorship of Westfield

including some children who were in wheelchairs. Being held in an outer part of Sydney, it was difficult to attract a large enough audience, so John Saunders hired buses and invited retired people and pensioners to watch this event. This was not only good entertainment for them, but it also filled up the stadium so that the children saw a great audience cheering them on. John insisted that just as much attention needed to be given to those who completed an event as to those who won. This embodied an old ideal of the Olympics: that the important thing is to participate and not to win. Regrettably, in recent years this principle has been largely forgotten. After two years of the Westfield Challenge, John became involved in competitions for handicapped adults. In one of these, a man who had cerebral palsy, now known as the comedian Steady Eddy, took part in a swimming race. Although it was to take him about 30 minutes to get from one end of the pool to the other, he persisted with his swim, and everyone waited until he reached the other end. It was a most inspiring moment.

The greatest promotional event that John Saunders was connected with was the Sydney-to-Melbourne foot race or ultra-marathon, which became known as the Westfield Run. The idea of having a long-distance run was brought to Saunders by the marketing department; they initially suggested to him that there should be a run from one Westfield Shoppingtown in Sydney to another. John quickly replied, 'Why not think bigger, and have the run from Parramatta Shoppingtown in Sydney to Doncaster Shoppingtown in Melbourne?' Apparently, a number of people initially decried this as being something of a hare-brained idea. However, Saunders contemplated it and hatched the plot with Westfield's then marketing executive John Craig, and they decided to go ahead with it.

The inaugural Westfield Run was from Sydney to Melbourne in 1983. Neville Wran, who was premier of New South Wales at the time, started the runners off. He was apparently quietly doubtful that many of them would get past the outskirts of the city. The potato farmer Cliff Young won it at the age of sixty-one, and became famous overnight. John Saunders got to like Cliff Young immensely, because he gave his prizes away to others whom he thought more worthy; this gesture of Young's humanity struck a chord with Saunders. The second Westfield Run was the only one which went from Melbourne to Sydney, and was started by the then premier of Victoria, John Cain, with the runners welcomed in Parramatta by Neville Wran. This event was won by Tony Rafferty from Melbourne. Subsequently, another prominent ultra-marathon runner, Janos Kouros, won the event for several successive years.

From the second year on, the run was managed by Charlie Lynn; he had previously been in the army, and was most interested in organising running races. As a result of his great organisational skills, all the runs went like clockwork. John Saunders was very much involved with the run. He was always there, both at the start and the finish, and often handed over the trophy. Saunders became very involved and interested in the mateship and camaraderie that developed among the runners, and he was very proud of his personal involvement. Charlie Lynn also managed to involve many reformed drinkers and other addicts to undertake the run, and this gave a new lease of life to many of them.

Saunders very quickly recognised the promotional potential of the event, and persuaded its organisers to call it 'The Greatest Run in the World'. It was certainly the longest, the hardest, and possibly the richest, and was done at a time when ultra-marathons were not even heard of. All the runners wore the Westfield logo on the front and back of their T-shirts.

Hailed as the 'World's Greatest Race', the Westfield Run was greatly supported by John Saunders and quickly became the Annual Westfield Run. It was held from Westfield's Parramatta Shoppingtown to Westfield's Doncaster Shoppingtown in Melbourne, and attracted great media attention. Here we see two well-known ultramarathon runners, Cliff Young and Geoff Molloy, displayed prominently in the Parramatta Advertiser

This provided incredible promotion for Westfield, because the run was televised each day, and much was made of it by the print media also. The Westfield Run was a wonderful win-win situation.

The promotional ideas of John Saunders are now legendary. I found it interesting to talk to his associates about this: they told me that John would listen carefully to each new idea presented to him, no matter how absurd it appeared to be, and no matter how derisive some of his associates were about it. Saunders accepted some new promotional projects and refused most others, but he always listened very carefully. I think it was Albert Einstein who once said something to the effect that, 'If an idea at first does not appear to be completely crazy, one might as well ignore it'. John Saunders was no Einstein, but he was certainly on the great scientist's wavelength when it came to promotional ideas.

On Failure and Quitting

Of course, not all the major projects that John Saunders was connected with turned out to be successful. As we have seen, he had immense persistence and was, at times, extremely stubborn. However, when a project was not successful, was losing money, and was becoming commercially unviable, Saunders recognised reality and quit without throwing good money after bad. When he perceived that a project had failed, he would tell his team that they could 'start the Kaddish', or mourner's prayer. If a deal had gone sour, and any further effort to recover money was, in his view, useless, he instructed his accounting team to give up and cut their losses. In this situation he would translate into English a somewhat coarse Hungarian saying: he would suggest to the accounting team that working further on money recovery would be like 'trying to get a fart out of a dead horse'. Failure was not welcome, but John faced up to it with realism and, importantly, with a sense of humour.

The Human Touch

John Saunders' style of relating to people in general, and to business associates in particular, was one of his greatest assets. Whenever meeting anyone new, John would characteristically say very little initially, mainly listening to what the other person was saying. It seems that by instinct and observation he understood where people were coming from—including their needs, prejudices, strengths, and weaknesses. Largely as a result of this listening and understanding, he could talk to anyone at any level: to the cleaner in one of the shopping centres; his friends; his staff; other business leaders, such as Sir Frank McDowell, Sir Edgar Coles, Sir Tom North, and Mick Grace; politicians and prime ministers; Henry Kissinger; and even Prince Charles. Listening quietly and modestly, John Saunders' genuine interest in their life, together with his boyish sense of humour, put most people at ease and resulted in many close personal relationships.

In fact, the personal relationships that both Saunders and Lowy enjoyed with the heads of major retailers in Australia became at least one factor in Westfield being able to persuade the big retailers into coming to the new large regional centres they were building. The major retailers in turn were able to de-emphasise their downtown department stores, and to develop strong regional shops at Westfield centres—to their mutual benefit and to the benefit of the suburb-dwellers. This was pure Milton Friedman economic theory in practice, and both John Saunders and Frank Lowy very clearly understood the immense significance of their association with Australia's major retailers.

It is also important to recall once again that both John Saunders and Frank Lowy had an image of total integrity and honesty. This meant that, added to close personal relationships, retail leaders also had a strong feeling of security and trust in Westfield and in its two managing directors. There was also a strong feeling of trustworthiness among those who had financed their ventures—which included their Australian and later Swiss bankers, life assurance and insurance companies, and superannuation funds and their shareholders.

The relationship between Westfield and the smaller retailers in the shopping centres was largely undertaken by John Saunders. He regularly visited the Westfield shopping centres around Sydney, usually during weekends, usually unannounced and usually taking with him, often unwillingly, one of his children. He knew the retailers by name, and spent a few minutes with many of them, discussing not only business but also life. When in other cities, he would do the same round of visiting the small retailers in the Westfield shopping centres. I myself had many experiences of making these unannounced

John Saunders in a hard hat
with two of his executives,
David Dinte and Bernard
O'Hara, at a building site

visits with John Saunders in Melbourne and Brisbane, often finishing up with Saunders eating a large cake at one of the food stalls around four o'clock in the afternoon.

The special relationship John Saunders had with his staff is yet another important secret behind his business success. Although quiet by outward appearances, he was a lover of life and had a genuine interest in other people. And, as we have already seen, he was able to relate to people at all levels of life.

Recruitment was often done on the basis of gut feelings and intuition, rather than after a careful examination of the applicant's curriculum vitae, or on recommendations made after exhaustive interviews by personnel agencies, or other similar 'head-hunters'. Frank Lowy made his assessment of the applicant independently, and this was yet another example of the wonderful interaction the two men had in coming to a decision. They made mistakes over the years, but mostly they had successes. We have already seen how John Saunders employed the first manager of The Shore Inn and the first manager of the bluemetal quarry, and how he invited Judy Hall to Australia to advise on food presentation. If someone had the right basic qualifications for a job, John and Frank gave him or her an individual interview and decided very quickly.

Youthfulness was an important factor in their recruitment decisions, particularly as the philosophy of the two men was always 'to start them young'. They liked to see how new staff developed, and wanted to bring them up under their personal guidance so that they could grow with the firm—just as Saunders and Lowy were themselves developing and adapting to changes as Westfield grew over the years. With the growth of Westfield in recent years, recruitment is now conducted along more formal lines involving interviews and questionnaires. A recently retired Westfield executive commented, 'If Saunders and Lowy had applied for a job with Westfield now, they probably would not be successful.'

John Saunders knew the name of everyone working with him; if he forgot a name, he always made quite sure that he knew it before speaking to the person. He knew about each employee's family and children—about their hobbies, aspirations, needs, and problems. Just as he visited Westfield shopping centres and spoke to everyone, he also made almost daily unannounced rounds of the Westfield offices, talked to the staff about work, and chatted about their personal life also. He knew or found out about any deaths among staff of close family members, and usually attended the funeral, standing quietly in the background. He sent flowers to the wives of his executives who had surgery or gave birth.

The door to John Saunders' office was always open, as was Frank Lowy's. Both men were very approachable if a member of staff had an idea, question, or problem. This was in marked contrast to many similar organisations, where new ideas had to go through the red tape of various administrative procedures. Decisions were made quickly as to whether an idea should be accepted or rejected or put on hold. John was also regarded as being very good at delegating important responsibilities. However, this only happened after he had developed a trust in the person. Once he delegated, he expected the project to be done on time, and he did not usually look over the shoulder of the executive. On the other hand, his staff knew that with the delegation of responsibility they also needed to have all the answers to any questions about progress, and they also had to have all the details at their fingertips about any ideas or problems with which they approached John. This sense of independence is an important motivator for excellence in performance among the executives of any organisation—a fact which John Saunders would have known instinctively.

Although John Saunders had no hesitation in telling someone if a performance was below par, or if a mistake or blunder had been made, he was also a person who came forth with praise for a good initiative or a job well done. This praise may have come in the form of a gentle touch on the shoulder while doing his daily wandering among the staff in the offices, or it may have been a handshake or a laudatory word, or a small gift, or a plane ticket for a holiday, or a bonus at the end of the year.

John Saunders had an extraordinary capacity to make a person feel special. Bill Szabolcs, Westfield's architect between 1964 and 1983, said of him: 'He was a nice guy—clever, visionary and, foremost, he had good people skills.' Jim Doe, who recently retired as an executive of Westfield and had a long association with John Saunders, said: 'He had the capacity to make ordinary people feel extraordinary, and this was one of his greatest assets.' This sentiment was echoed by others who had a long association with him. Brian Woolstone, the first chief architect of Westfield, said:

> John gave of himself to his associates, and in return they would give more. He was like a fertiliser for plants, so they were able to grow. He understood, respected and openly encouraged expertise and creativity among his associates. He gave them 'yiches', Yiddish for a pedigree or prestige. This allowed them to be themselves and give of themselves, much more than they otherwise would. This is the way John enriched their lives and also gained from this himself. He had this gift of being able to surround himself with people who would make his vision come true.

Although in his inimitable way John engendered a great esprit de corps at Westfield, it should not be assumed that the life of a Westfield executive was 'cakes and ale' all the way. While he was a great stimulator and motivator of staff at all levels, he was also a powerful controller. The John Saunders principle of getting value for money very much extended to his staff. He asked every shopping-centre manager to know precisely the turnover in every shop—which was part of their job—but also to know what was going on in the district, and expected them to be on first-name terms with the local mayor, the chief of police, and other important locals. Once a new project was begun, John set deadlines which were tight and at times unrealistic, and he knew this. He believed that, without a deadline, 'People just keep working away and never finish anything'. When I told him that writing his biography would take about one year, he replied characteristically, 'Nine months, I think.' When a task needed to be done, John Saunders had the ability to inculcate a sense of urgency in everyone around him. Something about him made people want to do their best for him, and more.

There was a type of poor performance that irritated John Saunders enormously, and he usually solved the problem by setting an example. John was brought up with the philosophy—and he brought up his own children the same way—that 'you should never ask anyone to do a job you would not do yourself.' On one occasion, when he made one of his many surprise visits to a large shopping centre, during which he talked to many of the retailers before talking to management, he found that the toilets were dirty and had not been cleaned that day. Talking to the centre manager, he asked why the toilets were dirty. 'It's because the cleaners are on strike', he was informed. Saunders was there with his daughter Betty, and the two of them went to the cleaners' cupboard, and got out some gloves, buckets, squeegees, and detergents. Betty cleaned the female toilets and John the male toilets. Funnily enough, there were never any dirty toilets in this particular centre subsequently.

On another occasion, whilst making a surprise visit to check on The Shore Inn Motel on a Saturday evening, it turned out that the person who washed the dishes had had an altercation with the chef, and both of them walked out on a full restaurant and a full bar. John got one of the assistant chefs to do the cooking, while he rolled up his sleeves and washed the dishes for the next four or five hours, missing dinner at home. After this incident, somehow the manager was able to have a chef and a dish-washer on duty all the time.

The John Saunders' formula for business success may not stack up well with current business-management theories, yet his human approach to business and management makes good sense. Not only has Westfield been enormously successful, but its success has been achieved with a minimum of controversy. John Saunders regarded the men and women on Westfield's staff as a part of an extended family. Westfield executives such as Jim Doe, Bernard O'Hara, John Craig, and others have told me that they loved going to work each day, and that the feeling was there, at least in part, because of John Saunders.

When Prince Charles opened the Royal Coaches Exhibition at Indooroopilly Shoppingtown, he asked Saunders about the secret of his success. John quietly and modestly answered that it was about hard work and the challenges involved in overcoming difficulties. He would give this answer to others, also, especially on any occasion associated with the media. When in a less formal situation, among his friends or close associates, John Saunders would admit that success did not come easily. With his heavy Hungarian accent and a smile on his pink, shiny cheeks, he would say, 'If it was easy, everybody would be doing it!'

HRH Prince Charles opening the Royal Coaches Exhibition at Westfield, Indooroopilly, shaking hands with John Saunders and asking him the reasons behind his business success

CHAPTER 14

FAMILY

Rabbi Harold Kushner in his book *To Life* gives us a wonderful personal account of what it is to be a Jew. In contrast to Christianity, which we can look on as having its origins as a religious organisation with set goals and beliefs, Judaism began as a people and a community; religion followed later. Unlike Christians, Jews do not need to be baptised. They are born into the Jewish community, and think of themselves as Jewish even when they are not religiously observant. Children of Jewish mothers are automatically Jews as part of a historical community going back to Abraham, Isaac, and Jacob. Jews think of themselves as part of a huge extended family going back for many, many generations. A Jew may not agree with or even like some members of his extended family nor the extended 'historic Jewish family'; nevertheless he or she feels bound to them by family ties and tradition. And so it was for John Saunders.

The *Oxford English Dictionary* defines a patriarch as 'the male head or ruler of a family or tribe'. Undoubtedly the head and ruler of his family, Saunders demanded respect for his views, and consultation when important decisions had to be made. He controlled the actions of family members, or tried to do so, particularly when there was any possibility or hint of instability or disintegration in his family. Yet John Saunders could not be described as a 'family man' in the traditional sense. He loved his family, but he certainly did not rush home after a day's work to put his feet up and relax with his wife and children. Both daughters recall that in their early years their father usually arrived home when they were already in bed.

John's first marriage to Eta was apparently happy, and he enjoyed a reasonable family life. However, with Eta's illness and with Westfield demanding an increasing commitment from him, home life suffered considerably for John—as well as for Eta and the children. Eta's premature death in 1970 was devastating for John Saunders, and left him in a state of grief, with feelings of despair and guilt. John's second marriage to Klara Koch in 1974 was blessed by a daughter, Monica. However, the marriage ended in separation in 1988, and then divorce. A 'patriarch' he was; alas, a 'family man' he was not.

John's sister Lilly, who was older by eighteen months than John, arrived in Sydney in 1960 with her husband, Miklós Somogyi, and their daughter, Judy. In 1963, John helped them financially to start up in business when they opened a shoe repair and travel goods store in the Hornsby Westfield shopping centre. Amazingly, Miklós, a warm-hearted and charming family man, happened to have been in the same-forced labour camp under the Nazis as my father. Miklós died prematurely, and his death was a great loss to his family. John's younger sister, Gita, was married to Pista Klein ('Pista' is a nickname for 'Steven' in Hungarian). They also had one daughter, Suzie. Gita recovered from the serious complications of her gall-bladder operation—which I described in the opening chapter—and returned to running two shoe shops with her husband. Although she had always looked on John as a father figure, her brother became even more important to her after the death of her husband. John, for his part, loved his two sisters equally, and he went to a lot of trouble to treat them and to appear to treat them in exactly the same way.

John Saunders had three children—Betty, Mark, and Monica—and loved them equally and profoundly. As one would expect from a patriarch, his love for his children did not stop him from trying to control their behaviour and activities so that they behaved in a way he thought was appropriate for them. Betty has few early memories of her father, because she was usually in bed by the time he came home

Sisters Lilly Somogyi (left), Gita Klein (centre) with John Saunders at a HopeTown School function

from work. One of these memories involves her father's shoes. John Saunders had his shoes specially made because of a very broad forefoot, and as a result the shoes were usually quite squeaky. Betty remembers being able to go to sleep only after she had heard his shoes squeak when he came into her room to kiss her goodnight. 'Squeaky shoes', she would think. 'Daddy's home, I'm safe, and I can go to sleep peacefully now.' Another early memory is of her father bringing home presents, often lollies and sweets; since then she has associated the feeling of security with sweets. Betty's early memories are of her father working during the week and taking her around shopping centres during the weekends while he was making his many unannounced inspections of various Westfield Shoppingtowns.

Two other dramatic experiences for Betty, which she feels have contributed to some early feelings of insecurity, were the unannounced arrival of brother Mark and her accidental discovery whilst playing with the Lowy children that she was an adopted daughter. John's second marriage to Klara Koch was at first wonderful for Betty, because Klara represented everything a girl in her teens would want in a mother—she was young, direct, and lots of fun. Betty says that she became something of a rebellious teenager, perhaps in response to parental control, and this created friction. It may have been one of the reasons for Betty's early marriage, which ended in divorce.

After her divorce, Betty met her present husband, Daniel Klimenko. At first, Daniel represented serious problems for John Saunders: he was not Jewish, he was a few years younger, he was a tradesman, and he had a Ukranian-born father. This last was probably particularly difficult for Saunders to accept, because Ukranians had often been the guards in concentration and labour camps during the Nazi occupation of Hungary. Although her father totally rejected Daniel initially, Betty stuck to her guns and, little by little, acceptance followed. Daniel later converted to Judaism, and has become an observant Jew. Betty says she knew that everything would turn out fine between John and Daniel when, after his conversion ceremony, they were all standing around the backyard pool, and the rabbi and John pushed

John Saunders with son Mark

Daniel, fully clothed, into the water. She looks on this as Daniel's 'mikva', a ritual bath for Jewish women at the end of their monthly menstrual cycle or after childbirth.

Betty can now see past the controlling influence her father had over her for many years, and can appreciate the positives. He taught her several important lessons in life. He would say, 'Keep a good name; that will be a credit to you, and good credit is everything', and also, 'Never get anyone to do anything you wouldn't do yourself'. She has a mature view about John and the way he kept secrets, and how he suppressed so much that he perceived to be unwelcome and unpleasant. On the positive side, she saw this as something that gave him strength of character and allowed him to persist in the face of adversity. On the negative side, Betty saw his habit of suppressing and not acknowledging problems as something which could and sometimes did make her father sick, both physically and emotionally. Interestingly, her views are very much in keeping with current scientific medical research concerning the development of several illnesses. She told me:

Daddy had an incredibly strong will to live, especially in the last ten years of his life, which I believe was due to his wish to keep the family together. Another side of Daddy was his mischievous nature. He would regularly sneak up behind me and put a block of ice down the back of my frock. Once when we were walking in Jerusalem along the Via Dolorosa, he managed to get a stick from somewhere, tied a white handkerchief on it, and waved it in the air, and literally misled a group of Japanese tourists who started to follow him. Yet another side of Daddy's character was that of a modest person who best enjoyed the simple life, a man who wanted to live in anonymity in the shadows.

By the age of thirty-eight, Betty Saunders-Klimenko had come from having been a slightly insecure 'daddy's little girl' and a rebellious teenager, to feeling a genuine love and reaching a deep understanding of her father. In spite of their differences over the years, each understood the strengths and weaknesses of the other, and at the end there was true paternal and filial love between them. Betty has three sons—Anthony and Ricky Salamon from her first marriage, and Matthew from the second—and all three were much loved by their grandfather.

Mark Saunders was first noted as having learning difficulties when he was about three or four years old. At the beginning, John did not accept that Mark had a problem or, if he did, he certainly did not acknowledge it. As Mark got older he went to the Devereaux School in Santa Barbara, California, where he spent two years. When he returned from California, Mark re-entered life, as it were, and has worked full time since—first at a television station doing clerical work, and subsequently in the workshop and maintenance department of the Terrace Tower Group of Companies. He is happy at work and proud of his job. John Saunders cared enormously for Mark's welfare, and was the single most important person in Mark's life. Mark respected, revered, and feared his father. Although at times he found him far too controlling of his behaviour, he worried not only about his father's approval but also about his health. What cannot be ignored is that John's incredible persistence was the single most important reason for Mark being able to lead a reasonably full and happy life.

During her pregnancy, John's second wife, Klara, suffered greatly from nausea and vomiting. On one occasion she was in Los Angeles with John and, whilst in a taxi, she became nauseated and had to get out. As she was leaning over the curb, John looked up and said, with one of his little smiles, 'If she's a girl, we'll call her Monica' (the cab had stopped at Santa Monica Boulevard). Monica it turned out to be: she was born in August 1978, and has grown into a beautiful, intelligent, active young woman, with a good feeling

A happy John Saunders with two loving daughters: Monica on the left, Betty on the right

A mischievous John Saunders with daughter Monica at a fancy-dress birthday party

for business and a mischievous sense of humour—similar to that of her father's. Her first recollection of her father is at about age four, when she would see him for just a few minutes each evening when he came home from the office, and briefly at breakfast the next morning. The subsequent separation and divorce of her parents was extremely stressful for Monica. Much later, during the 1990s, Monica got to know and love her father. Monica is like John in the way she thinks about life and about business. Like John, she does not seek too much formal learning, and prefers a practical, common-sense approach.

There was a fascinating difference in the way John Saunders loved Betty compared to the way he loved Monica. 'Dad's love for Betty was expressed like the love of a father for a daughter, tickling her back, bringing her lollies and chocolates', Monica told me. 'His love for me was shown by Dad imparting his wisdom and know-how in business.' At the age of sixteen, Monica went to Israel for a holiday with a school group. Whilst other parents were sending phone messages or hand-written faxes to their children about home events, John sent Monica balance sheets showing that there had been an 8-per-cent increase in the turnover of the Sydney SupaCenta. Nothing else was on the fax, although it was signed, 'Love, Daddy'.

John Saunders loved his family, and listened to all their complaints and requests patiently. Many of their requests apparently related to money matters. As we have seen, John regulated expenditure at a practical level by tightly controlling the money supply. He made everyone around him accountable for every dollar spent. This tight control was sometimes resented, as one would expect; it was often upsetting, or at least annoying. However, these family responses did not concern John Saunders too much. The philosopher

John Saunders and Sir Zelman Cowen, past governor-general of Australia, accompanying Betty's three children (l-r: Matthew, Ricky and Anthony), at a wreath-laying ceremony to mark the fiftieth anniversary of liberation after the Second World War. Betty Saunders-Klimenko is seen smiling, behind them, on the left of the picture

John Saunders surrounded by his children and grandchildren. Back row from left: Monica, Mark, Betty, grandson Anthony. Sitting on the ground, grandson Ricky; and, standing next to Saunders, grandson Matthew

Nietzsche supported the Saunders' approach: 'This is the hardest of all, to close the open hand out of love, and keep modest as a giver.'

Jews usually have a strong sense of their common heritage and values, and of their common responsibilities to all other Jews. John Saunders, who was no exception, was proud of his Jewish origins. In his religious politics, just as in secular politics, he was at heart a progressive liberal. He disliked right-wing orthodox fundamentalism as much as he disliked ghetto mentalities, and was opposed to those Jews who did not forgive and who lived in the past. He was upset by what he perceived to be the shift to the right in Israel, yet he generously supported both Orthodox and Progressive causes in Israel as well as in Australia. After each display of intransigence by Israeli leaders, which upset him, he became adamant that he would not give again. But every time his good-heartedness prevailed, and he gave generously to his extended Jewish family until the end—and even after.

CHAPTER 15

BOSOM FRIENDS

Bosom friends are those who know our hearts.

Bosom friends are those who may be separated by hundreds

of miles, yet still have implicit faith in us and refuse to believe

rumours against us; those who in given moments advise us as

to what to do and what not to do and those who at the critical

hour come to our help and sometimes undertake of their own

accord to settle a matter or make a decision without for a

moment questioning whether by doing so they

open themselves to criticism.

CHANG CH'AO, ABOUT 1650

John Saunders touched the lives and hearts of many, and had an amazingly wide array of acquaintances. John would have said of many people, 'Yes, we are friends'; in turn, they would have said, 'Yes, John Saunders is a friend of mine'. Yet, while these would be real relationships, the people involved would not be John Saunders' bosom friends. Among his early friends in Australia were the Korda brothers, Les and Imre, and their wives, who helped John escape from Hungary to Austria, through Slovakia. 'They were most charming people, the Kordas', John told me, 'and in my view they were in the high society of Sydney. They were educated, and one was a noted violinist, so we were on different social levels.'

However, differences in social standing were no bar to John's mischievous behaviour with his friends. Les Korda tells the story of how proud John was of The Shore Inn Motel. On a rainy day, soon after its opening in 1963, he persuaded Les and Klara Korda to go and see it. He bet one hundred pounds that Les would not jump into the pool with his clothes on. 'I took off my watch, removed my wallet and other papers and gave them to my wife, Klara, and then jumped in. John took us home in his air-conditioned car. I had my suit dry-cleaned for seven shillings and sixpence, so I reckoned I made some money on this deal. However, it was the only bet I ever won from John.'

Other early friends were Alex and George Pongrass (anglicised from Pongrácz), whom John had known in Hungary as an adolescent. After the war John helped them to escape from Hungary to Austria through Slovakia, using the BRICHA organisation headed by Les Korda. They settled in Sydney in the early 1950s, and retained their connection with John. However, there were differences in their philosophies, and in their perceived social standing; whilst these friendships remained warm to the end, they did not really blossom over the years.

Friendship is one of the most democratic of human relationships: the prime minister of a country is on an equal footing with a friend who may be a plumber or a television repairman. That great Chinese philosopher and sage, Mencius—who believed that humans are innately good, although they need proper conditions for their moral growth, including friendship on an equal basis—said, 'Friendship does not admit of assumptions of superiority'. John Saunders was fond of the Korda and Pongrass families, and they were friends. But he perceived the friendship not to be on an equal basis because of their different philosophies on business and life, and because he perceived that they had a more elevated social standing.

John Saunders first met Cantor Michael Deutsch in 1949 in the Rothschild Hospital in Vienna, which was then the hostel for displaced Jews. Michael recalls John as a fun-loving man, and they both had in common their love of pretty women. By 1949 there were many elegant women to be seen in Vienna, but the two refugees from Eastern Europe did not get any closer than a look. Michael has a beautiful singing voice, and whilst in Vienna he would go to restaurants and sing to the diners for a free dinner for himself and his friends. He became a cantor at the Temple Emanuel in Sydney, and remained friendly with John, referring to him as one of his best 'chavers', a 'cobber' in Hebrew (the two words may have the same linguistic origin). The two men remained loyal friends to the end, although not bosom buddies. At the valedictory dinner, when Saunders left Westfield in 1987, Neville Wran remarked in his speech that, 'Here we have John Saunders retiring, but Cantor Deutsch is still singing for his supper!'

Dr Alexander (Sanyi) Pollack was another longstanding friend of John Saunders. He was the doctor who called me in Melbourne to provide a second opinion when John's sister was very ill in Sydney in the 1970s (see chapter one). Dr Pollack was born and practised medicine in my hometown of Kassa in Hungary, and was in fact a friend of my parents. (When I interviewed him in connection with this biography, he recalled that many years ago my mother took me along to see him about a skin rash I had developed, and told him

Bevan Bradbury, previously Chairman of G J Coles and then of Coles Myer, teaching John Saunders and the author, unsuccessfully, the rudiments of golf in Queenstown, New Zealand

that she didn't know what the rash was. We had a good laugh, because Sanyi
Pollack told me that he didn't know what it was, either. It reminded both of
us of an old joke often told against dermatologists. A young woman goes to
a dermatologist with a rash on her arm. After examining her, the dermatologist says, 'Mm, young lady, have you had this rash before?' 'Yes, doctor,' she
replies. 'As a matter of fact, I have had it before.' 'Well', the doctors says, 'I'm
afraid you've got it again.')

Sanyi Pollack met John and Eta Saunders in the mid-1950s at a social
function. At first, their relationship was exclusively social. After Eta's death,
John gradually became a patient of Sanyi's. At first, this was because John was
rather low after his wife's death; then, some years later, he was found to have
adult-onset diabetes. Sanyi knew that John had the 'full hand' of risk factors
for heart disease—he was a smoker, had a poor diet, was overweight, was
diabetic, had high blood pressure, and for some years had been under considerable life stresses most days of the week. Sanyi also realised that John had
a great determination and will to live which had helped him in the past to
survive against great odds. Theirs was a genuine friendship, based on mutual
trust and loyalty. However, while it was uncomplicated by any demands or
competition, it was unequal in some ways—largely because of the superimposed professional relationship between a doctor and his patient.

Bevan Bradbury, who was a leading businessman, and committed member
of the Liberal Party, shared a long friendship with John Saunders. Their friendship, which was based in part on their business association and in part on their
common belief in Australia's bright economic future, was genuine and warm,
and was only cut short by Bradbury's untimely death. John's friendship with
Bob Hawke, which I have described in an earlier chapter, was also warm and
at times close. But with Hawke's assumption of high public office as prime
minister, the closeness of the friendship understandably suffered.

What about his friendships with women? John Saunders never hid his
admiration for an attractive woman with charm whenever he saw or met
one. Even in his last years, when his heart, his diabetes, and the need to take
medication to lower his blood pressure took its toll on his potency, he still

looked around admiringly when he passed a beautiful woman. At the same time, he was neither a sexist nor a man who regularly pursued or engaged in casual sexual encounters with women. He was in fact quite romantic—a side of his character few knew about. I was with him once when he asked the resident gypsy musicians to play for a woman sitting alone in the corner of a restaurant in Budapest, just because she seemed so sad. We left the restaurant soon after that, and John did not even introduce himself to her. He told me on many occasions that he enjoyed seeing beautiful women happy, just like Chang Ch'ao apparently felt in the seventeenth century:

> One should see flowers when they are in bloom, should see the moon when it is full, and should see beautiful women when they are gay and happy. Otherwise our purpose is defeated. Without the company of beautiful ladies, flowers and the moon would be wasted.

Many women found John charming, and some even thought that he had sex appeal. Was it his wealth? Women found him attractive after the war in Hungary, in Blacktown, and even when they were not aware that he was a millionaire. Was it his pink cheeks and cheeky smile? Was it the way he looked at women with open admiration? He certainly had an aura about him; there was a bit of magic there.

Did John Saunders have strong feelings for the women in his life? Did love elude him, as it often seems to with very successful men? Did patriarchy, great success, and the exercise of authority condemn him to renounce love? I know that John Saunders felt deep emotions, but it seemed to me that he had great difficulty expressing them. He certainly loved his first wife, Eta, and was shattered for some time by her untimely death. Years later, he loved a young woman doctor but was not free to marry at the time. He developed serious heart disease, and by the time he was free he had had heart surgery. His lady friend desperately wanted to have a family but felt it would be too much to ask of John, so they parted. It was so sad to see these two ships pass in the night. He was an unabashed admirer of women; yet it seems that, apart from the love and friendship of his first wife, the love and deep friendship of women largely eluded him.

So who were the bosom friends of John Saunders? Who were those he could relax with in an atmosphere of mutual trust? Who shared his feelings of complete loyalty, uncomplicated by competition, jealousy, or demands, and established friendships with him on an equal footing? To whom could he unburden his problems, and they theirs? With whom could he share his joys and successes, reaffirm his moral values, share witty comments and risqué jokes, and discuss the really important things in life, such as women and politics? After removing myself—since my view of our friendship could not possibly be unbiased through the writing of this book—I am left with six men, just and true: Sam Moss, Andrew Lederer, Frank Lowy, Feri Vadász, Fredi Pasternak, and Neville Wran.

The two expatriate Hungarians, Andrew Lederer and Sam Moss, became friends of John Saunders soon after his arrival in Australia. Although they have quite different personalities, their friendship with Saunders was similar in many ways. They are both successful businessmen: Andrew is a smallgoods manufacturer, and Sam is in textiles and clothing. They were of a similar age to John and, like him, both had a Hungarian and Jewish background and were survivors of the Holocaust. They both saw John as an entertaining man—as wonderful company, never boring, and full of humour. They both saw him as a soft-hearted and kind human being, and neither ever saw John do anything unkind to anyone in the forty years that they knew him. 'I couldn't have had a better friend', was what both men told me, quite independently. They saw John as an exceptional businessman—particularly as he had had to give up formal education early in life—and as a person with an immense natural intelligence and common sense who had 'a good nose for business'. Andrew Lederer also believed that John Saunders paid a very high price for success by growing up in the 'school of life', because this meant he sacrificed his personal life.

From time to time, John Saunders gave medical advice to his friends, claiming to have an ND (Nearly Doctor) degree. On one occasion, Andrew Lederer thought he was having heart problems because of left-sided chest

Two of John Saunders' oldest friends in Australia, Andrew Lederer and Frank Lowy, wishing him well at the Westfield Valedictory Dinner in November 1987

pain situated over his heart. This happened at a time when John Saunders, Frank Lowy, and Andrew Lederer were building a house together on a farm in Goulburn. One weekend they were planting trees in the drive. After Andrew complained of chest pain and suggested he had heart problems, John quietly asked him to drive in some stakes. After he had been doing this hard work for about ten minutes and felt no pain, Professor Saunders, ND, said, 'Bandi [his nickname], you are bullshitting me! There is absolutely nothing wrong with your heart.' This was indeed a very successful therapeutic trial, and Andrew forgot about his heart after that incident. These two long-standing friendships were based on similar backgrounds and philosophies of life. Each man knew the heart of the other. Moral, social, and philosophical values could be reaffirmed; old jokes could be retold; hearts could be unbur-dened of trouble and sorrow; and success and joys could be shared. These two friendships gave John Saunders enormous pleasure, and, I suspect, a kind of reassurance that life was worth living.

The friendship between John Saunders and Frank Lowy seemed, on the surface, to be rather similar to that with Andrew Lederer and Sam Moss. They were, after all, both from the same part of the world, had the same background and ethnicity, similar moral, social and religious values, and a similar sense of humour. The two men always had complete trust in and loyalty for the other, and great respect for each other's abilities in business matters. As we have seen, they recognised their complementary skills in business: John's for ideas and persistence, and Frank's for organisation and financial know-how. These qualities were germane to their enormous success in business.

The closeness of their friendship suffered eventually, probably because of the very thing which brought them together—their business partnership. Inevitably there would have been currents, well under the surface, of some competitiveness between the two men. Initially it was clear that John Saunders had much more business experience and much more life experience than Frank Lowy. This meant that, in the first few years at least, John's opinion often carried more weight when important decisions had to be made; even if Frank was to some extent opposed to a particular decision, I suspect he would have let it be. As the years went by, and the partners' success with Westfield grew, this condition of inequality would have disappeared as far as Frank was concerned. But this subtle change in the balance was probably not recognised, at least at a conscious level, by John Saunders.

The two men were both strong and independent thinkers. Whilst their approaches would have been very similar, at least in the first decade or two of their association, it is almost predictable that Frank Lowy would have thought more and more in terms of globalisation, the multinationalisation of business, and joint projects. John Saunders, on the other hand, would have been concerned more with issues to do with improved efficiency and changes in technology, and would have remained with a 'more of the same' philosophy. Events after 1987 bore out this difference in attitudes very clearly. Of course, this is an incomplete and facile summary of a deep friendship that lasted over forty years. It is easy for a biographer to look at this with the value of hindsight, using an instrument which in medicine we call a 'retrospectoscope'. I will discuss this friendship more in the next chapter.

Feri Vadász, the leader of the group of men in the internment camp in Garany, and then in Auschwitz and subsequently in Dörnhau, eventually settled in Budapest as a communist party official, and continued his work as a writer and journalist. John Saunders and Feri Vadász parted company in 1949, feeling their ideological differences keenly at the time that John escaped from Russian-dominated Hungary. Although Feri knew that John was somewhere in Australia, they lost contact for several years; both men probably had feelings of guilt and regret because of their previous falling-out. Eventually John made contact with Feri, and they wrote to each other several times. Then John went to Budapest on a number of occasions in the 1960s. As time passed and the fortunes of John Saunders improved, he invited Feri to Australia on four occasions—the last one being in May 1995, when he hired the Concert Hall of the Sydney Opera House to celebrate fifty years of liberation from the camps. John would telephone Feri in Budapest on an almost weekly basis. John told me that 'the passion of Feri Vadász has always been politics, so it was a great disappointment for him to witness Russian tyranny in Eastern Europe, even though he probably had blinkers on while this was happening. It was an even greater disappointment for him to see that communism in Russia and in Eastern Europe had failed so miserably.' Feri now admits that John was right, and that he saw what Feri couldn't see in 1949 concerning Russian tyranny.

When I visited Feri Vadász in 1997 in Budapest, he talked little about communism. At the age of eighty-one, his brain was working very well. He retained a philosophical attitude towards the aches and pains and other problems of old age. 'At eighty-one, I am more worried about that which does not hurt than that which hurts', he said, referring I presumed to the silence of cancer. He was very pleased with life at that time, after having had a prostate operation, because 'I can now pee like a young boy'. Feri could see the stark contrast between John's successful business career and his personal life, which was studded with sadness and tragedy. Yet Feri could also see that John had somehow been able to repress and get on top of these life problems; he was able to lead a full and often enjoyable life, experiencing great pleasure living in Sydney, and travelling every year. This was not even to mention John's eye for a pretty woman.

The friendship between John Saunders and Feri Vadász was certainly devoid of demands, competition, and jealousy. Yet it was unusual, in that the two men had different ideologies. They were separated by many thousands of kilometres, their social and financial states were very different, and yet they enjoyed a wonderful, almost spiritually enriching and deep friendship. It was a friendship born from unspeakable suffering that they had endured during their two years together in hell. 'Our bond is even stronger than that which exists between brothers', Feri told me in 1997.

Feri Vadász, John Saunders, and Fredi Pasternak, three friends and Holocaust survivors of the internment camps of Auschwitz and Dörnhau, celebrating the fiftieth anniversary of the liberation of Europe's concentration camps

Earlier, we left the fourteen-year old Fredi Paszternák at the liberation of Dörnhau in May 1945, looking after his sick father who had had a serious encounter with typhus. John Saunders had a lot to do with both Fredi and his father. He helped to save Fredi's life; as well, when Fredi's father was losing heart in Dörnhau, John was the one who kept up the spirits of the older men by telling them the BBC news—some of which he either made up at times, or conveyed in a much more optimistic light than was warranted by reality. After liberation, Fredi and his father returned to their small home town of Tállya. Here they were reunited with the young man's mother and two sisters, who had also survived. Paszternák senior was able to resume operating his flour mills and vineyards.

Fredi did not see John Saunders after liberation, because he went to Budapest to finish his secondary education, and then remained there to do his medical training at the Budapest Medical School. He then escaped from Hungary during the 1956 revolution and migrated to California, anglicising his name to Pasternak. He became a consultant in obstetrics and gynaecology at the Cedars Sinai Medical Center in Los Angeles, with a flourishing private practice. He is also a professor of gynaecology at the University of Southern California, and is currently writing a book on medical experimentation performed by the Nazis during the Holocaust. He met John Saunders again in 1988 in Los Angeles, 43 years after liberation. It was an extraordinary encounter, and due entirely to chance: Fredi's name came up while John was dining in Los Angeles with a mutual friend. As Fredi Pasternak recalled:

> I was a happily divorced man, having a wonderful relationship with a well-known singer who gave many concerts in the United States and out of the country also, and who had a large house in Los Angeles. Whenever she was in Los Angeles I stayed with her, and at other times when she was out of town I stayed in my own apartment. Late one night and on an occasion when I was with my friend—it was close to midnight—my answering service told me that a Mr John Saunders would like to talk to me. This was rather strange because, first of all, being a gynaecologist, I don't have men consulting me, and secondly, I knew

there was another Pasternak in Los Angeles, a Dr Glen Pasternak who was a thoracic surgeon. Our messages had often crossed in the past.

I asked the answering service to tell Mr Saunders that I was the wrong man and that he was looking for Dr Glen Pasternak. They called me back in two minutes and said, 'No, he is looking for you and he insists on talking to you.' I called the number, although I did not know who John Saunders was. The phone was answered by a man who said, 'I am Jenö Schwarcz from Sátoraljaujhely', and I knew immediately who he was. 'I really must talk to you right now', he said.

I told him that I was most excited about this, but I had an immediate problem in that it was almost midnight and I had a difficult operation to do at 7.15 the following morning, and that it would be most irresponsible of me to spend the rest of the night talking to him, and then turn up to do the surgery, which I could not cancel at this late stage. John was quite upset, and insistent that we meet immediately, but I managed to talk him out of it.

We got together the following afternoon at the Beverly Hilton Hotel, where John was staying. When I arrived he was pacing up and down the corridor in front of the lift well, and it was a most wonderfully emotional and exciting occasion. We talked for many hours. Subsequently we met on many other occasions in Los Angeles, in Budapest when we were both visiting there, and I also went to Australia at his invitation on two occasions—once when HopeTown School was extended, and the second time in 1995 when he celebrated the fiftieth anniversary of the liberation of concentration camps, held at the Sydney Opera House.

My heart often ached for John, because there was such a discrepancy between his very successful business life and the often tragic, sad, and unsuccessful private life. I know that John was a most intelligent person, so I am quite sure that he saw the failure of his private life much more clearly than he

John Saunders with Dr Fredi Pasternak, now Professor of Gynaecology in Los Angeles, on a motor yacht on the Great Barrier Reef in Australia

admitted to, and that it gave him a lot of pain. His challenges and successes in business were great sources of pleasure, but out of business hours his consumption of sugary foods, his smoking, and some fleeting associations with women all gave him only short-term joy. He suppressed or channelled these negative feelings into business challenges, foods full of sugar, and smoking. In spite of all this sadness, disappointment, and illness, he remained an extremely warm person who made me very happy whenever I saw him. He always made me laugh.

Fredi Pasternak later married a Hungarian-born paediatrician, whose nickname is Bubbi, with whom he has a warm and loving relationship. Whenever John Saunders came to their apartment in Los Angeles, he would say very early in the evening, 'As I can do most things with you, I am going to take my shoes off.' This was one of his great pleasures, because he had a particularly wide forefoot, and even specially made shoes became uncomfortable after a few hours of wear. When John was visiting Melbourne, my then wife Sue and I took him to Fanny's, a restaurant which at that time was regarded by gourmets as having the best cuisine in Australia. The food was certainly always excellent, and the place understated and elegant, although a little too precious for my liking. After we sat down, John surreptitiously took his shoes off. During the dinner his feet swelled a little, so that when we were ready to leave he found it almost impossible to put his shoes back on. Unperturbed, he suggested Sue and I have another cognac and another coffee whilst he asked for a large dessert spoon—which he snuck into the heel of his shoes, using it as a shoehorn.

Although the two men did not meet often, John Saunders counted Fredi as one of his close friends. An important medium of their friendship was fun and humour, usually expressed as jokes about the past and about life itself. John respected the achievements and intellect of Fredi Pasternak, and Fredi reciprocated in his friendship with almost filial loyalty, respect, and great warmth towards John. John Saunders had a deep need for this kind of support, so this friendship was immensely important to him.

Friends young and old at a HopeTown School function. From the left: Bubbi and Fredi Pasternak, Frank Lowy's eldest son, David, Bevan Bradbury, Andrew Lederer, Neville Wran, and John Saunders

If only examined superficially, the deep friendship that developed between the prominent Labor politician Neville Wran and the shopping-centre magnate John Saunders may be hard to understand. Wran got to know Saunders in 1974 when he was the leader of the opposition in the New South Wales Labor Party, a party which promised a new look and new policies after a long-overdue change from the reign of the conservative state government. Wran in fact became premier of the state in 1976, and remained in office for a decade. During this decade he delivered the goods for New South Wales: he used the Sydney Bicentenary celebrations to brush up Sydney, creating more museums and galleries, and making Macquarie Street, The Rocks, and Darling Harbour much more pleasant places. Neville Wran says that all this allowed Sydney to become a 'complete city'.

Initially, there must have been an instrumental quality to their friendship: early on, each saw the other as a winner who had the ability to indirectly advance his own future aims. But the friendship became established on the basis of shared sentiments. Both men loved Sydney, and believed that it was a great privilege to be able to live there. Both men loved Australia and its lifestyle. Both men were true democrats. This meant that their friendship was always on an equal basis, untroubled by any demands of the ego or of competition. John Saunders admired Neville Wran's straight talking, his decisive action, and his vision—not only for Sydney and New South Wales, but for the whole of Australia. Wran admired the ability of John Saunders to make business decisions instinctively, especially his unerring ability to make complicated calculations mentally about the potential profit and loss in a prospective land development. Neville Wran confirmed to me that, in business, he felt that John Saunders and Frank Lowy were like chalk and cheese. John was instinctive in his decisions, whereas Frank was the precise, detailed figures

John Saunders, Neville Wran, and the author cycling in the Botanical Gardens of Queenstown in New Zealand during a summer holiday. The three men cycled, played tennis, cooked, walked and sorted out all the world's problems during the week

man. This was an extraordinary combination of talent. Wran admired
Saunders because he was such a 'naturally generous man', very forgiving, a
person who did not hold a grudge. His forgiveness extended to almost
everyone. Wran viewed John's persistence—an outstanding Saunders characteristic—as demonstrating a degree of innocence, in that he would never
give up and never say 'never':

> John Saunders genuinely loved Sydney, and I cannot remember another person
> who loved that city more, apart from myself. The only other thing I want to say
> about John is that he was mad about Australia. He loved to be near the beach
> and he liked to walk on the beach and go into the water, and he liked the space
> we have. He was a great Australian, he loved its lifestyle, and on a Sunday he
> would get into a pair of casual shoes, light pants and a coloured shirt and go to
> a barbecue, and that was his idea of a good day.

In *The Best of Friends*, a study about extraordinary friendships among
heterosexual men, David Michaelis quotes Duncan Spencer, who had made
a record-breaking transatlantic voyage with George Cadwalader in a twenty-
foot boat: 'I think friendship satisfies everyone's need for unconditional
love'. Unconditional love, warmth, understanding, forgiveness, a strong
sense of loyalty, a relationship that was on an equal footing with the other
person —these were the hallmarks of what John Saunders was seeking in a
true and close friendship, and these were also the qualities that he brought
with him to every deep friendship that he had.

With it all, John never lost his sense of fun, his sense of humour and mis-
chievousness, so that his companion was rarely weighed down with the gravity of any situation for too long, no matter how serious. I can so clearly see
right now his cheeky little smile shining through those pink cheeks whilst in
the depth of some major personal anxiety or source of despair that we were
discussing, and I can hear his broad Hungarian accent: 'Gabi, now let's look
at it this way … ' When John was very ill, I asked him what he would do dif-
ferently if he could live his life all over again. He simply said, 'Spend more
time with my friends.'

CHAPTER 16

FRANKIE AND JOHNNIE

Although John Saunders and Frank Lowy genuinely loved each other as brothers, their close relationship started to change—probably in the late 1970s—in subtle and imperceptible ways. This change gathered momentum, and surfaced in the mid-1980s when they began to have informal discussions about finding ways of separating their assets and thereby working towards dissolving their 33-year-old partnership. Why would these two men, who perhaps had the most outstanding business partnership ever encountered in Australia, want to make such a dramatic change—especially at a time when Westfield was growing so rapidly, with 21 shopping centres in Australia, seven in the USA, two hotels, and a large office block complex?

When I talked to them about this, neither was quite certain about the reasons behind the decision. Both men, for their own reasons—which even they may not have been conscious of—felt it was time to end their business marriage. I can only speculate on what may have been behind the decision to separate. For a storyteller, this watershed is very important: the possible reasons for the separation illuminate the two men's personalities and character; and they can also explain, at least in part, subsequent events.

Although the partnership was always on an equal footing, probably there were subtle forces working within Frank's mind. Frank Lowy was very much a family man who had three rounded and able sons who were all interested in coming into the business. John Saunders was eight years older. He was usually the ideas man, at least in the early years and, although modest and self-effacing in public, he was a man who pursued his goals with great focus and relentless persistence. Not only was Saunders older, but he also very much looked and acted the part of the controlling patriarch: he had an aura and a confidence about him when dealing and talking to people at all levels of society. Lowy, on the other hand, always had and still has a youthful appearance, looking younger than his years.

John Saunders related the following story to me. Back in 1954, when John and Frank ran their now-famous grocery store and delicatessen in Blacktown, the partners supplied food in large quantities to many of the migrants in the area, and also to several work camps in the region. The work camps were mostly inhabited by migrants employed by the New South Wales Electricity Commission and the Department of Main Roads. Saunders and Lowy were selling so much tinned food to the camps, such as tinned peas and baked beans, that one of the senior salesmen of the large canning company wanted to see what the secret was behind a little grocery store buying such huge quantities of their products. When the salesman turned up, Frank and an assistant happened to be serving, as John was out.

'I'm from the company that supplies most of your canned foods', the salesman said. 'Can you tell me where the boss is?'

'I'm the boss', said Frank.

'No, I mean the real boss. Where is he?'

Although John related this incident with a

John Saunders and Frank Lowy in the early years of their friendship and partnership, happily riding painted wooden horses at a shopping centre

chuckle, and without any malice, it is not hard to imagine that it could have been wounding for Frank when it occurred. No doubt there were other similar incidents that were embarrassing and even upsetting for the youthful-looking Frank Lowy. Underneath his apparent reticence, Lowy is a strong-willed person. On occasions, especially in their earlier years, he might have acquiesced to the wishes of the more forceful Saunders. However, as time progressed and as Westfield became increasingly successful, the need for fuller self-expression in the making of business decisions was probably rising in Lowy's consciousness.

So, apart from all the other logical reasons, there may have been unconscious reasons for Lowy to feel that, at the age of fifty-five, it was time for him to be independent of Saunders' patriarchal and to some extent controlling influence. Frank Lowy knew that he was a fast learner in grasping new

economic, organisational, and management concepts in a corporate structure—concepts which in the 1980s were essential for the continuing growth
of Westfield. Lowy usually wanted action quickly; Saunders, as is the case
with most creative people, needed time and space when decisions had to
be made.

Frank Lowy's perception that there was a subtle imbalance between the
two men, and that this needed to be corrected, is likely to have been felt
instinctively by John Saunders. This may have been the most important reason for their separation. Lowy told me that he experienced a certain sense of
freedom after their separation, and it was only then that he first understood
that Saunders, however unwittingly, may have been putting some kind of a
brake on him.

Frank Lowy's perception that John Saunders to some extent kept him
down in the later years appears to have been vindicated by the 25-fold
increase in the worth of Westfield since the two men dissolved their
partnership—although, it should be said, this amazing growth may well
have occurred if the partnership had remained intact. In the 1980s, John
Saunders to some extent looked backwards, building on well-tested past
successes, whilst Frank Lowy looked forward, at least as far as expansion
was concerned. This is not the place to get too deeply involved in the sociol-
ogy of large shopping centres versus smaller shopping centres and strip
shops, or huge corporations versus smaller corporations; but it seems that,
at the time, John Saunders felt that bigger is not necessarily always better.
We'll never know.

John Saunders probably had other reasons for contemplating the drastic
change that would be involved in dissolving the partnership. There were family upheavals; he was beginning to have health problems, with high blood
pressure; he was overweight; and then he had diabetes diagnosed. He also
had had a previous heart attack. However, these alone are unlikely to have
been more than contributory reasons for his thinking about separation. I
strongly suspect that the instincts and gut feelings that John Saunders relied

on so much all his life also came into operation: these would have told him that there was an imbalance between his own family, without an obvious immediate successor, and Frank Lowy's family, with three young, able sons all interested in following in their father's footsteps. It would be very hard to imagine that John Saunders—a man for whom gut feelings had been so dominant a force in making decisions throughout his entire life—would not have felt this growing disparity.

During 1986 the two men made several further attempts to formally separate their assets, but at least in the beginning it seemed that such a move was not commercially possible. They tried several alternatives and also sought professional advice, but no-one could come up with a solution. Then, in the second half of 1986, John Saunders apparently made a dramatic decision. It seems that, without any prompting, push, or advice from anyone, he offered Frank Lowy the lion's portion of his Westfield shares. Was this decision completely thought through, or was John just testing the strength of the alliance?

> It was kind of out of the blue. He never really told me why he wanted to do it, although I felt that he may have realised it was best for him and his family to do something else at that time. In a way, there were too many Lowys, and the imbalance was there. I know that he had some problems within his family, and I don't really know how his health was at the time. He wanted hard assets so that he could deal with his life as he wished.

This was Frank Lowy's description of what happened. He later emphasised to me, 'I never believed that John would leave. I never pushed him.'

This dramatic decision of John Saunders apparently caught Frank Lowy by surprise, as he apparently could not imagine that John would ever leave Westfield. When he accepted the offer, I suspect it was John's turn to be surprised. This dramatic decision was, of course, not revealed. There apparently followed extensive, hard-nosed and at times acrimonious, commercially based negotiations over the details of the separation. It seemed to the two men that there was nothing morally wrong with this form of commercial bargaining, and they eventually agreed on the deal. The final handshake between these two men who had known each other for over thirty years, and who had nothing less than a perfect business marriage over this long time, was apparently amicable. Both men later emphasised to one and all that they had a long and very close personal relationship that they wished to maintain.

Around this time, John Saunders was diagnosed with a mild form of adult-onset diabetes—no doubt precipitated by a worsening of his already poor dietary habits, which in turn were one of his responses to an increasing level of stress. John always kept his problems to himself. I suspect this was partly because of his modesty, partly because he was such a private person, and partly because a positive attitude to life had always ruled his world. He kept too many secrets during his life, and this very likely eventually contributed to his ill-health. He certainly did not reveal, and probably did not even acknowledge to himself, that he was subject to many serious life stresses at the time of his separation from Westfield.

In fact, he had had a small heart attack whilst holidaying in Hawaii with Mark in 1981; after he had a coronary angiogram, it was suggested that he have surgical treatment. John decided against surgery. After 1981, he had bouts of discomfort in his lower chest and upper abdomen which were put down to 'indigestion'; in retrospect, it is very likely that these were anginal pains caused by a narrowing of the coronary arteries which supply the heart with blood. He was also found to have high blood pressure. But John Saunders kept all the serious life stresses in relation to his family, marriage, and business to himself. He also started to smoke a little more, his refrigerator was always full of food, he ate more sweets and, at times, he didn't take his medication.

In July 1987, at a time when his friend Bob Hawke won office for a third term as prime minister of Australia, Saunders was struck down by severe chest pain. The accumulated stresses of life had been too much for his poor heart, and he had a major heart attack. He was admitted to the coronary care department of St Vincent's Hospital in Sydney. An x-ray of the arteries to the heart, a coronary angiogram, showed a severe blockage in the three main arteries supplying the heart muscle. After his cardiologist, Professor John Hickie, asked for a surgical opinion, John was seen by Australia's leading heart surgeon at the time, Dr Victor Chang. Victor advised a triple bypass operation. He told John that it was very important to have the operation performed as soon as possible. Initially John brushed it off and said, 'Look, the pain is gone. There is just a little bit of tightness there in the chest. I think I'll go home, think about this operation, and take a holiday in New Zealand'. I talked to his cardiologist and looked at the angiograms: even with the untrained eye of a gut surgeon, I could see quite marked narrowing in all three major coronary arteries.

But it was not easy to persuade John to have the operation. His usual medical practitioner and friend, Dr Pollack, talked to him for a long time, as did John's wife, and I—all to no avail. Finally, we invoked Neville Wran, a close friend with great persuasive powers over John, who ultimately talked him into staying in hospital and having the operation. Victor Chang kindly called me after surgery to say that it had been a difficult job: John's blood vessels below the bypass were not in the best of shape, but he had done his best. In the event, John's triple bypass lasted much, much longer than did Victor Chang—who, four years later, almost to the day of the operation, was mindlessly gunned down by bandits in Mosman, Sydney. Dr Chang was at the height of his career, and his death was a great loss to Australian heart surgery.

John Saunders recovered well from the bypass operation after an initial period of feeling rather low. This type of depression is reasonably common after coronary-bypass surgery. As well, for the first time in his life, John now had to have insulin injections in order to control his diabetes. This was something that John hated initially, but became accustomed to within two or three months. Most importantly, his angina disappeared and his physical and mental powers recuperated remarkably in the face of all the continuing major stresses in his life.

The details of the separation from Westfield, and that between John Saunders and Frank Lowy, were largely completed in 1987: John formally

*A parting shot. Frank Lowy and
John Saunders shaking hands
in front of their portraits by
Louis Kahan, at the time John
Saunders relinquished his role
in Westfield*

relinquished active participation in Westfield in November of that year. This
occurred at a time when the bottom fell out of share markets around the
world. Although Westfield was also hard hit, the share-market crash did not
stop Frank Lowy and Westfield from giving John Saunders a glittering valedictory dinner in the ballroom of Sydney's Regent Hotel. Everybody who was
anybody in the business world of Australia was there—as was John's family,
and all his friends from Sydney, and from elsewhere in Australia and overseas.

The prime minister, Bob Hawke, was represented by his then wife, Hazel,
and he also sent a pre-recorded videotape of himself talking about John
Saunders, which was projected during the evening. Mr Hawke paid tribute
to a great Australian who was unspoilt by his material success. He said that
John Saunders was a firm and loyal friend to him and to many others, and
that he had an important concern for the welfare of under-privileged

Australians —as shown by his establishing HopeTown School for minimally disabled children. He concluded most movingly, 'You've been an adornment to this country. This is not an end, but a change in career direction. I thank you on behalf of so many Australians, the country you made your own.'

The evening was hosted by Gordon Elliott, a television personality who had returned from the United States especially for the occasion. He first introduced Frank Lowy, who told the audience that he first met John Saunders in 1953 when John ran a delicatessen in the Sydney Town Hall railway station underpass and he was a smallgoods salesman. 'You were one of my customers', Frank said. 'And what a customer! I learned a lot from you. You were experienced and I was just a rookie. You liked my family and children, and encouraged all my children to become involved with Westfield. There was never a question when you wanted to sell your holding that it was to be sold to anyone else but me, and I am very grateful for this.' Frank Lowy told us that John Saunders' achievements could not be seen only in the buildings associated with him; it was much more important to know about his compassion, vision, wisdom, and inspiration to others in the past and in the future. 'We are still friends, and will remain so in the future', Frank Lowy said. 'We will be coming to you for advice and guidance, which I am sure you will offer to us most generously.'

Neville Wran was called to the podium. 'John, I have recently also taken a change in direction', he said. 'I welcome you to the Pensioners League!' He told us that John was a great achiever, a great Australian, and a great friend. Neville Wran also said:

> John Saunders joined a band of Australians who came to this country after the Second World War penniless, and usually with little or no English, and by hard work, determination, grit, ambition, and the simple need to survive and succeed, did succeed. These were men such as Arvi Parbo, Frank Lowy, and Peter Abeles. These men gave us new direction and a new feeling. When the history books are written about post-World War II Australia, John Saunders will be one of these men—a man with great instinct and foresight, mixed with immense compassion. John knows people well and is prepared to help them. He is some-

thing of a softy; and yet he, with Frank Lowy, was able to build an enormous corporation of national and international standing.

One other characteristic of these men, such as John Saunders, is their love of Australia. Just recently on a Sunday afternoon I was walking near Hyde Park toward William Street, and there were four flags flying on one building—two Australian and two flags of New South Wales. These flags were all on top of 80 William Street. Men like John Saunders are characterised by the love of their adopted land. The Lowys, the Brenders, and the Saunders are some of those people who have made our country great.

John Saunders then came to the podium amid thunderous applause. He said the following, in his broad Hungarian accent:

Thank you. I have never been a genius at public speaking. This night brings an era to its close. It is a decision I made almost three years ago, and I have to confess I am a little bit sad. It is time to attend to my personal and private business matters and commitments. In between, perhaps I'll find time to put my feet up. However, a good visitor knows when it is time to leave without being asked. The key to my successful partnership with Frank was based on respect, determination, honesty, loyalty, and trust. We never used a scale to measure our individual achievements. Each one had a particular talent which we put together to make joint decisions.

Frank used to tell me [pretending to make an aside remark, off the record], 'If you do it my way, it will be all right' [Saunders smiles; there is lots of laughter]. I have always believed that determination, a positive attitude, confidence, and believing in yourself are important for success, and this makes up for everything. I thank everyone who has been part of Westfield, or in some way associated with Westfield—business associates, bankers, politicians, accountants, lawyers, competitors, members of local government. I thank Frank, the executives, management, the cleaners, architects, engineers, switch operators, secretaries, and everyone else at Westfield, which has a wonderful team. They are all excellent people.

I now propose a toast—with a glass which I haven't got [waiter hurries over with a bottle of champagne, and pours a glass for John]. Now that's style ['It's champagne', says the waiter]. That's nice; it's cheaper than water [much laughter]. I salute you, and thank you from the bottom of my heart. Thank you. I drink to you one and all, and cheers. I also want to pay tribute to the wonderful country of Australia, with its freedom, equal rights, and no restrictions. I feel very honoured, and I believe I have some reason to be self-satisfied on this occasion. My next chapter begins at 80 William Street [laughter and much clapping], when a new and different challenge and experience begins. Thank you. Thank you very much.

As we were leaving the Regent Hotel at midnight on Monday 16 November 1987, I had this wonderful feeling about John Saunders going contentedly into retirement. I guess many thought, 'Well, there he is: good old John Saunders, at last retiring comfortably to live a life without stress'. The arrangements that were eventually put into place involved John Saunders selling most of his Westfield shares to the Lowy family, and acquiring ownership of Eastgardens Shoppingtown (which had been opened by the governor of New South Wales, Sir James Rowland in October 1987), which he then leased back to Westfield. Saunders also gained a vacant block in Crown Street, and an office block at 80 William Street called Terrace Tower that had just been built. He also acquired The Shore Inn Motel. The three properties—Terrace Tower, Eastgardens Shoppingtown, and The Shore Inn—were to be John Saunders' main assets, which he was to administer with three or four staff.

We were all heading back home to start our usual work the next day, already imagining John quietly managing his office block and other investments, and spending lots of time in his beloved house in Queenstown, New Zealand. As he enjoyed walking, being outdoors in the fresh air, and was known to have green fingers in the garden, some of us—if we were given to flights of fancy—could also imagine that he was about to take up golf and start growing roses.

The American quilt presented to John Saunders on his retirement by Richard Green, President of Westfield USA Inc, in a moving ceremony in 1987. Each of the seven USA Westfield shopping centres is represented by a square which was hand-stitched by the employees as a warm tribute to John Saunders. It now hangs in a prominent spot at 80 William Street

CHAPTER 17

THE SECOND EMPIRE

So if you really want to see me some more,

Just cross the road and enter my door.

JOHN SAUNDERS, NOVEMBER 1987
WESTFIELD VALEDICTORY DINNER SPEECH, REGENT HOTEL, SYDNEY

Most of us probably missed the significance of that little throw-away ditty at the end of John Saunders' valedictory speech at the Regent Hotel, said quietly with his pink cheeks shining and with his characteristic little smile. We all thought that a man of sixty-five who four months earlier had had a triple coronary-artery bypass, with his second marriage breaking down, having family and health problems, and losing what he called 'my baby', Westfield, could not do anything else but retire and tend to his assets.

In fact he took his own advice, and in November 1987 went across Crown Street, up to the eighteenth floor at 80 William Street to head the Terrace Tower Group of Companies. The newly built office block was distinctive and unique, with beautifully scalloped terraces, and almost immediately became a Sydney landmark. It has a huge '80' on three sides that can be seen glowing north, south, and west. Saunders had little difficulty in letting the sixteen floors of office space. The building also has a bank, restaurant, and other shops on the ground floor.

David Dinte, Sam Samuels, Peter Polgar, and Bernard O'Hara were the four men Saunders recruited as executives for the fledgling Terrace Tower group. John met David Dinte at David's wedding in 1985 when he married Judy Junger, the daughter of an expatriate Hungarian couple who were John's friends. John enjoyed David's humorous wedding speech, much of which was directed at Hungarians living in Australia. At the time, David had just finished the college of law, and was practising as a solicitor. The two men only spoke for two or three minutes at the wedding, in the course of which John asked David how he enjoyed his job. David's reply was, 'I am bored'. The groom, who was about twenty-three, described himself as a young 'pischer' (the Yiddish term for a squirt). He was very surprised when, some time later, he got a call from John suggesting a meeting at Westfield Towers. 'How would you like a job in which you wouldn't be bored?' he was asked.

When they met, John Saunders hired David Dinte then and there to become the manager of the newly formed Terrace Tower group. David started first in a small office in Westfield Towers at 100 William Street, a few

John Saunders behind his desk on the eighteenth level of Terrace Tower, with a beautiful view of his beloved Sydney Harbour. It is hardly the image of a man about to retire from business

months before John's official retirement. He says he learned everything he knows in business from John, and looked up to him not only as his boss but also as his friend and as a father figure. David's father had died a few months before he started working with John.

The combination of John Saunders and David Dinte was heaven sent. Saunders was looking for a young man with talent and ambition, someone who was not pre-conditioned in his business thinking and philosophy. For his part, Dinte—after having spent five years to gain two degrees, one in law and another in economics—was looking for a challenging commercial opportunity. Mutual trust and respect quickly developed. The two men had a similar sense of humour, and over the years their working relationship also became a personal friendship.

The chairman of the newly formed Terrace Tower Group of Companies in a typical pose with the then manager, David Dinte, during one of their daily business meetings. David Dinte is now the managing director and chief executive officer of the group

David Dinte is a hard worker and an enthusiast for whom every day at work is a pleasure. He regularly used to tell John that he was still not bored. He embraced the golden opportunity that was offered to him, and is fast becoming one of the important forces in the Australian business community. His appointment was a wonderful illustration of John Saunders' recruitment of young talent—fostering a young man, coaching him, sharing his knowledge with him—and eventually giving David Dinte the opportunity to be the chief executive officer of a thriving organisation.

Sam Samuels was working as a chartered accountant with a Sydney firm when he was recruited by John Saunders to work as the financial manager of Terrace Tower. Apart from being very meticulous, as behoves a chartered accountant, what is outstanding about Samuels is his total integrity. He is a stickler for the truth. He impressed John Saunders right at the beginning of their relationship when he told him: 'I am the sort of person who is absolutely frank, and I will always tell you exactly what I think.'

Sam later threw an interesting light on John's character. He believes that John always needed time to be able to trust people, because he was not sure whether a person wanted to associate with him because he was drawn to his personal qualities or to his wealth and influence. This assessment always took John some time to make. However, once he trusted a person, he relied on him, delegated work to him, and did not look over his shoulder. The other side of the coin was that this person remained completely accountable to Saunders for the decisions he made. Sam likened John's ability to focus on the main issues at hand as being akin to putting alluvial muddy water through a sieve, identifying any small flakes of gold at the bottom, and ignoring the rest. Sam also understood that John wanted value for his money, but that at the same time he was very generous with people whom he believed to be his friends. As did many of Saunders' executives, Sam looked on John as a father figure and as a friend, and believed that he worked with John rather than for him. He says that he loved him dearly, and would have gone well out of his way to do anything he could for him—not only in business, but outside office hours as well.

Peter Polgar, a charming man of Hungarian extraction, came over with John Saunders from Westfield. However, soon after, he left Terrace Tower to take up another position. He was an important and enthusiastic part of the team whilst Terrace Tower was in its early stages of development.

John Davidson, a previous centre manager of Eastgardens Shoppingtown, joined Terrace Tower a few years later as manager of property development and acquisitions. The way in which John Saunders recruited him is worth recounting. One Friday morning the two men met accidentally while Davidson was on his way to a final interview for a new job. Saunders invited him to have a coffee with him after the interview. Davidson was successful in his job application; nevertheless, while he was having a cup of coffee with John Saunders, he was asked to 'come and work at Terrace Tower'. John Davidson accepted without even asking about the precise nature of the job, nor the terms nor the salary.

He said, 'John, before starting, I promised my wife that I'd take a bit of a rest.'

One of the several informal planning meetings of the group during the development of the prestigious Crown Gardens apartments situated directly behind the Terrace Tower headquarters at 80 William Street. John Saunders is talking to David Dinte, just to the left of the architect's model of Crown Gardens

'That's fine with me,' Saunders replied. 'So what are you doing on Saturday and Sunday? Take your rest, and it's fine with me if you start next Monday.'

John Davidson did start two days later, and has remained one of the important executives of the Terrace Tower group.

Bernard O'Hara was first employed by Westfield in 1970 as a site clerk. Subsequently he was given the job of being one of the people involved with purchasing, and then with letting and negotiating contracts for Westfield. An expatriate Englishman, he migrated to Australia in 1968 via New Zealand, and over the years developed a special affinity for John Saunders. 'In spite of all his success and wealth, John always remained an ordinary bloke, someone who had the ability to talk to the man on the street, as well as to the prime minister and anyone in between', he told me. When Saunders invited O'Hara to come to Terrace Tower to do the letting and the contracts, the decision was quite simple for him: he joined Saunders without a thought to the contrary. He thinks his affinity with Saunders was due to the fact that he always related to the ordinary person, and Bernard considered himself to be just that, with a 'not too high and not too low' level of self-esteem. He found it very comfortable to be around John, and for John to be his boss. Bernard O'Hara remains an important part of the organisation and, because of his warm heart and sympathetic nature, was active in assisting John Saunders' philanthropic activities.

A few months after the Terrace Tower Group of Companies got going in 1988, Australia celebrated its bicentenary. It turned on a spectacular event in John's much-loved Sydney Harbour, in the presence of Prince Charles, with many tall ships arriving in the harbour from various parts of the world. As well, the Queen opened the new Parliament House in Canberra. With the prime minister, Bob Hawke, in attendance, the glittering occasion took place in the presence of state governors, premiers, politicians, media chiefs, and other Australian mandarins of business, including John Saunders.

Overseas, George Bush was elected as the next president of the United States, just as America entered a serious economic downturn. Within Australia, many high-risk investments started to go bust after the stock-market crash, taking with them merchant banks and state banks in South Australia and Victoria which had loaned substantial sums to investment propositions of doubtful value.

This was the era that brought down formerly notable business leaders such as Alan Bond and Christopher Skase; it was the era that made 'entrepreneur' a dirty word for the first time. It is a great pity that this French word took on a sleazy meaning in the late 1980s, because in its original sense it refers to an honourable activity—to a contractor who takes on a reasonable risk in creating a new development in the community, thereby aiding its progress. John Saunders was a genuine entrepreneur. It is, of course, interesting and salutary that neither Westfield nor the Terrace Tower Group of Companies went bankrupt, or even came close to it, as they were solidly managed, and had substantial and sound financial underpinnings.

In the face of a global financial downturn that included Australia, Saunders wisely decided to go slowly in the late 1980s, and to observe developments in business. During this time he was also experiencing a sense of loss—and some collateral pain—after separating from Westfield. As might have been imagined, Lowy's sons rose quickly in the Westfield organisation. But Saunders, an old-fashioned person who believed in giving respect to family and to elders, felt that he did not get the respect or acknowledgement he deserved from these young men. He was disappointed and hurt; as his friend Bob Hawke had put it in another context, Saunders was in a state of 'sad bitterness' because his counsel was not sought. John Saunders could not understand that the lack of consultation may have been part of a more general 'young bull–old bull' struggle, and also that a somewhat lower level of respect for and acknowledgement of one's elders had become the norm in our society.

John Saunders was also disenchanted with Frank Lowy: in part because of the difficulties involved in reaching their settlement; in part because he had expected Lowy to consult more with him subsequently; and in part because it seemed to him that suddenly a wall had sprung up between them, after they had been so close for over a generation. John Saunders felt upset that he was not invited to some Westfield functions. Lowy says in his defence that he principally didn't ask Saunders back so as not to hurt his feelings. Whatever the reasons, John Saunders felt hurt, disappointed, and bitter; unfortunately, he did not reveal any of these feelings to Frank Lowy or to Lowy's sons.

At the same time as this perceived barrier developed between the two men and their families, John's marriage to Klara broke down. They separated permanently in 1988 and then divorced. The marriage breakdown, separation, divorce settlement, and custody problems and their aftermaths—together with the problems of the Westfield separation—were major stressors for John Saunders. But John repressed all of these events. Having in the past done extensive research into the relationship between stressful events in life and subsequent illness, I am convinced that the sum of all these stresses played an important role in the ill-health that John experienced after the 1980s. This is not to ignore the fact that there were other important reasons for his ill-health, such as his eating habits, his smoking, his high blood pressure, and his diabetes.

In 1990, economic doom and gloom was widespread in Australia. But for John Saunders it was a time to look for new challenges in business; his gut feelings told him an economic recovery was not far away. After the separation John had acquired The Shore Inn, to which he had been very attached for sentimental reasons. Unfortunately, due to the economic crisis of the late 1980s, small seminars and conferences organised by industry, business, and the public service declined sharply in the whole of Australia. This adverse development, along with the stubborn reality of a surplus of hotel rooms in Sydney, meant that The Shore Inn was losing more and more money each year. John decided to sell the property, but it took him some time to work out the best way of disposing of this valuable piece of real estate. Eventually he converted the hotel into studio apartments, and sold them on a strata-title basis in 1995 and early 1996. These apartments on the north shore of Sydney remain very successful and popular. Saunders' timing turned out to be excellent, because this was just the beginning of the shift to inner-city living in Sydney.

It is amazing that John Saunders could often get a good profit out of an enterprise, apparently by coincidence. This happened so consistently that I am sure that what looked like lucky timing to an outsider was in fact driven by his finely honed instincts and gut feelings. It was an early member of the Rothschild dynasty who apparently once said, 'There are only two things you need to know in business: one is when to buy, and the other is when to sell.'

Eastgardens shopping centre was opened in October 1987, just a month before John Saunders' retirement from Westfield. As we have noted, John

The entrance to the Eastgardens Shoppingtown, which John Saunders leased back to Westfield

leased it back to Westfield to manage. This shopping centre became one of his most successful acquisitions; in fact, it is expected that by the year 2004 the equivalent of the entire population of Australia will have gone through its doors. The Terrace Tower group also acquired, in August 1994, the SupaCenta in Moore Park, Sydney. At the time of its acquisition the SupaCenta was a moderately successful shopping centre for appliances, furniture, hardware, and other similar goods. With refurbishment, repainting, and good advertising it has become extremely successful, and has undergone major expansion.

As before, John Saunders went 'where the people are'. Having observed Sydney's population expand northwards to the beautiful central coast of New South Wales, he acquired land at Tuggerah in 1994. On this he built a successful business park, and next to it a SupaCenta. He also undertook a successful land-subdivision venture in Woodbury Park on the central coast during the 1990s.

*Inside Eastgardens
Shoppingtown*

John Saunders acquired a piece of land behind 80 William Street upon his
separation from Westfield, which was initially destined for a moderately
priced hotel. However, there was such a surfeit of hotel rooms in Sydney in
the early 1990s that Saunders wisely scrapped quite advanced plans for the
development. As they say in Japan, 'A good Samurai knows when to run'. He

turned around, and instead, with the help of David Dinte and Bernard O'Hara, in 1996 planned and built over one hundred luxury apartments with central gardens, a swimming pool, a gymnasium, and other wonderful facilities. Most of the apartments had million-dollar views of Sydney Harbour, the harbour bridge, and the Opera House.

This was a time when not only Sydneysiders but also well-to-do migrants and Asian investors looked on apartments of this type as a convenient luxury residence and investment. Amazingly, 40 per cent of the apartments were sold off the plan; the rest went by the time the building was completed. The building, called Crown Gardens, is directly behind Terrace Tower at 80 William Street, and is adjacent to Westfield Towers and the Boulevard Hotel. A view from the north, from near the New South Wales art gallery, shows these four buildings well. The two on the left are Westfield's, and the two on the right are John Saunders'; he was, as he said he would be, just across the road, 'doing business as usual'.

Taken during the fiftieth anniversary celebrations of the liberation of Europe's concentration camps, when John Saunders hired the Concert Hall of the Sydney Opera House for an unforgettable night. John is here with two old friends and fellow Holocaust survivors, Feri Vadász (right) and Dr Fredi Pasternak (left). Behind them on the right are Westfield's headquarters and the Boulevard Hotel, and on the left is 80 William Street, the headquarters of the Terrace Tower Group

The past and the present. Taken from the Art Gallery of New South Wales, the past is represented on the left by Westfield headquarters and the Boulevard Hotel, and the present and future in the two buildings on the right, with Crown Gardens Apartments in front and the Terrace Tower Group headquarters at 80 William Street behind

In the United States, Saunders had acquired an office block at Encino, California, which was only a moderate commercial success. Because of this, and the low returns in the United States at the time, many advised him to keep away from the United States as an investment location. Typically, receiving this kind of advice became the very reason that John Saunders went ahead and looked for a good investment in the States. He made many enquiries and received several offers of properties along the west coast, but most of these were not worth considering. He then met Steve Johnston, whom he engaged to acquire property, and Terrace Tower opened an office at the Beverly Hilton in Los Angeles. Johnston had previously worked for a large firm involved with many office buildings, so he had contacts all along the west coast. In 1993 he showed Saunders an office block in Portland called the Bank of America Financial Center. John travelled to Oregon and liked Portland itself, as it is a beautiful town. His research had revealed that its population was growing very rapidly, and again his gut feelings told him to buy the property.

Portland has been an incredible commercial success; currently, it is 99 per cent let. However one explains the connection, the building also has two physical characteristics that drew Saunders to it. First, it has a lot of marble in it; John loved to look at and feel marble. (He once taught me how to tell whether something that looks like marble is genuine or not. One puts the back of one's hand on the marble surface: if it feels cool or cold, it is genuine.) Second, the building, situated in Oregon, also uses a lot of oregon beams; John also loved timber. Woodwork had been one of his hobbies over the years (and, of course, he had a wood-manufacturing business in Hungary after the Second World War). Together, these characteristics gave him additional, sentimental reasons for buying the office block in Portland.

As if all this were not enough, John Saunders bought an office block in Canberra in October 1996, which he then leased to Commonwealth government departments. He also bought a block of land in a good position in Queenstown, New Zealand, with a view to obtaining commercial rezoning and then building a shopping centre upon it in the future.

By its tenth anniversary, after having been established at the end of 1987, the Terrace Tower Group of Companies had become a thriving organisation. The combined worth of the group had trebled and, despite a corporate climate characterised by staff cuts, it had increased its staff numbers fifteenfold. This hardly represented the holding pattern which many thought John Saunders was about to enter when he made his Westfield valedictory dinner speech in 1987.

Throughout his joint leadership of Westfield, John Saunders was a quiet but significant supporter of worthy causes. He gave money each year to the Deaf and Blind Society. After a few years of receiving substantial donations

Bank of America building in Portland, Oregon, USA, seen through one of the spectacular glass-domed entrances

The lobby of the Bank of America building in Portland, full of marble and beautifully inlaid wood

from Saunders, the chairman, Sir Garfield Barwick, asked him on to the board of directors. Saunders also supported Israel anonymously and generously over the years. He donated $500,000 to Moriah School in Sydney to build a modern high-tech science centre, which was named the John Saunders Science Building. He also helped very significantly to realise the dream of Rabbi Brian Fox of Temple Emanuel, now in Manchester, England, to establish in Sydney the first progressive Jewish day school in the world to have classes ranging from kindergarten to matriculation. The Emanuel School now has an enrolment of 600 children. John Saunders was most generous, endowing the administration building, which now bears his name. He also enlisted the support of his good friends Joseph Brender and Sam Moss to endow the main lecture building.

John Saunders' most important philanthropic contributions were directed to the establishment of the HopeTown School and the Sydney Jewish Museum. HopeTown School happened mainly because John's son, Mark, had early learning problems. An important factor in Mark being able to overcome his problems was the two years that he spent at Devereaux Special School in Santa Barbara in California. John thought it might be a good thing to start such a school in Sydney. Initially there were a lot of difficulties, so he thought that, instead, he might start a kind of holiday camp for deprived children. However, it was hard to get quality staff for just a few weeks each year, so he reverted to his original ambition.

A fifty-acre block of land for the proposed school was eventually found in Wyong, about two hours' drive north of Sydney. When Saunders put his mind to establishing buildings on the site, he remembered a joint venture in a coal mine in North Queensland that had been entered into by Westfield, BP, and Thiess Brothers. Although the consortium had found coal, the project had been abandoned because there were already much richer and more profitable coal fields elsewhere in Australia. They had left behind a number of unused houses that had been erected for the personnel doing the drilling. It was these that John managed to buy from the joint partners for a total cost

An aerial view of HopeTown School near the Wyong Creek, close to the beautiful mid-coast of New South Wales

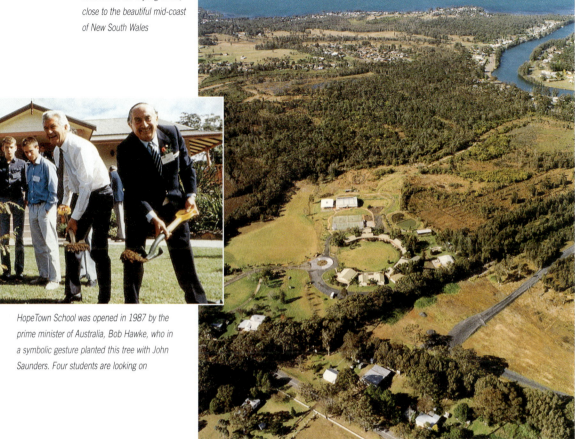

HopeTown School was opened in 1987 by the prime minister of Australia, Bob Hawke, who in a symbolic gesture planted this tree with John Saunders. Four students are looking on

An extension of HopeTown was opened in 1991 by the then premier of New South Wales, Nick Greiner, seen here with John Saunders—both men clearly enjoying the occasion. Here also is the charm of the Saunders smile, and the disarming posture of the arms and shoulders, so characteristic of him

Great jubilation among students and teachers alike at
HopeTown when the tractor arrived in 1991. It was donated
to the school by the Variety Club

At a HopeTown charity ball was
its founder and chairman, John
Saunders; deputy chairman,
Neville Wran; the school's
principal, Mrs Elaine Quilty;
and television personality,
Kerri-Anne Kennerley

of $3,000, which was very cheap. The transport company TNT brought them down to New South Wales after Saunders spoke with the chairman, Sir Peter Abeles. Again, he got a very good price—this time for the transportation costs, for a journey of over 1,500 kilometres. John Saunders' associates modified the buildings, making them functional for the school, so that it had a residential component as well as an office building.

HopeTown was opened in 1987 by the then prime minister, Bob Hawke. In a wonderful and touching opening ceremony, the two men, John Saunders and Bob Hawke, together planted a small tree, symbolising the hoped-for growth of the new school. As it turned out, HopeTown has been a model school in Australia for minimally disabled children. It aims to have children in the school for six to twelve months, in order to give them skills so that they can get back to regular schooling or obtain a suitable job, instead of being possibly thrown on to the human scrapheap. The school's success rate in achieving these aims has been nothing less than miraculous—of the order of 80 per cent.

Much of this success is attributable to its principal, Elaine Quilty, a woman who is passionate about the children, the school, and its aims. She has enlisted the support of an equally talented and enthusiastic group of teachers. After establishing the school, John Saunders subsidised it to the extent of about half a million dollars every year. In 1999 the New South Wales Department of Education assumed responsibility for the educational component of the school, thereby assuring its future. Elaine Quilty continues as school principal.

For many years, as a good Jew and a Holocaust survivor, John Saunders had thought about promoting the idea of a museum and Holocaust centre: he wanted to tell young Australians about the wonderful history of Australian Jewry, and at the same time remind them of the horrors of the Holocaust. By 1990 he felt that it was time to act, and to bring the Holocaust and its impact to the forefront of our consciousness. For some years there had been a small museum in Sydney, and there was also a group called 'The Holocaust

Sir Peter Sinclair, governor of New South Wales, Lady Sinclar, and John Saunders outside the Sydney Jewish Museum, after the museum was opened by Sir Peter in November 1992

A happy and proud John Saunders pictured here with the author at a celebration to acknowledge him as the founder and benefactor of the Sydney Jewish Museum and Holocaust Centre

Survivors Group' which had discussed the idea of building a museum about the Holocaust. Saunders attended one or two of their meetings. The group believed that such a centre would cost about $50,000 to establish. Saunders knew full well that it would cost much more; and, as action among the Survivors Group seemed a little slow for him and progress somewhat vague, he decided to build and finance the centre himself.

John Saunders started to look for a suitable place in Sydney, and eventually found the Maccabi Centre, which was a Jewish cultural and sporting centre that had been opened in 1922 by the great Sir John Monash—in the year Saunders was born. He got together with Jim Doe, who was still working at Westfield, as well as with David Dinte, Michael Bures, Kylie Winkworth, Bernard O'Hara, and Marika Weinberger. The group spent a lot of time drawing up plans and visiting overseas Holocaust centres before building the museum. The entire process and project was sponsored and supported financially by John Saunders.

The group also spent much time researching the historic aspects of Australian Jews and of the Holocaust. Sourcing and acquiring pictures, videos, clippings from newspapers in Europe and the United States, and the actual newspapers themselves was a

very creative process which John supported passionately. Eventually it cost nearly
six million dollars out of John Saunder's
pocket to build and set up the museum.
Subsequently it cost Saunders almost one
million dollars a year to support it.

The Sydney Jewish Museum and
Holocaust Centre was opened in November 1992 by the governor of New South
Wales, His Excellency, Rear Admiral Sir
Peter Sinclair. Coincidentally, Steven
Spielberg's *Schindler's List* was released not
long after the Sydney Jewish Museum was
opened. The museum has been an enormous success. It depicts the history of
Australia's Jews—beginning with the
arrival of the first fleet in 1788—and
reminds Australians not only of the horrors of the Holocaust but also of those few
brave men and women who helped
European Jews, the 'righteous gentiles'
during those tragic years in Europe. As a
fitting reflection of the spirit in which
John Saunders acted to establish the muse-

Part of the interior of the Sydney Jewish Museum during a major event

um, the centre features a quotation from the eighteenth-century Irish states-
man and philosopher, Edmund Burke: 'The only thing necessary for the triumph of evil is for good men to do nothing.'

Each year over 10,000 students from non-Jewish schools visit the museum to learn about the importance of religious and racial tolerance. This is a
significant issue in present-day Australia. The affable Rabbi Jeffrey Cohen is
supported by able staff in tending to the welfare and day-to-day activities of

The great contributions made by John Saunders to Australian business as well as to philanthropy were first recognised in 1989 when he was awarded the Australia Medal (AM), here presented by Sir Laurence Street. John Saunders received the Order of Australia (AO) in 1992

this thriving museum. One leaves the building filled with hope and optimism about the future, even whilst having been reminded of the horrors of the past.

Until the publication of this book, not many people knew or would have believed that John Saunders spent almost two million dollars a year, out of his own pocket, supporting philanthropic causes. Some might say that he could afford this—which is true. Yet nobody made him behave so generously, while many others who are wealthy give little or nothing towards worthy causes in our community.

In May 1995 John Saunders hired the Concert Hall of the Sydney Opera House for an unforgettable celebration of the liberation of Europe's concentration camps, and the end of World War II. The hall was filled to its 2,000-seat capacity, and amongst the audience were many young people, Jews and non-Jews alike. John Saunders invited many Australian and overseas luminaries. A message of goodwill was sent by the United States' president Bill Clinton, and delivered by Edward Perkins, the US ambassador to Australia.

John Saunders hired the Sydney Opera House Concert Hall in May 1995 to celebrate the fiftieth anniversary of the liberation of Europe's concentration camps. Seen here is part of the audience in the lobby of the Opera House

At the Sydney Opera House celebration. From the left: Mrs Bessmertnykh and Dr Bessmertnykh from Russia; Edward Perkins, US ambassador to Australia; Kim Beazley, finance minister, representing the prime minister of Australia; General Alexander Haig of the United States; Lord Geoffrey Howe, former British deputy prime minister; David Dinte, then general manager of the Terrace Tower Group of Companies; and Charlie Lynn, New South Wales parliamentarian

A happy John Saunders pictured here with Dr Bessmertnykh and General Haig after the Sydney Opera House celebration

John Saunders shaking hands with the United States' ambassador to Australia, Edward Perkins, at the Sydney Opera House tribute, after Mr Perkins had read a goodwill message from US president Bill Clinton

The US film-maker Steven Spielberg also sent his best wishes. The evening was hosted by John Saunders' friend Justice Marcus Einfeld.

Representing the Allied forces responsible for the defeat of Nazi Germany were the former United States secretary of state, General Alexander Haig; the former Russian foreign minister, Dr Alexander Bessmertnykh; and the former British deputy prime minister, Lord Geoffrey Howe. The three statesmen reiterated the key message of the evening: 'Lest we forget.'

Kim Beazley spoke, representing Paul Keating, the prime minister of Australia. This was followed by a wonderful speech from the leader of the opposition (and future prime minister), John Howard. As well, survivors spoke, the Holocaust was illustrated visually, and there was an uplifting musical programme from the SBS Youth Group and the Jewish Choral Society.

John Saunders, optimistic as always, looking to the future but remembering the past, told us of his hopes that this night would remind 'future generations not to repeat the atrocities of fifty years ago, and that Australia will continue to be a tolerant and peace-loving society. This is my hope and vision.'

On leaving the Opera House, an elderly survivor was overheard to say: 'Now I can die happy, knowing that the memories have been passed on.' This commemoration was a deeply moving occasion.

Victor Chang's triple-bypass graft of John Saunders' coronary arteries held up well for almost ten years, and much better than Victor himself predicted. Victor, who was a brilliant surgeon, didn't know about the John Saunders' survival factor. Every individual is unique, and we must never reduce the chances of survival in any one person to statistics or biological equations. However, the high-risk factors in John Saunders' life, which I discussed in the previous chapter, eventually caught up with him. He suffered a further heart attack at the end of 1996. After examining him, all the experts agreed, and John was pleased to hear, that it was inappropriate to treat his heart condition surgically. In fact, further surgery was not possible.

John Saunders recovered from this further assault on his heart, following intensive medical treatment, and improved sufficiently to get back to work by early 1997. Although his doctors predicted a lifespan of not more than six months, John defied the odds once again. He was taking a week's holiday on Australia's Gold Coast in early September 1997 when he was again struck down by chest pain. He had to be admitted to a Southport hospital, and was placed on an intensive life-support system. He was given a few days—a month, at the most—to live.

When I went to Queensland and saw John Saunders in hospital, I really thought this was it for my dear friend. However, even after many years of knowing him, I too forgot about the John Saunders' survival factor. During this grave illness, John Saunders—this amazing survivor—made several important, independent decisions regarding his treatment that clearly helped to prolong his life. For example, he refused an indwelling bladder catheter for fear of a kidney infection, quite rightly, but agreed to a central intravenous line. After extensive discussions with me about the risks and advantages of transferring to a major hospital in Sydney, he eventually agreed— but only if a pressurised, comfortable plane was available. His old friend and partner, Frank Lowy, gladly came to our assistance, as did Professor Michael O'Rourke, a cardiovascular physician, who oversaw the transfer. In fact, John remained active to the end in evaluating his own treatment.

We now know from medical research that one of the characteristics of unexpectedly long survivors of serious illness—such as advanced cancer or advanced heart disease—is that they take responsibility for and control of their illness. After extensive medical and lay consultation, they decide eventually for themselves which line of treatment they are prepared to agree to. We now also know that these long survivors of serious illness often operate at an intuitive level, and that they are at peace and completely comfortable with themselves as they do so. This description fits John Saunders to a tee.

Although it took a few weeks in hospital for John Saunders to improve, he went home, attended his office for brief periods of time, and very much enjoyed his family and friends who, together with his faithful personal carer, Ilike Halász, provided wonderful daily social support for him. Fortunately, as was his way, John had trained his business team in his own mould, so that he only needed to work as a consultant in the now very successful Terrace Tower Group of Companies.

This man who, ten years before, had been farewelled with pomp and ceremony, and had been put out to pasture, had once more come to the top. In spite of everything, he had once again become one of the wealthiest and most influential men in Australia. John was certainly wealthy financially. But he was even wealthier spiritually, because he was surrounded by his family and friends. He celebrated his seventy-fifth birthday on 22 November 1997, weak in body but still sharp in mind, with all his close friends and family. We were all there paying homage: his family, Neville Wran, Frank Lowy, Sam Moss, John Landerer, David Dinte, Sam Samuels, John Hickie, Alexander Pollack, and myself. John summoned up extraordinary strength. Like Phoenix, the mythical bird, he had risen and emerged from the ashes to enjoy his last birthday and complete his seventh life. His birthday party was held, just as he would have wished, on a wonderful, sunny Sydney afternoon. He died peacefully twelve days later.

There is one last story about John Saunders that I would like to tell: it is, characteristically, a story about his optimism. At the end, John knew that he was very ill. In spite of this, he looked forward excitedly to celebrating his seventy-fifth birthday. For the occasion he asked his tailor to measure him for a new suit, and insisted that he make two pairs of trousers. John Saunders wanted to have a second pair handy after he had worn out the seat of the first pair.

CHAPTER 18

CODA AND AFTERGLOW

It was a wet, dark, and gloomy Sydney morning. The hall of the Chevra Kadisha in Woollahra was packed; there was not even standing room available. John Saunders' sisters, children, and nieces were in deep mourning. The prime minister, John Howard, was there. So were the leader of the opposition in the Senate, Senator John Faulkner; two past premiers of New South Wales, Neville Wran and Nick Greiner; and several other political and business leaders of Australia. Frank Lowy was trapped in Israel because of a general strike. However, his two sons who reside in Australia, David and Steven, were there also.

John Saunders' dear friend, the Reverend Michael Deutsch, the Cantor at Temple Emanuel, gave a moving eulogy in which he recounted the story of their friendship, and how John was his best 'chaver'.

Rabbi Franklin then told us about the similarity between John Saunders and the Jewish teacher of the first century, Hillel Habibli, the Babylonian. Hillel rhetorically posed three questions to himself, questions that wonderfully distilled the essence of John's life. The first question he asked was: 'If I am not for myself, who is?' This certainly expressed the amazing ability of John Saunders to survive in the face of so many adversities: losing his father, taking responsibility for the family business as a child, and surviving the concentration camps of Garany, Auschwitz, and Dörnhau; coping with the transitions from living under Russian tyranny to being a displaced person and a penniless migrant in Australia; and then enduring the more typical although severe life stresses of the loss of his wife, family problems and upheavals, the separation from Westfield, his divorce, and serious illness.

The second question Hillel asked was: 'If I am only for myself, who am I?' John Saunders was a man who looked beyond his personal needs and private universe, in the process touching many hearts and minds, and helping many individuals, groups, and organisations over the years.

The final question Hillel asked himself was: 'If now is not the time to act, when is the time?' John Saunders, more than anything else, was a man of action. He admired and valued men and women whose behaviour was consistent with the notion that, in life, action was much more important than words. He had a little plaque on his desk that read: 'There are three kinds of people. Those who make things happen, those who watch things happen, and those who wonder what happened.'

David Dinte, John Landerer, Andrew Lederer, Sam Moss, Alex Pongrass, Neville Wran, and I solemnly took the coffin from the Chevra Kadisha into the hearse. On this dark, wet day the cortege passed through Sydney to the cemetery. The coffin was lowered into the ground slowly and, in the pouring rain, the dirt was shovelled over the man who had meant so much to us. Just a small temporary sign indicated who was underneath. It simply said, 'John Saunders'. There was much weeping and grieving.

The coffin of John Saunders carried by the pallbearers on 10 December 1997. From the front: Professor Gabriel Kune , Mr Andrew Lederer OAM, Mr David Dinte, Mr Sam Moss, Mr John Landerer CBE AM, Mr Alex Pongrass AM, and Mr Neville Wran AC QC (Reproduced by permission of The Sydney Morning Herald*)*

As I was walking around the gravesite I wondered, as thousands of others must have done on similar occasions: is that all there is to a great man's life? Just being dropped into the ground with some earth shovelled over the coffin, and a tiny sign indicating his name? Did John Saunders pay too big a price for his success? Was it all really worth it? In the midst of this grief, I saw a strong light coming through the rain. Yes! I thought. His family and many friends and acquaintances will remember him for a long, long time. The lessons he taught his business associates will be passed on. The buildings, hotels, shopping centres, HopeTown School, and the Jewish Museum, as well as the thriving Terrace Tower group, will remain as visible evidence of his achievements. I thought of Christopher Wren's son placing the inscription about his father on St Paul's Cathedral in London, which said, 'If you wish to see the monument to this man, look around you'. At that moment I could also see the achievements of John Saunders as a lasting reminder of this man.

There is no doubt that John Saunders was an extraordinary man. There were two major streams in his life. One was full of immense business success and a genuine love for his family, friends, and associates. The second stream was that of personal sadness, bitterness, and tragedy. Although he had qualities that some people found difficult, it is remarkable that, during my twenty-year friendship with him, and after interviewing scores of people before and even after his death, I met none who spoke ill of John Saunders. Nor could I find a single enemy of this man.

But what sort of a man was he? I do not have a clear or simple answer. Even after a long and close friendship, after talking to him extensively and virtually vivisecting him for the last twelve months of his life, after talking to his family and friends, and after trying to weigh up his life since his death, I cannot come to a clear conclusion about him. In many ways he was a man of paradox. He loved his personal freedom immensely; yet he was patriarchal and controlling, highly demanding of his family and business associates, asking everyone to be accountable to him—not only with their spending but also with their actions. He squeezed every last cent out of every deal and every financial arrangement; yet he was very generous to his friends and to those in genuine financial difficulty.

At the same time as being master of the purse strings with his family, he was one of the most important and generous philanthropists in Australia. At heart a true liberal with a social conscience, he appeared apolitical on the surface—even to the extent of usually donating equal amounts to Labor and the Liberals. He was persistent to the point of being pig-headed when pushing an idea or a project—apparently not realising that, while this characteristic was of great value in business, it was sometimes the source of serious problems in his personal life.

In his role as a patriarch he was usually kind-hearted and thoughtful, but he could be quite hard on his family if there was any hint of family instability. He admired and supported those who were in public life and exercised high political office, but summarily dismissed those he perceived to be arrogant in their behaviour. John Saunders enjoyed the company of charming women. He had an outstanding talent for business. He was a great teacher, often by example, of business and business management. Yet he hung on to a homespun philosophy of the economy, and resisted some of the newer concepts of corporate structure and organisation.

He was always modest, warm-hearted, and eventually forgiving, even to those who had done him great wrong. He loved the freedom of Australia, the beauty of Sydney, the informal quiet life out of business hours. Away from the limelight he would relax, walk, talk with friends, and laugh at jokes—even the old ones. He embraced Australia and everything it offered with gratitude and passion, and contributed immensely to the country's prosperity and vitality. More than anything, he was a great survivor in the face of many and extreme adversities. And more than that, he demonstrated by his achievements the mind-boggling power of an individual to live beyond himself. He had an amazing ability to suppress negative thoughts and feelings. This helped him enormously to survive in the face of adversity; but, paradoxically, this very characteristic eventually cost him his good health and his life.

Now this tubby, pink-cheeked little man with the cheeky smile and big heart is gone. He was a real 'mensch'—a man of character, integrity, and dignity. He was a modest, warm-hearted, generous man: philanthropic, dismissive of all humbug, loyal to his friends, mischievous, humorous, happy, relaxed, and comfortable with himself. He was a man who enjoyed the charm of women. He was sentimental, patriarchal, stubborn, controlling, and instinctive. He was a tough businessman, a risk-taker, a genuine entrepreneur, a true liberal and democrat, a great survivor in life, and a visionary with hope and optimism for the future. It could be said of John Saunders, as Hamlet did of his father, 'He was a man, take him for all in all, I shall not look upon his like again.'

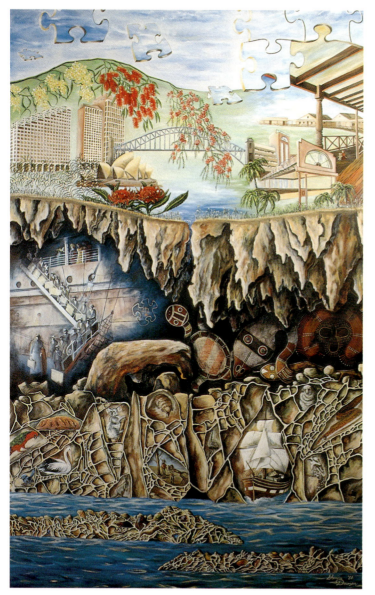

This 1986 painting by the Australian artist Sharon Davson is a wonderful mosaic symbolising some important parts of the life, passions, and achievements of the late John Saunders. The migrant ship arrives in Sydney, disgorging its passengers. John's much-loved Sydney Harbour and the Opera House are seen. Native birds, animals, plants, marine life, as well as Australian landscapes, abound. Westfield Towers, The Boulevard Hotel, Terrace Tower, and Eastgardens Shoppingtown symbolise some of the achievements, whilst HopeTown School embodies the Saunders' vision, hope, and optimism for the future

BIBLIOGRAPHY

Baker, Mark Raphael. *The Fiftieth Gate: a journey through memory*, Flamingo, Sydney, 1997
An Australian-born son reconstructs the events and mystery behind his parents surviving the Holocaust

Braham, Randolph L. *The Politics of Genocide: the Holocaust in Hungary*, vols 1 & 2, Columbia University Press, New York, 1994
History of Hungarian Jews in Hungary in the twentieth century, including the Holocaust, liberation, restitution, and retribution. Very detailed

Brasch, Rudolph. *Australian Jews of Today*, Cassell, Australia, Sydney, 1977
Among studies of outstanding Australian Jews, there is an interesting vignette of John Saunders

Bryson, Bill. *Made in America*, Secker & Warburg, London, 1994
A vivid description of the history of shopping in the USA (see Chapter 12) from corner stores to department stores, supermarkets, shopping centres and, finally, to shopping towns

Frankl, Viktor E. *Man's Search for Meaning* (revd), Pocket Books, New York, 1984
A personal explanation of the spiritual and psychological aspects of human survival, based on experiences in Auschwitz

Friedman, Milton. *Capitalism and Freedom*, University of Chicago Press, Chicago and London, 1962
Discusses the basis of his theory and economic model of competitive capitalism. Also discusses the power of money supply and the positive relationship between economic freedom and political freedom

Horne, Donald. *The Lucky Country: Australia in the sixties*, Penguin Books, Ringwood, Australia, 1964
An account, revolutionary in its time, of the development of Australia in the post-war era

Koestler, Arthur. *The Thirteenth Tribe: the Khazar empire and its heritage*, Hutchinson, London, 1976
A fascinating account of the rise and fall of the Khazar empire, tribes which practised Judaism. A dissident Khazar tribe, the Kabars, together with the Magyars, invaded what is now called Hungary at the end of the ninth century, where they have remained ever since

Kune, G A. 'The Influence of Structure and Function in the Surgery of the Biliary Tract', Arris and Gale Lecture, *Annals of the Royal College of Surgeons of England* 47:78–91, 1970
Results of research describing anatomical dissections and cholangiograms examined in which the surgical significance of the subvesical duct of Luschka is discussed and emphasised

Kune, Gabriel A. *Current Practice of Biliary Surgery*, Little Brown, Boston, 1972
Textbook of gallbladder and bile duct surgery read by John Saunders' doctor, Dr Alexander Pollack, which led to the author's meeting with John Saunders

Kune, Gabriel A & Bannerman, Susan (eds). *The Psyche and Cancer*, University of Melbourne, 1992
Describes conference proceedings of how the human psyche might influence the development and response to the treatment of cancer and other chronic illness. The characteristics of unexpectedly long survivors in the face of advanced disease is also discussed

Kushner, Harold S. *To Life*, Warner Books, New York, 1994
An account of the origins, history, and culture of Jews. A personal account of what it is to be a Jew

Levi, Primo. *If This is a Man*, Orion Press, London and New York, 1959
A graphic and powerful account of life in a concentration camp, written precisely and with some detachment—as one would expect from Levi, who was a chemist

Lin Yutang. *The Importance of Living*, William Heinemann, London, 1938
Describes Chinese philosophy on the reasons to be alive and on the enjoyment of life, particularly from a Chinese, Confucian, and Taoist perspective.

McQuillan, T, Manolas, S, Hayman, JA & Kune, GA. 'Surgical Significance of the Bile Duct of Luschka', *British Journal of Surgery* 76:696–698, 1989
An anatomical, pathological, and clinical account of the consequences of damage to the small subvesical bile duct first described by Luschka and emphasised by the authors. This duct is of special relevance in the biography (see chapter one)

Michaelis, David. *The Best of Friends: profiles of extraordinary friendships*, William Morrow, New York, 1983
Describes the importance, conflicts, and pleasures of close male non-sexual friendships in the lives of fourteen men, including John F Kennedy, Buckminster Fuller, John Belushi, and Dan Ackroyd

Moshinsky, Mark. *Mietek Gringlas: a biography*, The Gringlas Family, Melbourne, 1989
A grandson's biography of his grandfather, Mietek Gringlas, who survived the Second World War in the

Russian army, but whose family died in the Holocaust. It is a story of a man rebuilding his life successfully in Australia in the face of many personal and family tragedies

Murray, William H. *The Scottish Himalayan Expedition*, J M Dent & Sons, London, 1951
Interesting perceptions about commitment, persistence, and determination

Nietzsche, Friedrich. *The Bird of Tragedy and the Genealogy of Morals*, Anchor Books, New York, 1956
Describes, among other philosophical concepts, the proposition that the release of instinctual forces in a positive way is healthy and is not immoral

Pick, Hella. *Simon Wiesenthal: a life in search of justice*, Weidenfeld & Nicolson, London, 1996
The story of the Holocaust survivor and Nazi hunter, who continues to fight against what has been called 'Holocaust amnesia'

Ross, John (ed). *Chronicle of the Twentieth Century*, Chronicle and Penguin Books, Ringwood, 1990
Historical references of events in Australia and the world

Sas, Meir. *Vanished Communities in Hungary: the history and tragic fate of the Jews in Újhely and Zemplén counties*, Memorial Book Committee, Toronto, 1986
Describes the 2000-year history and fate of Jews in Zemplén County and Sátoraljaujhely up to 1944

Vernon, PE (ed). *Creativity*, Penguin, Harmondsworth, 1970
The nature of the creative process is discussed from several perspectives; I found some views particularly illuminating in relation to the subject of this biography

Watt, Donald. *Stoker*, Simon & Schuster, Sydney, 1995
The story of a young Australian soldier captured by the Germans who ended up in Auschwitz for seven months, and was made to stoke the furnaces

Wilson, Derek. *Rothschild: a story of wealth and power*, Andre Deutsch, London, 1988
An amazing portrait of the banking dynasty over the centuries, right up to the present time

Zandman, Felix. *Never the Last Journey*, Schocken Books, New York, 1995
The story of a Holocaust survivor who has risen literally from under the ground to become one of America's foremost scientists/inventors/entrepreneurs

INDEX